THE UNIVERSITY
OF CHICAGO
CONSORTIUM ON CHICAGO
SCHOOL RESEARCH

RESEARCH BRIEF FEBRUARY 2013

FROM HIGH SCHOOL TO THE FUTURE

The Challenge of Senior Year in Chicago Public Schools

Melissa Roderick, Vanessa Coca, Eliza Moeller, and Thomas Kelley-Kemple

TABLE OF CONTENTS

1 Executive Summary

Introduction
9 Preparing for Postsecondary or Coasting to Graduation?

Chapter 1
17 What Coursework Should Students Take Senior Year?

Chapter 2
27 Making Sense of Senior Year in the Chicago Public Schools

Chapter 3
49 Getting In and Staying

Chapter 4
63 The Sum of Its Parts

Chapter 5
91 Interpretive Summary

99 References

103 Appendices

119 Endnotes

Publications: From High School to the Future

The following CCSR publications are related to the *From High School to the Future* series.

From High School to the Future: Making Hard Work Pay Off, April, 2009. Melissa Roderick, Jenny Nagaoka, Vanessa Coca, and Eliza Moeller

From High School to the Future: The Pathway to 20, October, 2008. John Q. Easton, Stephen Ponisciak, and Stuart Luppescu

From High School to the Future: ACT Preparation—Too Much, Too Late, May, 2008. Elaine Allensworth, Macarena Correa, and Steve Ponisciak

From High School to the Future: Potholes on the Road to College, March, 2008. Melissa Roderick, Jenny Nagaoka, Vanessa Coca, Eliza Moeller; with Karen Roddie, Jamiliyah Gilliam, and Desmond Patton

Working to My Potential: The Postsecondary Experiences of CPS Students in the International Baccalaureate Diploma Programme, March, 2012. Vanessa Coca, David W. Johnson, Thomas Kelley-Kemple, Melissa Roderick, Eliza Moeller, Nicole Williams, and Kafi Moragne

Update to: *From High School to the Future: A First Look at Chicago Public School Graduates' College Enrollment, College Preparation, and Graduation from Four-Year Colleges*, October, 2006. Elaine Allensworth

From High School to the Future: A First Look at Chicago Public School Graduates' College Enrollment, College Preparation, and Graduation from Four-Year Colleges, April, 2006. Melissa Roderick, Jenny Nagaoka, and Elaine Allensworth; with Vanessa Coca, Macarena Correa, and Ginger Stoker

---

This report was produced by UChicago CCSR's publications and communications staff: Emily Krone, Director for Outreach and Communication; Bronwyn McDaniel, Communications and Research Manager; and Jessica Puller, Communications Specialist.

Graphic Design: Jeff Hall Design
Photography: Cynthia Howe
Editing: Ann Lindner

02.2013/1,000/jh.design@rcn.com

ACKNOWLEDGEMENTS

In the late winter of 2005, CCSR researchers asked students in 12 junior English classrooms to join a longitudinal study of students' experiences in making the transition to college. In three neighborhood high schools, we recruited students from three IB classrooms, three AP classrooms, and six regular English classes. We told students they were the experts who could help us understand what works, what needs to be improved, and how to make Chicago high schools do a better job of supporting students as they make the transition to college or work. We told students that they would not get any benefits from participating, but asked them to join us in helping Chicago schools become better for their younger brothers and sisters and for all students who would come after them. In a testament to the character of CPS students, more than 85 percent of the recruited students volunteered to join the study—so many that we could not, unfortunately, include them all. For over three years, students gave up lunch breaks, talked to us about their experiences and plans, and continued to make time for us in their busy schedules, even after they graduated. Their teachers allowed us to visit their classrooms, gave up free periods to be interviewed, and voluntarily filled out individual assessments of each student in our study. We are indebted to these students and teachers for the many hours of time they volunteered and to the principals and staff of the high schools in which we worked, who allowed this study to happen and supported it over two years. The students, teachers, and other school staff truly were the experts who guided our quantitative analysis and provided critical insights. In the end, we hope we have delivered on our promise to these students and have assembled their experiences and our analysis into a report that will assist CPS educators and policymakers in building effective systems that bridge the gap between students' college aspirations, their college access, and their college success.

Along the way, many individuals helped shape this report. It is a testament to our colleagues that we have so many people to thank. The heart of this report is found in its student voices and we want to thank all those who conducted student interviews, including Jonah Deutsch, Jamiliyah Gilliam, and Macarena Correa, as well as Karen Roddie for her significant contributions to our qualitative analysis. We also owe a debt of gratitude to our colleagues who provided feedback, guidance, and support through all stages of this project, helping us clarify our findings, refine our argument, and build a cohesive report out of a wide variety of methods and data. In this regard, we especially want to thank CCSR leadership, (John Easton, Elaine Allensworth, Penny Sebring, and Sue Sporte); the project staff who helped guide and edit the report (Jenny Nagaoka, David W. Johnson, Nicole Beachum, Faye Kroshinsky, Kersti Azar, Billie Jo Day, and Tasha Keyes); colleagues who took on the essential but difficult tasks of doing the technical read of the report (Matthew Holsapple, Courtney Thompson, and Marisa de la Torre); and CCSR Steering Committee members, Lila Leff and Raquel Farmer-Hinton, who read an earlier draft of the report and provided incredibly helpful comments.

Emily Krone and Bronwyn McDaniel, the public informing staff at CCSR, were instrumental in helping us edit and produce this report, while simultaneously developing effective impact and informing strategies. We want to thank both Emily and Bronwyn for their many contributions to our work.

The purpose of this research is to help inform practice. And there are also many practitioners who have guided this report. First and foremost, we owe a great debt to Greg Darnieder, currently serving as a Senior Advisor to the U.S. Secretary of Education, who, as the director of the Postsecondary Initiative, saw the value of data and research and was invaluable in both starting this project and guiding our work. Kelly Sparks and Gudelia Lopez were amazing partners in designing our CPS postsecondary database and in helping to align the research with a set of validated research-based indicators that CPS could use to support high schools in tracking their progress. We miss their leadership at CPS.

We have, however, the additional advantage of working with some of the most cutting edge educators in high school reform in the country, through our partner project, the Network for College Success (NCS). NCS directors and coaches (Mary Ann Pitcher, Sarah Howard, and Elizabeth Monge-Pacheco) provided invaluable feedback on everything from the readability of graphs, to the question of what the implications of the findings might be for high schools across the city. NSC staff held us to high standards and challenged us often in ways that made the report better.

Some of the issues in this report are difficult to grapple with, particularly around issues of employment. We are tremendously indebted to Robert Schwartz, Aarti Dhupelia, and Jackie Lemon, who pushed our thinking by participating in a critical and substantive conversation about the findings of this report, which is being published separately. Similarly, we want to thank Heidi Shierholz of the Economic Policy Institute. Heidi was generous with her time and provided us with detailed breakdowns of trend in youth employment data that proved critical in framing the problem faced by students who don't go to college.

Finally, we would especially like to thank the administrative staff at the School of Social Service Administration—Keith Madderom, Gidget Ambuehl, Suzanne Fournier, Anita Goodnight, John McDonald, John Adamczewski, and Sid Ulevicius—who provided ongoing and important support for this work. SSA's staff always made us feel that our work was important and never made us feel like we were asking too much.

The study is funded by grants from the Bill & Melinda Gates Foundation, the William T. Grant Foundation, and the Spencer Foundation. The research reported here on AP and honors coursework was supported by the Institute of Education Sciences, U.S. Department of Education, through Grant #R305R060059 to the University of Chicago. The opinions expressed are those of the authors and do not represent views of the Institute or the U.S. Department of Education.

Executive Summary

Historically, senior year has been a time of finishing up graduation requirements as most students entered the work force after high school. But in this new economy, most students now hope to go to college and those who are not entering college face a rapidly eroding labor market for young adults with only a high school education.

In a 2010 address to the College Board, U.S. Secretary of Education Arne Duncan laid out a vision for high school that advances the Obama administration's goal of the U.S. once again leading the world in educational attainment. In this new economic landscape, Duncan argued:

> "High schools must shift from being last stop destinations for students on their education journey to being launching pads for further growth and lifelong learning for all students. The mission of high schools can no longer be to simply get students to graduate. Their expanded mission, as President Obama has said, must also be to ready students for careers and college—and without the need for remediation."[i]

There is no grade in which the magnitude and complexity of this shift becomes clearer than in senior year. Historically, senior year has been a time of finishing up graduation requirements as most students entered the work force after high school. But in this new economy, most students now hope to go to college and those who are not entering college face a rapidly eroding labor market for young adults with only a high school education. This changing educational landscape means that students' coursework and activities in senior year are becoming increasingly important.

If the new purpose of high schools is to be a "launching pad rather than a last stop destination," what does that mean for senior year? In our previous CCSR report, *Potholes on the Road to College*, we looked at this question from the perspective of whether students were effectively participating in college search and selection. In this report, we turn to students' academic experiences senior year. We analyze the coursetaking patterns of more than 50,000 CPS students in the graduating classes of 2003 to 2009. We look at the impact of senior year coursetaking on college enrollment and persistence. We describe the post-graduation outcomes of CPS graduates with extremely limited access to college.[ii] Finally, we draw on data from detailed interviews with seniors in three CPS high schools to take an in-depth look at students' experiences during senior year.

The bottom line is that there is much work to do if CPS is to shift the focus of twelfth grade from finishing graduation requirements to preparing for college and employment or training. Too many students who enter twelfth grade qualified to attend a four-year college are not participating in coursework that would signal to colleges that they are taking an academically focused senior year. Too many students enter senior year unqualified for college and without a viable pathway to employment. Too often, senior year in CPS looks like it is serving the needs of students 30 years ago, rather than the needs of students today. Perhaps most

> **[SENIOR YEAR IS EASY]** because the way our school is set up. Each year you're losing classes. You start off freshman year with seven classes...so it's like of course it's going to be hard your first year. But as you go along, you lose classes, so that burden becomes lighter...It's just the amount of work that you're getting. You're not getting as much as you're used to.
>
> — FRANKLIN, SENIOR YEAR EXPERIENCE

importantly, across nearly all types of coursework, students themselves portray their senior year experience as unchallenging and, for some, wasted time.

A central theme of this report is that there is no single answer to the question, *"What is a good senior year?"* Students are coming into senior year with very different needs. In order to look at differences in needs across students, we group students by their college qualifications at the end of eleventh grade (**see box below**). Some students enter twelfth grade with high GPA's and test scores that make them positioned to attend a very selective college, while others are graduating with such low qualifications that their college choices are most likely limited to two-year colleges. These students might need very different supports and academic experiences. Thus, throughout this report, we focus on identifying the set of issues that educators need to grapple with for students on different trajectories.

HOW WE GROUP STUDENTS BY COLLEGE QUALIFICATIONS

1. Very high grades and test scores (access to **very selective colleges**);
2. High grades and test scores (access to **selective colleges**);
3. Strong—but not elite—qualifications for admission to four-year colleges (access to **somewhat selective colleges**);
4. Very low grades and test scores (access to **non-selective college**);
5. Extremely low qualifications for admission to open-enrollment schools only (access to **two-year colleges only**).

KEY FINDINGS

CPS graduation requirements ensure that all students take a common set of courses from ninth to eleventh grade. It is in senior year that the expectations for and experiences of students become differentiated by race/ethnicity, achievement, and especially by high school.
In 1997, CPS led the nation by raising graduation requirements to align with minimum coursework requirements for college entrance (three years of math, social studies, and science; and four years of English). Most of these requirements are finished by the end of eleventh grade, leaving little guidance about what courses students should take senior year. As a result, there is great uniformity in what most students take during the first three years of high school but wide variation in what they take senior year.

- More than 70 percent of white and Asian American high schools graduates in our sample took four or more courses in core academic subjects during their senior year, compared with 54 percent of African American and 58 percent of Latino graduates.

- Only one-quarter of African American and 29 percent of Latino graduates in our sample took at least one AP class in twelfth grade. In comparison, nearly half of white and 68 percent of Asian American graduates had taken at least one AP class. Similar patterns are observed for fourth-year math.

National estimates of coursetaking also demonstrate the same pattern of widening gaps in the proportion of graduates taking advanced coursework. In this report, we attribute the differences in coursetaking patterns by race/ethnicity in Chicago to: (1) differences in coursetaking by achievement and (2) differences in coursetaking across high schools. The combination of

> **I THINK I'M JUST LEARNING HOW TO THINK BETTER.** Looking back, before we had to memorize, memorize like dates and all these things. Now, it's more about thinking and analyzing and taking facts that you don't have to memorize—you just see them in books—and then coming up with ideas. We spend so much more time talking, discussing things, and writing that I'm learning how to think better.
>
> NADIA, IB SENIOR YEAR EXPERIENCE

these two factors means that African American and Latino students in Chicago are much less likely than white and Asian American students to be participating in a senior year that appears to be preparing them to be competitive in college admissions.

There is no clear set of expectations or consensus on what most seniors who are positioned to attend a four-year college should be taking their senior year. The exception is the most highly qualified CPS students, who generally take an advanced course load. The highest-achieving CPS seniors—those students who enter senior year positioned to attend a very selective college—are generally participating in a senior year that includes a fourth year of math and one or more AP or International Baccalaureate course. This group, approximately 6 percent of graduates, is concentrated in selective enrollment high schools and specialized programs (e.g., International Baccalaureate programs) where students are expected to prepare for and go to college.

In sharp contrast, there seems to be no organizing framework and common set of expectations for students who might be positioned to attend a selective or somewhat selective college. These students, approximately 50 percent of CPS graduates in the cohorts we studied, enter senior year on track for entrance into the majority of public universities in Illinois and a wide variety of private schools.

- Among students who begin senior year positioned to attend a somewhat selective college, only 60 percent took four or more core classes in their senior year, less than half (43 percent) took a fourth year of math, and just one-third took an AP course.

This lack of advanced coursework may have important implications for college admissions. College admissions officers we interviewed emphasized the importance of senior year coursework in admission, enjoining students to take a senior that is *"as rigorous or substantial as possible."*

Given this focus on seniors' strength of schedule, this report looks beyond specific courses to focus on

Senior year coursetaking is unevenly distributed by race/ethnicity

	Percent Taking Four or More Core Courses	Percent Taking Fourth-Year Math	Percent Taking One or More AP Courses	Percent Taking Two or More Vocational Courses
All CPS (N=90,041*)	59%	39%	30%	30%
African American (N=42,162)	54%	34%	25%	37%
Latino (N=30,672)	58%	36%	29%	25%
White (N=11,264)	70%	47%	43%	18%
Asian American (N=5,792)	77%	68%	57%	14%

Note: Numbers in this table come from 2003–09 CPS graduates (N=90,041) who were not enrolled in special education and not in alternative or charter high schools. The sample does not include students who took fewer than four courses in their senior year.

*Some ethnic groups were excluded from this N due to the small numbers of students in those groups.

students' overall experience senior year. We characterize the academic focus of seniors' overall schedule—the transcript those admissions officers would receive.

The majority of CPS seniors have schedules that could be characterized as focused on completing graduation requirements rather than preparing for college. Their schedules fall into five distinct coursetaking patterns. Importantly, these patterns are not simply a result of different achievement patterns. In fact, CPS seniors with the same qualifications are often taking different course schedules. The lack of commonality in coursetaking among students positioned to attend a four-year college is most striking for students who enter senior year with access to somewhat selective colleges. Across high schools, seniors in this group were nearly equally as likely to be taking an Elective Heavy senior year, an Advanced Placement senior year, or a Vocationally Focused senior year:

- A small group of students (6 percent) are focused on making it to graduation and need senior year to make up courses and finish requirements. We categorize this group of students as "Making Up Courses."

- Approximately one in five students with access to a somewhat selective college is finishing vocational program requirements and taking multiple vocational courses in addition to non-core graduation requirements. We call this group of students "Vocationally Focused."

- The most common pattern, which we term "Elective Heavy," consists of students who are taking multiple electives in both core (social studies and English) subjects and non-core (music, art, and physical education) subjects.

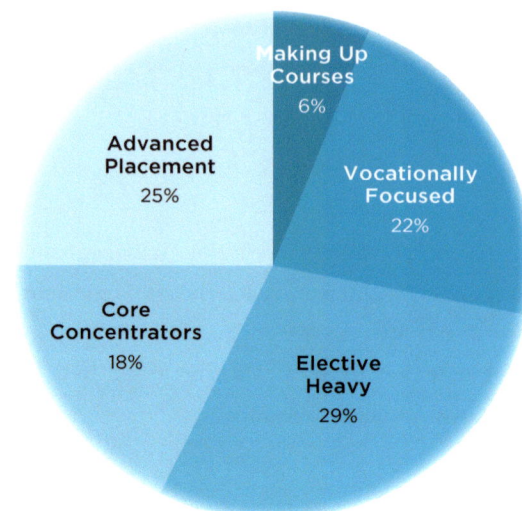

Students who enter senior year qualified for a somewhat selective college have no dominant pattern of coursetaking in senior year

Access to Somewhat Selective Colleges

The stereotype of senior year is that students are choosing easy courses and "coasting to graduation" and thus that the differences in coursetaking we observe reflect differences in students' motivation. What we find instead is that whether students who enter senior year positioned to attend a somewhat selective college fall into an Elective Heavy, an Advanced Placement, or a Vocationally Focused class schedule was largely determined by what high school they attended.

- Among students who are qualified to attend a somewhat selective college, the proportion of students taking AP varies from a low of less than 10 percent in some high schools to a high of nearly 90 percent.

> **[IT'S] JUST BORING.** We ask [our teacher], and he just says it's up to us to know what to do…and I'm just sitting there, like, "Why do they do this to us?"… [we] just sit there sometimes for two whole periods.
>
> SHAYLA, CULINARY AND HOSPITALITY COURSE

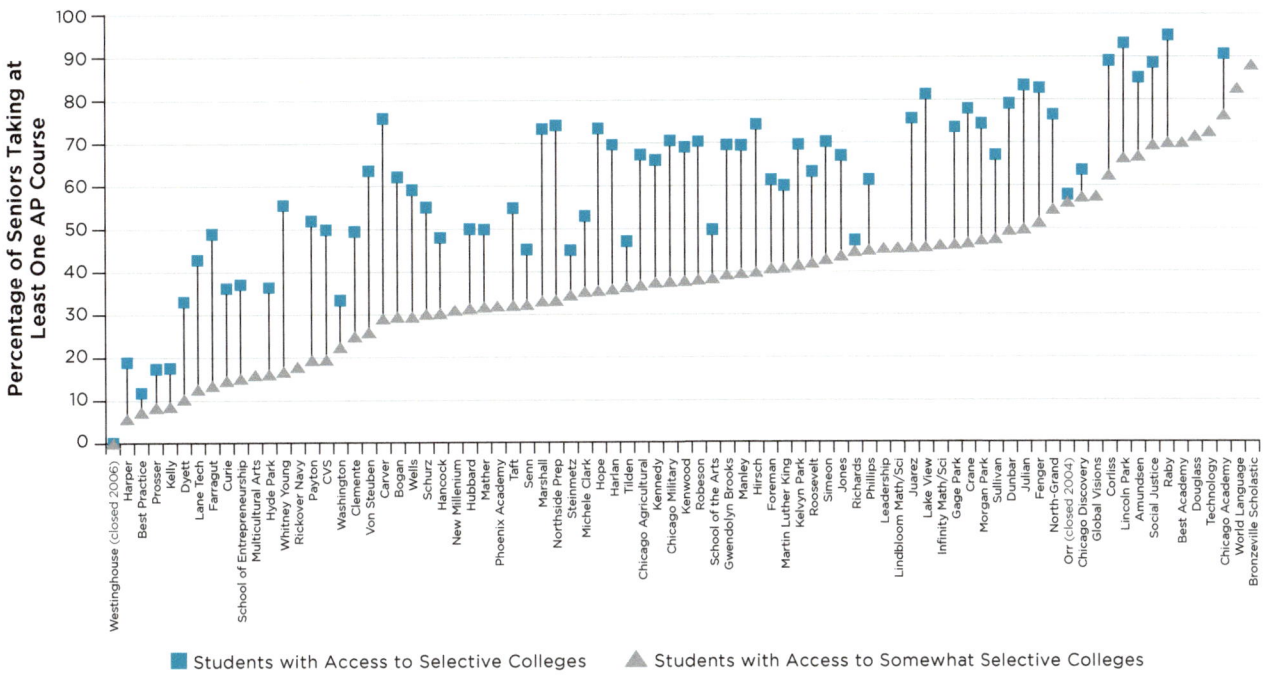

Participation in AP coursework varies widely across high schools, even among similarly qualified students

■ Students with Access to Selective Colleges ▲ Students with Access to Somewhat Selective Colleges

Note: Numbers in this table come from 2003–09 CPS graduates who were not enrolled in special education and not in alternative or charter high schools. Data points were only included if school had 15 or more students in a given category.

Taking Advanced Placement courses and a fourth year of mathematics may shape college access but is not associated with improved retention in college once students are enrolled.

If coursetaking in senior year is associated with college enrollment and retention, then these differences across high schools in their expectations for students may have very real implications for their college access and performance. Estimating the impact of coursetaking on college outcomes is complicated by the fact that students who take AP courses or a fourth year of math may be the most motivated students and thus would have done better in college anyway. To address this problem, often called selection bias, we use an innovative methodology of matching students across schools to estimate the effect of senior year coursetaking on the likelihood that students will enroll in a four-year college, a selective or very selective college, and, once in college, whether they are continuously enrolled for two years. Without using these controls for selection, we would overestimate the effects of advanced coursetaking.

After addressing this problem of selection, senior year coursetaking, particularly taking AP courses, is associated with an increase in the likelihood that students will attend colleges that they are qualified to attend.

- Among students who enter senior year positioned to attend a somewhat selective college, those who took an AP course were substantially more likely to enroll in a four-year college. Those who took a fourth year of math were also more likely to enroll in a four-year college.

- Among students who enter senior year positioned to attend a selective college, taking two or more AP courses is associated with a substantial increase in the odds of enrolling in a selective or very selective college (i.e., making a college match).

However, while coursetaking is strongly associated with college enrollment, there is no association between taking AP courses, fourth-year mathematics, or four core courses and retention in college. Though we find no effects on college retention, our findings may miss other critical effects of taking advanced coursework. Without college grades and coursework placement, for example, we cannot look at whether

Executive Summary

> **"I GOT THREE REAL CLASSES AND THE REST OF THEM ARE BLOW BY'S.** First period I have Spanish. Second period I got World Literature, and 3rd period I got Physics. The rest of my day is a blow off...4th period I got PE, 5th period band, and 7th period is just a work study class. My class is supposed to be with carpentry and architecture, and I have a job at a grocery store."
>
> — KYLE, AN HONORS STUDENT

participation in fourth-year mathematics or AP courses allowed students to do better in terms of course performance (grades) or avoid remediation.

Making a shift from twelfth grade as the endpoint to twelfth grade as a launching pad will require a fundamental rethinking of senior year on the part of educators.
A surprising finding is that regardless of achievement level and regardless of whether students took advanced courses, the overwhelming majority of the seniors in our qualitative study describe senior year as unchallenging. They characterize senior year as easier than previous years. They describe multiple classes in which little work is required, and often said that they learned so little in senior year that they might as well have skipped the grade.

The primary strategy that CPS has pursued in making senior year a college-preparatory experience is expanding access AP courses. This strategy partly works. Students described their AP classes as being more challenging than other senior year classes and more challenging than similar classes taken in previous years of high school. They thought their AP classes were teaching skills and competencies that would be beneficial in the future.

The central problem with the AP strategy is that is insufficient. Many highly qualified students in our study enrolled in at least one AP course, in addition to whatever schedule was common for students at their school to take. However, adding one or two AP courses does not ensure a challenging senior year. This is in contrast to the experiences of students in our sample enrolled in the IB program who reported a challenging senior year filled with rigorous coursework and skill-building for college.

In addition, the AP strategy does not reach all students. For seniors not in AP classes, English IV often became an anchor, presenting clear standards and goals for students' learning in their final year of high school instruction. Unfortunately, most other classes filling students' senior year schedules lacked this kind of focus. The coherent narrative that emerged in students' accounts of senior year coursework was one of minimal workload and low standards and engagement across the board.

Much of the reason that the students we interviewed found senior year to be unchallenging overall was because their days were dominated by unchallenging elective courses in both core (English, social studies) and non-core (fine art, physical education, and vocational) subject areas. Students described these classes as *"not real," "blow-off"* classes where *"nothing happens."*

Roughly 45 percent of CPS graduates begin senior year off of the trajectory to attend a four-year college with some level of selectivity. These students face rapidly deteriorating employment prospects.
Perhaps the most troubling challenge of this report is the high proportion of CPS graduates who leave high school with such low GPAs and ACT scores that they have only the most limited college options and extremely low odds of succeeding in any college. In a special supplement, "Not in College, Not Working, and Out of Options," we conduct an analysis using both employment and college enrollment data to track three cohorts of these students in the year after graduation. These are the graduates with the weakest skills who are most vulnerable in the job market and in college admissions. We draw on more recent national data on youth employment to discuss the range of problems facing these

students. Employment prospects for these students are further complicated by the fact that nationally fewer than 10 percent of Latino and African American high school students hold jobs, limiting the job skills they are able to gain while in high school.

- In the fall after graduation, the most common outcome for CPS students who have very low college qualifications was to be neither working nor in school. Those who do enroll in postsecondary education are unlikely to persist, and those who find work are substantially underemployed (analysis of the graduating cohorts of 2003-2005).

The current dramatic recession has exacerbated this problem. Nationally, the employment rate of recent high school graduates not enrolled in college has plummeted, from 76 percent in 2000 to 61 percent in 2011.

Concluding Points

Over the past several years, "college and career readiness for all" has become the mantra of education reform in the United States. At one level, this report would seem to take on only a very small piece of this large goal of college and career readiness. The challenges of senior year described in this report, however, demonstrate the magnitude of the problems educators face in creating an educational experience that truly prepares students for life after graduation. We hope that the analysis in this report will inform a discussion of how best to reform senior year, but also spark a conversation about the important challenges that precede and follow this pivotal period.

At first glance, some of the findings of this report may lend themselves to a rules-based solution. For example, given the wide variation in students' experiences across CPS high schools, requiring all seniors to take a fourth year of math has a certain appeal. However, the findings of this report suggest that the variation across high schools is evidence of a much deeper problem: the underlying lack of clarity among high school educators about what college and career readiness means and for whom. Coursework requirements may solve the problem of wide variation in students' opportunities across schools; however, such requirements may also create problems, such as putting lower-achieving students at risk of not graduating. Most importantly, however, imposing a rule-based solution does not address the overall poor quality and lack of challenge in senior year courses.

What most needs to change is the culture of senior year, and that will take more than changing requirements. For students who hope to attend college, senior year must be reinterpreted as more than the end of high school and should instead function as a bridge into college. Transforming senior year ultimately requires school leaders, counselors, and teachers to initiate a culture shift in the purpose of senior year. Teachers need to engage in a discussion of what skills and academic behaviors students will need in order to do well in college and how those skills and behaviors need to develop over time. As a first step, educators must become engaged in actively deciding not just what courses students should take, but how teaching within and across those courses will prepare students for postsecondary opportunities.

We need an equivalent shift in culture and a set of new institutional arrangements for those students who get to graduation with low grades and ACT scores. Teachers, students and families need to understand that graduating with a D average is no longer enough. The first priority is to intervene earlier and ensure that students do not get to senior year having just passed their courses. Senior year, however, also needs to be as much a launching pad for students who do not go to college as for those who are college bound. Although we are only able to provide a cursory sketch of these students and their post-high school outcomes, their experiences and the prospects they face in the labor market and postsecondary education are a bellwether of the extent to which the transformation in the economy has dramatically altered the landscape for young adults. It has revealed significant gaps in our education and postsecondary employment and training systems that need to be attended to if all students are to successfully transition out of high school. We must consider: What is the comprehensive strategy that would sets students who graduate high school without the likelihood of going to college on a path towards financial stability and viable life choices?

Educators might wonder where to place senior year on their list of priorities. At present, high school leaders have few incentives to address the issues highlighted in this report. High school educators are under enormous pressure to raise test scores, reduce dropout rates, increase attendance, and ensure safety. Fixing senior year would not necessarily solve any of those problems, and as such, might rate as a fairly low priority.

But that is not the case if we are interested in college readiness and access. "Fixing senior year" requires grappling with a number of questions that are crucial not just for twelfth grade but for grades nine, 10 and 11 as well: What sets of skills do students need to develop in order to make a successful transition from high school to college? How do those skills differ for different groups of students? What would it mean to create a truly transitional year? All of these questions provide an important opportunity to think critically about how to transform high schools from institutions largely focused on graduating students to institutions that equip all students for college and postsecondary training. We hope that the analysis and findings presented in this report will provide educators and policymakers with more useful tools to begin this important work.

Executive Summary Endnotes

i Arne Duncan "The Three Myths of High School Reform" Remarks of U.S. Secretary of Education Arne Duncan to the College Board AP Conference July 15, 2010, Washington, DC 20010. (Speaker may have deviated from prepared remarks.)

ii By linking this dataset to data from the National Student Clearinghouse, we are able to identify students' college enrollment and persistence, though we are unable to track more detailed information about students' performance in college, such as grades, remediation, or credit accumulation.

INTRODUCTION

Preparing for Postsecondary or Coasting to Graduation?

Senior year. It's an American iconography—a phrase that evokes images of proms, class rings, and yearbooks. In the decades following World War II, for most high school students and their families, senior year was the end of formal education and the beginning of a transition to work. It was a capstone of their education, and there was much to celebrate.

Beginning in the 1950s and continuing through the 1970s, the United States experienced dramatic increases in educational attainment, driven largely by improvements in the proportion of students who graduated from high school.[1] The proportion of young adults with a high school diploma or its equivalence increased from 54 percent in 1950 to 86 percent in 1980 among whites and from 22 to 73 percent among African Americans.[2] This rise in high school graduation rates and the extent to which increases in attainment were widely shared across racial/ethnic groups make it one of the great success stories in the history of American education. In this context, senior year became the culmination of a unique institution—the American high school—that helped shape an increasingly productive work force, rising income, and an economy that shared the wealth.[3]

But that was then. Over the past three decades, the earnings of college graduates rose while the earnings of young adults without college degrees declined. Getting a high school diploma is no longer a step to entering the middle class. With this new economic reality, a different transformation is occurring in high schools—one that may be equally important as the rise in high school graduation rates for the American education system. The United States has become a nation of college-goers. Between 1980 and 2008, the proportion of American high school graduates who enrolled in a two- or four-year college the fall after graduation increased from 49 to 71 percent, with most of the shift being enrollment in four-year colleges.[4] During that same time period, the proportion of seniors who hope to complete a bachelor's degree or higher rose dramatically across all racial/ethnic groups, with the largest increases occurring among low-income students.[5] Today, over 90 percent of Chicago Public School (CPS) seniors state that they aspire to obtain a two- or four-year college degree.[6]

There is a growing consensus that high schools must adapt to these changes. As U.S. Education Secretary Arne Duncan argued in a 2010 address to the College Board, "High schools must shift from being last stop destinations for students on their education journey to being launching pads for further growth and lifelong learning for all students. The mission of high schools can no longer be to simply get students to graduate. Their expanded mission, as President Obama has said, must also be to ready students for careers and college—and without the need for remediation."[7]

In this changing educational landscape, it stands to reason that students' coursework and activities in senior year are becoming increasingly important. If seniors aspire to attend college, a senior year lacking in serious academic coursework may place them at high risk of academic difficulty and remediation when they enter college. For students who have the potential to

attend more selective colleges, not taking advanced coursework and a college-oriented curriculum may make them less desirable applicants in an increasingly competitive college admissions pool, may place them at an academic disadvantage compared to students coming from higher performing school systems, and may cut off critical college majors if students are missing prerequisites. For students who are not college bound, senior year offers the last opportunity to ensure that students are linked to pathways to employment and training. For all students, senior year offers the opportunity to focus on the development of critical transitional skills that ensure students are ready to meet the academic and developmental challenges they will face as they transition either to college or to work. These possibilities all suggest that senior year may be a critical lever in addressing college readiness and performance, but first we need to understand what matters for which students in shaping specific outcomes such as college access, competitiveness in admissions, and college persistence.

The recognition that twelfth grade is a pivotal year that requires substantial attention is not new. Ten years ago, the U.S. Department of Education established a partnership with national foundations to form a National Commission on the High School Senior Year. The commission's final report called for dramatic changes in twelfth grade to improve alignment between high schools and postsecondary institutions so that senior year courses aligned with the requirements, challenges, and expectations of college environments and engaged more students in rigorous coursework.[8] A decade later, national coursetaking trends suggest that some of the commission's recommended changes have already occurred. In Chapter 1, we show that high school graduates across the nation are taking a more academically oriented curriculum, are accumulating more credits in major subjects, and are taking more advanced courses such as Physics, Pre-Calculus, or Advanced Placement (AP) offerings.[9]

The problem is that these changes in coursetaking are occurring unevenly. There have been dramatic improvements and a closing of racial/ethnic and income gaps in the proportion of high school students who participate in what is often termed a college preparatory curriculum (three years of mathematics, social studies, and science; and four years of English). At the same time, there is a widening of the racial/ethnic gap in the proportion of high school graduates who take advanced courses beyond the college preparatory curriculum. As we will demonstrate in Chapter 1, in CPS much of the difference between the college preparatory curriculum and a more advanced curriculum comes down to what courses students take senior year.

The bottom line is that senior year is becoming the grade in which the expectations for experiences of American students are becoming more—not less— differentiated by race, ethnicity, and income. In high-performing school systems, senior year has been transformed to a time of getting ready for college; a year filled with college applications and deadlines; and a year of taking rigorous courses to gain a step up in college admissions and prepare for the next phase of formal education. In 2009, *The New York Times* invited top academics from around the country to respond to the question: "Are there downsides to pushing many more students into taking these rigorous courses?" and in 2010, posted a video by director Vicki Abeles titled "Advanced Pressure—The Problem with Advanced Placement."[10]

While *The New York Times* queried about whether educators have gone too far in their expectations, a look at senior year in CPS paints a different picture. CPS has become a national leader in increasing enrollment in AP courses. But enrollment in advanced coursework is still not the norm in Chicago, even for students with strong academic performance. Less than half of CPS seniors currently take a fourth-year math class, only 35 percent take one or more AP classes, and 41 percent take less than four academic classes. From these numbers, it appears as though most CPS seniors are not "overburdened" in the same way as students in *The New York Times* story. How important are these differences, and what constitutes a "good" senior year in a school system as diverse as CPS?

Overview of the Report

A central issue we grapple with in this report is that there is no single answer to the question, "What is a good senior year?" The answer depends on whether the focus is on preparing students to enter college or on preparing students to make a more immediate transition into the workforce. It will depend on whether a student is positioned to attend a two-year college, a four-year college, or a more selective four-year college. And, it will depend on whether access to college or success in college is the ultimate goal. There is not one problem, one solution, or one particular group of seniors who need attention. For this reason, this report explicitly looks at senior year from multiple perspectives.

Chapter 1 begins by setting the context. We look at the CPS graduation requirements: What courses are CPS students required to take senior year? We look at the college context: How do CPS graduation requirements align with the expectations and minimal entrance requirements of colleges? And we look at the national context: How do the graduation requirements and coursetaking trends in CPS compare to trends nationally? The national context is important. As noted previously, one of the most significant trends in high schools is that the average American high school graduate is completing more total credits and a more academically focused curriculum than their counterparts were completing just 10 years ago. CPS was at the forefront of raising standards when, in the mid-1990s, it raised graduation requirements to align with the minimum coursework requirements of public four-year colleges in Illinois. Thus, for most of the last decade, most states and districts have simply been catching up to CPS. The most recent NAEP transcript study estimated that approximately 59 percent of 2009 high school graduates had taken a set of courses that CPS requires of all graduates.[11]

While CPS is far ahead of the nation in engaging all students in a set of coursework that would minimally qualify them to enroll in a four-year college, most of these core requirements are completed by the end of eleventh grade. A central finding in Chapter 1 is that neither CPS graduation requirements nor the minimum coursework requirements of colleges give any specific direction for what students should take senior year beyond a fourth year of English. At the same time, almost all colleges stress that they place heavy emphasis on evaluating the "rigor" of students' secondary school coursework in their admission decisions. This context, one of unclear and mixed messages, raises a set of questions that we return to often in this report. Which set of courses signal "rigor" to colleges? And to what extent is there a significant difference between the coursework that minimally qualifies a student to get into the application pool and coursework that enables a student to be competitive in an increasingly well-qualified pool of applicants? In the absence of very clear directives, high school educators and students are largely on their own in determining what courses seniors should take.

Chapter 2 examines how this lack of directives plays out across Chicago's school system by presenting a detailed analysis of what CPS students are taking senior year and how that differs across students, both by their college qualifications and by race/ethnicity and gender. We group students into common coursetaking patterns to develop a picture of what senior year looks like for different groups of students. Our analysis finds that most CPS seniors take a senior year schedule that could be characterized as "finishing up" graduation requirements and not going beyond the basics. They do not take math, science, or AP courses. When they are taking four or more core courses, these largely consist of social studies and English electives. One interpretation of these patterns in coursetaking is that students are choosing to take an easy senior year and are just coasting to graduation. The underlying picture, however, is not so straightforward. Some seniors are not going beyond the graduation requirements because they are making up core credits required for graduation. Some students are finishing vocational credits and non-core graduation requirements (arts, music, career education) and have little room in their schedule for additional courses. This means that there are no easy fixes because many seniors are constrained in their ability to go beyond the graduation requirements.

The findings in Chapter 2 shape the remainder of this report. Our analysis suggests that there are three groups of students that raise different sets of issues for CPS. First, the good news is that the highest achieving CPS seniors—students who enter senior year positioned to attend a very selective college—are engaged in coursework that ranks them in the top 10 percent of students nationally, and we see little variation in their coursetaking patterns across high schools. Ninety-two percent of the most highly qualified CPS students are taking four or more core classes; 80 percent are taking a fourth year of math as one of those core classes; and 85 percent take an AP class (with 60 percent taking two or more AP classes).

We do not observe this uniformity in coursetaking among students with access to somewhat selective and selective colleges, who together comprise slightly over half of graduates. For example, students with access to somewhat selective colleges enter senior year with the GPAs and ACT scores that position them for entrance into the majority of public universities in Illinois. Yet, 40 percent of these students take less than four core classes in their senior year, over half (57 percent) do not take a fourth year of math, and less than one-third take an AP course. Why would students who are positioned to attend a four-year college not take an academically focused senior year? The answer is that the choice of courses during senior year is driven less by decisions that students are making than by decisions that their high schools are making. For students who want to attend a four-year college, there is little agreement in CPS on what courses will provide the best preparation for this important academic transition.

Before looking at the college enrollment of students who enter senior year with qualifications to attend a four year college, we include a special supplement on the post-high school experiences of a third critical group: students who enter twelfth grade with such low grades and ACT scores that they will struggle to gain access to any public four-year college that is somewhat selective. These students comprise over 40 percent of CPS graduates. These are the students with the weakest skills who are most vulnerable in the job market and in college admissions. These students are the least likely to take an academically focused senior year. In Chapter 2, in the insert "Not in College, Not Working, and Out of Options," we conduct a special analysis using both employment and college enrollment data to track three cohorts of these graduates in the year after graduation. For this group, we find that the modal outcome in the year after graduation is that they are neither working nor in school. When these students do work, they are substantially underemployed. We bring in more recent national data on youth employment to discuss the range of problem facing these students.

The bottom line is that in 2011, high school graduates with low test scores—and particularly those with low GPAs—are in deep trouble. Students with poor academic records at the end of high school face limited college options and have little chance of success if they enroll in college. Their employment prospects are equally dismal. Since the dramatic recession that began in 2007, the employment prospects for more recent cohorts of graduates nationally have deteriorated further, leading to the conclusion that CPS students who graduate from high school today with limited college access are essentially "out of options."

In Chapter 3, we examine whether differences in norms and expectations for students across high schools are associated with differences in college enrollment and college retention. One of the most striking findings in Chapter 2 is that differences in senior coursetaking are largely driven by which high school students attend. This is particularly true for students who enter twelfth grade positioned to attend a selective or somewhat selective college. Because of the wide variation in senior coursetaking, we can identify groups of students across schools that look very much alike in terms of their academic characteristics and background prior to twelfth grade but who take different courses because of the school they attend. Using an innovative approach, we examine whether taking AP courses, taking a fourth year of math, and taking an academically focused senior year was each associated with a student's likelihood to enroll in a four-year college, to enroll in a selective or very selective college, and to stay continuously enrolled in a four-year college for two years.

What specific courses students take senior year is one way to assess the quality of the senior year experience. Being college ready, however, means more than taking the right courses. It is also about what happens within and across these courses. In its 2002 report *Greater Expectations*, the Association of American Colleges and Universities (AACU) concluded:

> The senior year of high school should ideally be a time for students to undertake work approaching, in nature and level, that expected in the first year of college. It should be time to synthesize, integrate and demonstrate the learning of the previous eleven years. For many students, however, the reality is quite different. For them, the senior year means rather a waste of time and a loss of educational momentum...[12]

Is senior year in Chicago a culminating and transitional experience for students or a "waste of time?" Chapter 4 focuses on this question by turning to the students themselves. We draw on data from detailed interviews with seniors in three CPS high schools to take an in-depth look at students' experiences during senior year. We present an analysis of whether seniors describe their coursework as challenging, and the extent to which they portray individual courses and senior year overall as a time in which they are working hard and learning.

The findings in Chapter 4 are provocative. The overwhelming majority of the seniors in our qualitative study describe senior year as unchallenging. They characterize senior year as easier than previous years. They describe specific classes in which little work is required, and they often feel like they learn so little in senior year that they might as well skip the grade—essentially confirming the conclusion of AACU. Chapter 4 identifies a range of issues that CPS educators must grapple with if students' senior year experience is to be improved. Most importantly, the findings from this chapter suggest that improving senior year in CPS requires paying as much attention to what happens within courses as to what courses students are taking.

The Challenge of this Report

Whenever a school system takes on a new problem and begins to look at the related data, it will uncover issues that are both disturbing and controversial. Many such areas are identified in this report. We want to applaud the administration at CPS and the leadership at the high schools for giving access to this data and allowing us into their schools. We agree that critical to solving problems is taking a look at where students and high schools currently stand. The issues we talk about in this report are not isolated to Chicago. Urban and low-income students throughout the United States face the same problems and barriers we identify for CPS students. This report presents a multifaceted and nuanced look at senior year. Our findings are complex and do not lend themselves to quick-fix solutions. Senior year must meet multiple objectives for different sets of students as they prepare to transition to the next stage of their lives. For all students, a strong senior year is defined not only by experiences of individual classes but also by experiences across classes. However, approaches to senior year must be differentiated to meet students' needs—this starts with research that does not elide the challenge this complexity presents.

While we raise important sets of issues for schools to grapple with, this report does not offer easy answers for what it would mean to provide all CPS seniors with the experiences they need to move from being minimally qualified to apply to college to being competitive and ready to engage in college level work. This is a significant challenge, but one that twenty-first century school systems must face if we are to bridge the gap between students' aspirations and their college access and attainment. While we do not offer concrete solutions, the goal of this report is to provide educators and policymakers with insight into a range of complex problems in ways that better equip them to move toward multifaceted solutions.

Previous CCSR Research on Postsecondary Outcomes

This Senior Year report is part of an ongoing study from the University of Chicago Consortium on Chicago School Research (CCSR). In 2004, CCSR began a multi-year, multi-method research project, The Chicago Postsecondary Transition Project. The quantitative project is tracking the post-high school experiences of successive cohorts of graduating CPS students and systematically analyzing the relationship between high school preparation, college choices, and postsecondary outcomes. This project also has a qualitative component, which began in the spring of 2005; researchers interviewed a diverse group of students from three Chicago high schools from eleventh grade until two years after graduation and examined differences in the educational demands of their classroom environments through a linked observation study of high school and college classrooms.

The series *From High School to the Future* has released reports that examine the challenges faced by urban students and the supports needed in attaining their educational aspirations:

From High School to the Future: A First Look at Chicago Public Schools Graduates' College Enrollment, College Preparation, and Graduation from Four-Year Colleges

In 2006, CCSR released its first major report from the Chicago Postsecondary Transition Project. The report focuses specifically on understanding why, despite high aspirations, many CPS students are not making the transition to college and why those who do are concentrated in two-year and nonselective colleges. A major finding of the report is that low ACT scores and, particularly, low GPAs are constraining students' access to college and undermining their success once enrolled. A second major finding of the report is that even those CPS students who enroll in four-year colleges are graduating at very low rates. Once again, course performance emerges as an important contributor because students with low grades in high school are very unlikely to graduate from a four-year institution once enrolled.

From High School to the Future: Potholes on the Road to College

Early in 2008, CCSR released a second report, which examined how well CPS students participate in the college search and application process and what barriers they face in translating aspirations into college attainment. In the report, we find that low access to social capital (norms, information, and clear structures of support) means that many CPS students have difficulty managing the process of identifying colleges that match their qualifications and interests. Despite their high aspirations, they are not taking the steps to effectively apply to colleges and navigate financial aid. A significant finding is that although most students have high aspirations to obtain a four-year degree, many do not even apply. Those students who do apply and get accepted often do not enroll. Applying for financial aid is the most significant predictor of whether students who are accepted actually enroll. Concerns about paying for college, misunderstandings about financial aid, and "sticker shock" are important explanations of why students who aspire to go to college ultimately never apply.

From High School to the Future: ACT Preparation—Too Much, Too Late

In the third report of this series, the second of 2008, CCSR researchers look at the reasons behind students' low performance on the ACT and what matters for doing well on this test. CPS students are highly motivated to do well on the ACT, and they are spending extraordinary amounts of time preparing for it. Four key findings emerged: (1) low ACT scores reflect poor alignment of standards and curriculum from K-8 to high school and from high school to college; (2) test strategies and item practice are not effective mechanisms for improving students' ACT scores; (3) ACT performance is directly related to students' work in their courses; and (4) incorporating the ACT into high school accountability is not an effective strategy for high school reform by itself, without accompanying strategies to work on instructional practice.

From High School to the Future: Making Hard Work Pay Off

Expanding on previous work, in 2009 CCSR released a report that focused on the importance of developing specialized supports for the college search and application process for highly qualified students. In the report, we find that nearly two-thirds of this group of students graduate from high school with access to a very selective or selective four-year college. A significant finding is that these strong qualifications do not translate into matched college enrollment. These highly qualified students face barriers to college enrollment that include lack of knowledge about the broad range of colleges available to them and about financial aid possibilities. If they do consider more competitive colleges, they often lack the structured support necessary to navigate the more complicated application.

Working to My Potential: The Experiences of CPS Students in the International Baccalaureate Degree Programme

This recently released report looked at the outcomes and experiences of CPS students in the International Baccalaureate Degree Programme (IBDP). CCSR examined the 12 small-scale IBDP programs in neighborhood CPS high schools across the city that serve predominately low-income, racial/ethnic minority students with little or no history of college-going. This report finds that the success of this program for this traditionally underserved population of students is significant. The analysis strengthens the story told about these students in *Hard Work* and broadly confirms the impression that the IBDP in CPS has given its graduates remarkable opportunities to succeed in postsecondary education. For high-achieving minority students from low-income communities, academically advanced students in the IBDP are more likely to go to college, more likely to go to a selective college, and more likely to persist in college than a matched comparison group. When in college, IBDP students report feeling prepared to succeed and indeed excel in their coursework, often stating explicitly that their experiences in the IBDP provided the specific skills and behaviors demanded of them in college.

This report and in further reports in this series, turn to students' academic experiences and the question of what challenges CPS educators face in raising their students' college readiness. A forthcoming report will examine the expansion of Advanced Placement courses throughout CPS high schools. Ongoing CCSR work focuses on classroom environments that may build students' readiness for college-level work.

CHAPTER 1

What Coursework Should Students Take Senior Year?

The Messages CPS Students Receive and the National Context

What courses should students take if they want to be competitive in college admissions, prepared for college level work, and ready for post-high school employment? This is a simple question with a complicated answer. One common policy prescription is to align high school graduation requirements with the expectations of colleges. CPS was at the forefront of this national trend when in 1997 it raised graduation requirements to align with the minimum entrance requirements of public four-year colleges in Illinois. This benchmark, however, provides little concrete guidance to seniors because most core requirements can be completed by eleventh grade, leaving little direction for senior year.

The CPS graduation requirements make senior year different than any other year. From freshman to junior year, CPS graduation requirements result, at least on paper, in little variation across students and schools in coursetaking in the major subjects—what we call core courses. Some juniors take honors or Advanced Placement (AP) courses, but usually these courses are advanced versions of the same courses taken by their classmates. This all changes senior year; students can meet minimal coursework requirements by taking a fourth year of English and a social science elective. As we will see in the next chapter, that results in wide variation across students and schools in senior year coursetaking.

The problem is that meeting minimal coursework requirements means only that students can apply to a four-year college. It does not mean that students will be competitive in the admissions pool or that they will be academically ready for college. Colleges, however, do not fill in the information gap; in fact, colleges send students ambiguous and mixed messages about what courses to take senior year. Most colleges not only list the minimum coursework requirements but also convey the importance of a strong senior year schedule that demonstrates motivation and a willingness to take challenging courses. It remains unclear what specific courses demonstrate to a college a student's mettle. The implicit message is that courses that make a student eligible to apply to a college may not be the courses that make a student an attractive candidate for admission.

In the absence of clear direction from either CPS or colleges, we might expect to observe widening gaps across students and schools in coursetaking. In the next chapter, we find just that pattern. This is not just a Chicago phenomenon; we see the same pattern nationally—a greater proportion of students are completing a high school curriculum that, like CPS's graduation requirements, meets the minimum coursework requirements of the majority of four-year colleges. Yet it is in the area of advanced coursework (e.g., AP or a fourth year of math) that we continue to see very low participation and growing gaps by race/ethnicity and income.[13] In school systems like CPS, taking advanced coursework in senior year accounts for much of the difference between meeting minimum admissions criteria and being competitive in admissions. In Chapter 3, we test this assertion directly by examining whether differences across schools in participation in advanced coursework is associated with college enrollment and persistence.

The next three chapters focus on making sense of how the lack of requirements and the mixed and ambiguous messages that students, teachers, and administrators receive ultimately shape coursetaking patterns, students' college enrollment, and their academic experiences in twelfth grade. This chapter sets the context for that analysis. We examine the messages that students receive from CPS graduation requirements and from colleges and universities about what to take senior year. We also set the broader context by describing trends in coursetaking nationally. This national context is important, both to determine where CPS seniors stand compared to their counterparts nationally and because many of the trends we observe in this report are reflected in coursetaking patterns throughout the nation.

CPS Graduation Requirements

What courses students take senior year largely depends upon the credits they need for graduation, norms of the high schools regarding course offerings, requirements of particular high school programs, and students' own interest and motivation. Students' most basic task senior year is to make sure that they are eligible to graduate. To graduate, CPS students must meet two sets of benchmarks. First, they must accumulate at least 24 high school credits. Second, they need to take and pass the specific courses that are required for graduation. **Table 1** shows CPS's current graduation requirements, which were adopted in 1997 when CPS ended remedial coursework and aligned new graduation requirements with the minimum entrance requirements of most four-year colleges in Illinois (see *College for All Summary*).

TABLE 1
CPS graduation requirements

Core Courses	
4 Credits of English	English I, II, III, IV
3 Credits of Math	Algebra, Geometry, Advanced Algebra/Trigonometry
3 Credits of Science	Biology and two of the following: Chemistry, Earth and Space Science, Environmental Science, or Physics
3 Credits of Social Science	World Studies, U.S. History, Other Social Science
2 Credits of World Language	Course I and Course II
Electives and Requirements	
2 credits of Fine Arts	Art or Drafting and Music
2 credits of Physical Education or ROTC	
2 credits of Career Education or ROTC	
3 credits of electives	

College for All Summary

In an attempt to increase academic rigor and prepare all students for college, CPS mandated new graduation requirements for all students in all high schools. Beginning with entering freshmen in 1997, the policy ended remedial classes and required four years of English; three years of math (Algebra, Geometry, and Advanced Algebra/Trigonometry); three years of laboratory science (Biology and two of the following: Chemistry, Earth and Space Science, Environmental Science, or Physics); and three years of social science (World Studies, U.S. History, and an elective). CCSR research has found that the policy had a number of both intended and unintended effects, most notably that, while the policy did expose many more students to college-preparatory courses, it failed to boost achievement.

One substantial result of the policy was a reduction in tracking. Allensworth, et al (2009) found that, after the policy's implementation, virtually all CPS ninth-graders were enrolled in both English I and Algebra I. The gaps in course enrollment by race and ethnicity that existed prior to policy largely disappeared afterwards. Science and math course completion rose significantly during this time period. Two years prior to the 1997 policy change, most CPS graduates had not passed more than one science course, and only 60 percent of students progressed as far as Algebra II in the math sequence. After the policy, nearly all graduates completed three years of science and math through Algebra II.[A]

However, while students were considerably more likely to earn English I, Algebra II, and science credits, researchers found no evidence of broader effects on academic outcomes as a result of the policy. Test scores in math and English were unaffected by the increase in college-preparatory coursework. Furthermore, grades declined in both subjects for lower-skill students, and these students were significantly more likely to fail ninth-grade English or math. Absenteeism also significantly increased among students with stronger skills. Students' science skills did not appear to improve, with five out of six CPS students averaging a C or lower in science courses after the policy change.[B]

If the intent of the new graduation requirements was to help more students make a successful transition to college, there is little evidence that this was achieved. The new policy also had unintended negative consequences for high-achieving students, who were actually less likely than before to take the science course sequence required at competitive colleges and less likely to progress to Pre-Calculus. Students were no more likely to enroll in college or remain in college after the policy. In fact, college-going rates actually declined slightly in the years following the policy, especially among students with the highest levels of achievement.

What is most striking about CPS graduation requirements is how little guidance they provide students about which courses to take as seniors. **Table 2** shows the suggested schedule from the CPS high school handbook for how students might distribute their requirements across their high school careers. In senior year, students must complete a fourth year of English; the handbooks also suggests that seniors complete the third required social studies course and the remainder of their elective requirements. An elective is defined as any course that is not specifically named as a graduation requirement but can be used to fulfill the three-elective requirement. Thus, senior year electives could include one or more of the following: a fourth year of math or science; an additional English or social studies course; a third year of world language; or an additional music, art, physical education, or career education class. Students could also take many of those courses as an honors course or AP class. Depending on what courses a student's high school offers, a CPS twelfth grade schedule could range anywhere from rigorous and academically advanced to undemanding and unchallenging. As we examine more closely in Chapter 2, this results in students having widely varying senior schedules—even among students with similar qualifications.

The Expectations of Colleges: What Makes Students Competitive in the Admission Process?

If CPS graduation requirements provide little direction on what students should take senior year, the problem is compounded by the ambiguous messages students receive from colleges. We used two sources of information to assess the messages that colleges send to students about the specific courses seniors should take and the overall importance of senior year coursework. First, we looked at the courses that colleges require and recommend through the most readily available sources of data (e.g., college websites, and college planning websites such as the College Board). Second, we interviewed admissions officers at colleges that are often attended by CPS students. We asked admissions officers what they were looking for in an applicant, how they used senior coursework in making admissions decisions, and what advice they gave to juniors about which classes they should take senior year (see *Expectations from Admissions Offices* on p. 20).

We find that colleges often do not present a clear standard for the coursework that they expect applicants to have completed in high school. To illustrate, for eight local colleges, **Table 3** presents the information

TABLE 2

The CPS high school graduation requirements give little guidance for what seniors should take

Sample General High School Course Schedule					
Subject Area	Freshman Year	Sophomore Year	Junior Year	Senior Year	Credits Earned
English	English I	English II	English III	English IV	4
Mathematics	Algebra	Geometry	Advanced Algebra and Trigonometry		3
Science	Biology	Lab Science	Lab Science		3
Social Science	World Studies	United States History		Third Social Science Course	3
World Language		World Language Year I	World Language Year II		2
Fine Arts	Art or Music		Music or Art		2
Career Education			Career Education or ROTC	Career Education or ROTC	2
Physical Education		Physical Education I/Health, or ROTC/Health	Physical Education II/ Drivers Education or ROTC II/ Drivers Education		2
Electives				Electives (3)	3

TABLE 3

Colleges send mixed signals about what courses students should take (required versus recommended)

College	Selectivity of College	How Important is "Rigor of Students'" Coursework?	English	Math	Science	Social Studies and History	Foreign Language
Dominican University	Somewhat	Very Important	(4 Rec)	(3 Rec)	(3 Rec)	(3 Rec)	(2 Rec)
Northern Illinois University	Somewhat	Very Important	4	2 (4 Rec)	2 (4 Rec)	3 (4 Rec)	1 (2 Rec)
Southern Illinois University, Carbondale	Somewhat	Considered	4	3	3	3	—
University of Illinois at Chicago	Somewhat	Very Important	4	3 (4 Rec)	3	3	2
DePaul University	Selective	Very Important	4	3	3	—	(2 Rec)
Lake Forest College	Very Selective	Very Important	4	3 (4 Rec)	3 (4 Rec)	4	2 (4 Rec)
University of Illinois, Urbana-Champaign	Very Selective	Very Important	4	3 (4 Rec)	2 (4 Rec)	2 (4 Rec)	2 (4 Rec)
University of Chicago	Very Selective	Very Important	(4 Rec)	(4 Rec)	(4 Rec)	(4 Rec)	(3 Rec)

Source: College Board website (www.collegeboard.com—Accessed 5/4/2012)

Expectations from Admissions Offices

We conducted in-depth interviews with admissions counselors at seven colleges* that are commonly attended by CPS students to understand colleges' expectations of students' senior year coursetaking. Admissions counselors from both public and private colleges were interviewed, and the schools ranged in selectivity (somewhat selective to very selective). In the course of these interviews, counselors shared the advice they give to college aspirants as they begin their senior year; their characterizations of ideal candidates for admission to their schools; their opinions of the relative importance of AP and other advanced courses; and general insights into the admissions processes. The information collected in these interviews demonstrates how easy it is for students to receive vague, and sometimes contradictory, signals from colleges about expectations of applicants.

Our goal in interviewing admissions counselors was to understand how students' choices in senior year coursework affect college admittance. Given the disparate and often ambiguous information on college websites, we hoped that the information gathered from these experts would help us to synthesize and clarify colleges' expectations of applicants. On the contrary, we found that these first-hand accounts of the dynamics of college admissions made the question of whether senior year coursetaking matters for admission even less clear. When asked what advice they would give students, the advice was often vague and there proved to be little consistency in answers. Though every interviewee stated a desire to see a challenging core curriculum attempted, the definition of that idea was vague and wide ranging: some emphasized the importance of a higher-level math course, while others noted the importance of grade trends, AP, or completing graduation requirements. In addition, the extent to which the participation in this advanced coursework—in most cases considered above and beyond the basic coursework required for admission—was considered important was unclear and inconsistent. In short, the signals coming from colleges were confusing.

Using a specific comparison helps to illustrate the confusion from a student's perspective. We interviewed admissions counselors from two colleges (here called Urban College and Suburban College), both private selective institutions, with stated minimum coursework requirements that are roughly comparable to the CPS graduation requirements. The

COLLEGE ADMISSIONS INTERVIEWS CONTINUED

interviews, however, indicated that a different set of criteria was used in assessing the strength or quality of the applicant's coursework. We asked the representatives what advice they would give to a rising senior making decisions about what courses to take. The counselor from Urban College suggested students *"consider grade trends"* and pursue a *"college-prep curriculum—for example, an additional year of math or science."* Recognizing that not all students are able to take AP, Urban College stated that a student performing *"consistently well in the coursework appropriate to their ability"* was more important than taking AP coursework. On the other hand, the counselor from Suburban College advised that the *"senior year academic course load be as rigorous or substantial as possible."* For Suburban College, AP matters in admissions. While the counselor did not expect that applicants will have a full AP course load, it was clear that, if a student's high school offers it, the college expects to see some AP on students' transcripts. Suburban College reviews high school profiles in the admissions process and assesses how many applicants from a particular school are taking AP courses—*"if we have a group of students coming from one school, and, just for example, there are three, and one has no AP courses and the other two have a combination of them, that person with no AP course is probably not going to fare as well."* While both schools might use the terms "college-preparatory curriculum" or "challenging senior year" to describe what they're looking for, these two very similar colleges convey two subtly different sets of expectations to applicants. To a student, this is not simply a semantic difference. Were a student to take the advice of Urban College, s/he might choose to focus on earning strong grades in core classes and not enroll in AP courses—a decision that would have negative consequences for the admissions process at Suburban College.

The specific role of AP in admissions further complicates the signals students receive from colleges. AP is not a requirement for admission at any of these colleges; however, the recognition of AP coursework being college-preparatory was mentioned at least anecdotally at every school. When asked for examples, it was common for the counselors we interviewed to volunteer a definition of rigor or challenge that was conflated with AP. Though their definition of a "challenging" or "rigorous" senior year course was not limited to AP, AP coursework was a nearly universally recognized signal of course challenge and quality. The two were concepts virtually indistinguishable, despite counselors' statements that AP was not a requirement for admission. In addition, it remained unclear, based on the counselors' responses, whether students would be penalized in the admissions process for not taking AP. Most counselors reiterated that AP was not a requirement for admission. But their deeper responses imply that AP serves as a credential, giving the counselors confidence that students have engaged in coursework that is preparing them for college. As described by one counselor, AP is *"a bellwether...because it's the outside kind of program, it tends to force a curriculum to be more rigorous because you know they're going to be working towards this exam,"* regardless of whether or not they take the AP exam. Discussing CPS students specifically, another counselor stated that evidence of AP coursework *"puts us more at ease that this student certainly is ready and able to handle college-level work."*

AP was never meant to be a universal definition for rigorous coursework, nor was it created to serve as a credential for admittance into college. The purpose of AP is to provide high school students the opportunity to qualify for advanced standing once in college (Lichten, 2000). In fact, only one counselor spoke plainly about AP; the admissions counselor from the least selective college in our sample stated that taking AP serves *"[students'] own agenda, they'll get college credit, if it transfers...but it won't affect their admission."* The discussion of AP in the interviews with admissions counselors indicates that, for some colleges, pursuing a challenging core curriculum is the minimum requirement expected for admission. There is a distinct difference between the qualified student and the competitive student. Without clearly established expectations, students are left to determine for themselves what constitutes competitive college preparation. This ambiguity further disadvantages applicants from large urban school districts, such as CPS, if confidence in their academic preparation hinges on a curriculum structure outside the district's control.

Note: *The seven colleges listed here are not the same as the schools listed in Table 3.

that students would see when visiting colleges' websites regarding requirements or recommendations for high school coursework. While all colleges acknowledge that the strength of an applicant's high school transcript is an important factor for admissions, a student would have a hard time determining what coursework a standard college would consider "strong." Some colleges, like Southern Illinois University, present a minimum of coursework that is necessary for students to apply and do not make any mention of whether coursework beyond the minimum is desired or even considered. Other schools, such as the University of Illinois at Urbana-Champaign, present lists of required courses versus recommended courses.

Across colleges, there is a lack of common language and expectations around high school coursework. For example, if students follow the curriculum recommended by the University of Illinois, they should take classes in all core subjects their senior year, including a fourth year of math, science, and world language. However, if students follow the minimum coursework requirements as needed for admission, they should only take one English course. There are two important implications of this ambiguity. The first is that the coursework requirements for colleges do not provide a substantially different set of expectations for students than do CPS graduation requirements, which means that there is still little direction for senior year. The second implication is that the minimum coursework that allows a student to get into the application pool at a particular school may be quite different from the transcript that signals to that college that the student is a competitive applicant and well prepared to succeed if admitted.

All of the institutional messages about senior year coursetaking are further complicated by the choice of taking AP courses. AP courses were not explicitly identified as recommended or required by either a college in our online review or an admission officer in our interviews. Over the past several decades, AP courses have become synonymous with the definition of a "rigorous curriculum," leading many districts like CPS to expand AP course offerings as a means of better preparing its students for college. For example, while not requiring AP for admission, the University of Illinois at Urbana-Champaign states on its website:

> Minimum subject matter requirements must be met… The rigor of the curriculum is strongly considered. Illinois appreciates applicants who take challenging courses, including honors, Advanced Placement (AP) or International Baccalaureate (IB) courses if available…. A strong senior schedule is also encouraged, as it also helps show the applicant's commitment to higher education.[14]

According to a College Board review, 85 percent of selective colleges and universities and 72 percent of nonselective institutions state that participation in an AP course "favorably impacts admissions decisions."[15] Eighty-three percent of colleges in the College Board's survey stated that they use AP in admissions "to determine how prepared a student is for the rigor of college academics" and 83 percent also stated that they use AP "as an indicator of a student's motivation/willingness to challenge him/herself."[16] Thus, colleges seem to use enrollment in AP as a signaling mechanism, which means that students who do not take AP courses may be at a disadvantage in college admissions. Almost all colleges use language like the above quote from the University of Illinois to convey to students the importance of taking a rigorous curriculum and strong senior schedule. It appears as though both high schools and colleges are focused on AP coursework as a way to help students make a successful transition to college, but how AP coursework impacts this process is unclear. In Chapter 3, we investigate the question of how AP and other advanced coursework affects college outcomes.

National Trends in Coursetaking: A Relative Comparison

CPS was at the forefront of raising standards when it increased its graduation requirements in 1997. But it is no longer alone. Many states and districts have followed suit.[17] One of the most significant trends in American education over the past 30 years is that the average high school student is taking more credits, more core courses, and more advanced coursework. From 1982 to 2005, the average number of credits a high school graduate accumulated rose from 21.6 to 26.7.[18] Almost all of this increase came from core academic courses; the average high school graduate in 2005 took an additional year or more of science, foreign language, and math (above Algebra I), compared to a 1982 graduate (see Figure 1).

These increases in coursetaking in core subject areas mean that many more students across the nation are positioned to be able to apply to four-year colleges. The National Assessment of Educational Progress (NAEP) tracks trends in coursetaking using data from a national sample of high school transcripts. NAEP groups students' transcripts into four categories: *a standard curriculum* (four credits of English; three each in social studies, math, and science); *a mid-level curriculum*, analogous to CPS's graduation requirements (a standard curriculum plus at least two courses in Biology, Chemistry, and Physics; and one credit of world language); *a rigorous curriculum* (a standard curriculum plus four years math including Pre-Calculus or higher, and three years of world language); and *below standard* (students who do not fulfill the standard curriculum).[19] In 2009, 13 percent of graduates in the NAEP transcript study took a rigorous curriculum, 46 percent of graduates completed a mid-level curriculum, and 16 percent took a standard curriculum.[20] This means that about 25 percent of graduates took a below standard curriculum.

The dramatic increase in the proportion of high school graduates who took at least a mid-level curriculum is one of the most significant changes in American high schools of the past 20 years. In 1990, less than one-third (31 percent) of high school graduates had taken at least a mid-level curriculum.[21] By 2009, the majority (59 percent) of high school graduates nationally met this mark.[22] Most important, as illustrated in Figure 2, the racial/ethnic gaps in the proportion of graduates who took at least a mid-level curriculum have closed over time. In 1990, less than one-fourth of African American and Latino high school graduates had taken at least a mid-level curriculum—a rate much lower than their white peers.[23] By 2009, however, the gap had closed between high school graduates who are African American and Latino and high school graduates who are white.

The story is less sanguine when looking at the proportion of high school graduates taking more advanced coursework (see Figure 3). At the higher levels of coursetaking, the opposite trend is occurring—racial/ethnic gaps are widening. White and Asian American high school graduates are substantially more likely than African

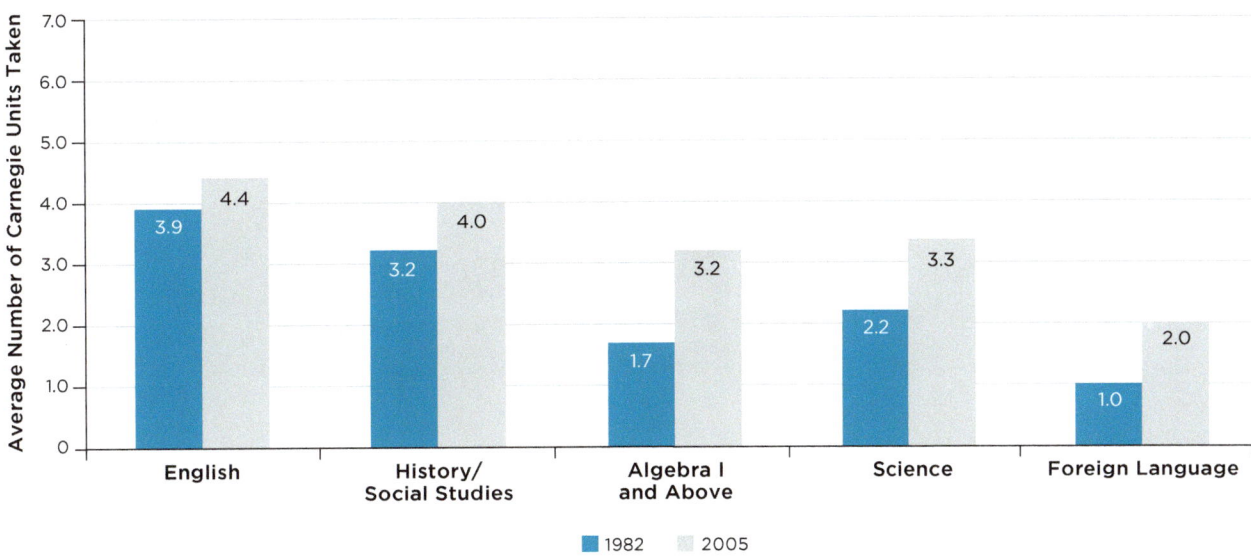

FIGURE 1

Nationally, since 1982, the amount of coursework completed by high school graduates has increased significantly

■ 1982   ☐ 2005

Note: Coursework is measured as the average number of Carnegie units earned by high school graduates. Coursetaking patterns were only slightly lower for African American and Latino students in every category. For example, in 2005 the average number of Carnegie units taken by graduates in Algebra or above was 3.2 for whites, 3.0 for African American and 2.8 for Latinos.

Source: U.S. Department of Education, National Center for Education Statistics, High School and Beyond Longitudinal Study of 1980 Sophomores (HS&B-So: 80/82), "High School Transcript Study"; and 1987, 1990, 1994, 1998, 2000, and 2005 High School Transcript Study (HSTS). (This table was prepared January 2007.)

FIGURE 2

Nationally, the percentage of seniors who had taken at least a mid-level curriculum has increased significantly across race/ethnicity

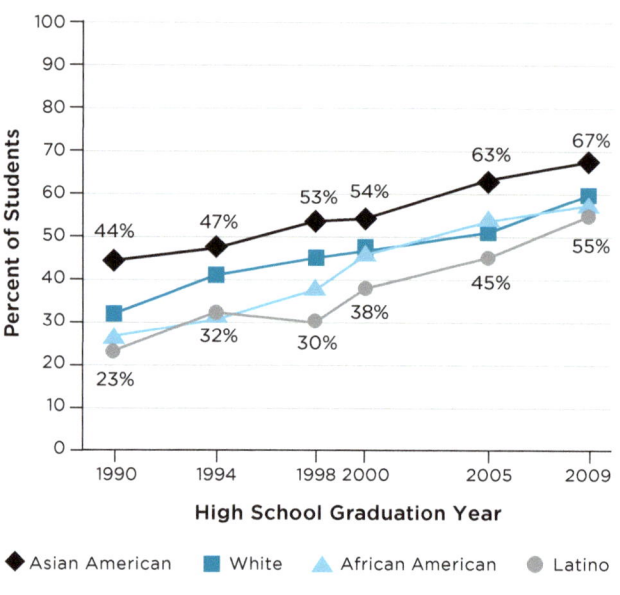

Note: This figure represents the proportion of graduates taking a mid or higher level curriculum 1990 to 2009.

Source: U.S. Department of Education, Institute of Education Sciences, National Center for Education Statistics, NAEP High School Transcript Study (HSTS), various years, 1990–2009.

American and Latino students to take an advanced math course (i.e., above the level of Algebra II/Trigonometry), nearly twice as likely to receive an AP or IB credit, and more likely to take advanced science.[24] These coursetaking differences mean that Latino and African American seniors are much less likely than their white and Asian American peers to have taken what the NAEP characterizes as a "rigorous curriculum." From 1990 to 2009, the proportion of high school graduates in the NAEP transcript study who had taken a rigorous curriculum increased from 5 to 14 percent among white students and from 13 to 29 percent among Asian American students.[25] By comparison, in 2009, only 6 percent of African American and 8 percent of Hispanic seniors in the NAEP transcript study were classified as having taken a "rigorous curriculum," a rate that remained unchanged since 2005.[26]

For most high school students, these advanced courses are taken in senior year. Thus, while we can conclude that nationally more students of all racial/ethnic groups meet the minimum requirements for entrance into a four-year college, coursetaking in the senior year is where we continue to observe differences

FIGURE 3

Nationally, the percentage of students taking advanced courses differs significantly by race/ethnicity

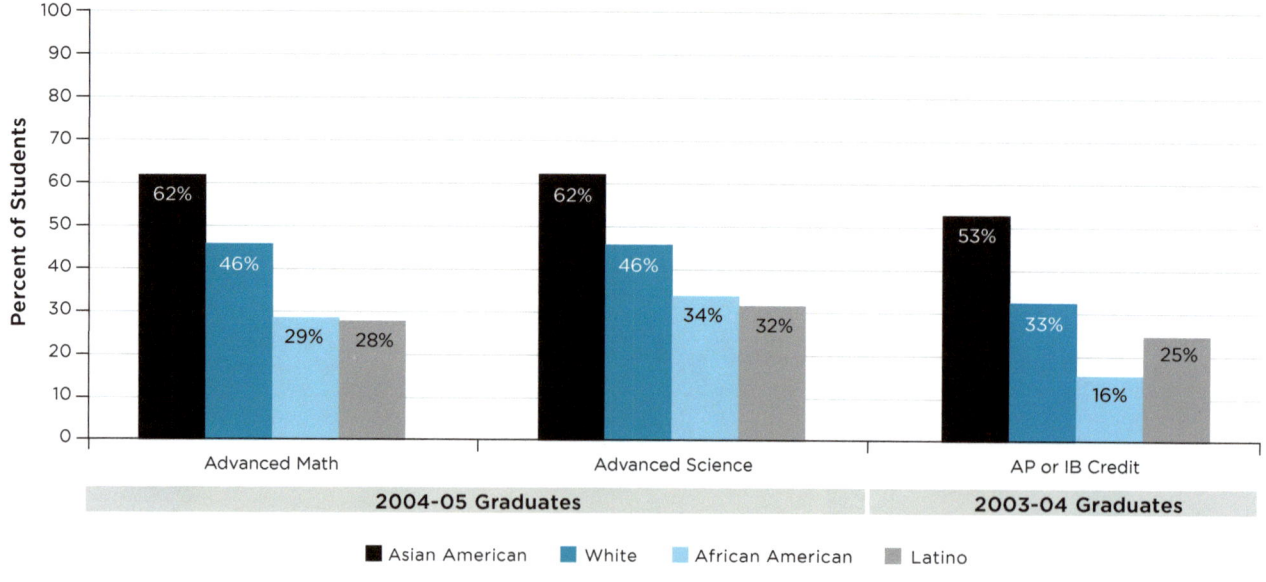

Note: This figure represents the percentage of high school graduates taking advanced courses by race for the years 2003-04 and 2004-05.

Source for Midlevel Curriculum, Advanced Math and Advanced Science: U.S. Department of Education, Institute of Education Sciences, National Center for Education Statistics, High School Transcript Study (HSTS), 2005

Source for AP or IB credit: Planty, M., Bozick, R., and Ingels, S.J. (2006). Academic Pathways, Preparation, and Performance—A Descriptive Overview of the Transcripts from the High School Graduating Class of 2003-04 (NCES 2007-316). U.S. Department of Education, National Center for Education Statistics. Washington, DC: U.S. Government Printing Office.

by race/ethnicity. If advanced coursetaking matters in students' likelihood of gaining admission to four-year colleges, Latino and African American students may be disadvantaged in that process.

Summary

By the end of junior year, most CPS students are making concrete decisions about about their college plans. They have taken their ACT, and the GPA that they will be reporting on college applications has been largely set. Their next step is to decide what courses to take in senior year. In this chapter, we looked at the messages students receive to guide that decision. What we found was a significant information gap and many confusing messages about what matters. CPS graduation requirements provide little direction to students other than to take English IV. Colleges send ambiguous messages, stressing the importance of taking rigorous senior year courses without being explicit about what those courses are—being particularly and problematically vague around the role of AP courses. Students need to understand the difference between being minimally qualified and being competitive in the application process—required versus recommended coursework—and how that difference matters for college admission and/or college success. Unless educators in the high school have answers, first-generation college students may be at risk if they feel as though a set of unwritten rules governs this process.

One of the most significant findings in our previous report *Potholes on the Road to College* was how much the college-going cultures of schools influenced whether students with college aspirations effectively participated in the college search and application. As we summarized:

> Across all of our analyses, the single most consistent predictor of whether students took steps toward college enrollment was whether their teachers reported that their high school had a strong college climate... Indeed, students who attended high schools in which teachers reported a strong college climate were significantly more likely to plan to attend a four-year school, apply, be accepted, and enroll.[27]

The influences of school culture and norms are even greater when it comes to coursework; seniors are dependent on their high school to offer the advanced courses. Most importantly, unlike students' participation in college application, high schools educators have direct control over what students take senior year; the school decides what courses to offer and how accessible those courses are. Closing the information gap may be a critical component of creating a college-going culture. Ultimately what matters most is how educators in their high schools—not the high school students—interpret these mixed messages. As we will see in the next chapter, CPS high schools are making very different decisions about what courses most groups of students should be taking in their senior year.

Finally, national trends in coursetaking tell two different stories. Encouragingly, the proportion of students who are taking a mid-level curriculum—one that meets the minimal coursework requirements of most four-year colleges—has increased significantly, concurrent with dramatic reductions in gaps across racial/ethnic groups. However, despite what is now almost equivalent aspirations for college completion, racial/ethnic gaps in participation in advanced coursetaking are widening. In many school systems, this gap is due to what students take senior year. In the next chapter, we find the same pattern in coursework in CPS. This context is important because it demonstrates that the problem of senior year is not unique to Chicago but reflects a set of critical issues that faces school systems across the country.

CHAPTER 2

Making Sense of Senior Year in the Chicago Public Schools

Throughout this report, we grapple with the question of what makes a "good" senior year. A starting place for that discussion is to get a clear picture of what senior year looks like in CPS. In this chapter, we use a quantitative approach to describe senior year on the basis of what courses students are taking. In Chapter 4, we address the same question using qualitative data, which allows us to examine the experience of students within and across these classes.

As we will see in this chapter, at present there is no typical senior year in CPS. What courses students take senior year differs widely across students and schools—whether their schedule is dominated by core courses (English, math, science, foreign language, and social studies) or non-core classes (art, music, physical education, and career education); whether they enroll in advanced courses like AP; or whether their schedule is filled with electives. The goal of this chapter is to make sense of these coursetaking patterns, explore the variation across students, and identify the main drivers that explain the variation we observe. This overview allows us to identify the set of issues educators and policymakers must grapple with in assessing whether senior year is meeting the needs of students.

If one looked at the senior year course schedules of the majority of CPS seniors, twelfth grade coursework would likely be characterized as focused on completing graduation requirements rather than preparing for college. Some students are trying to make it to graduation and need senior year to make up courses and finish requirements. Approximately one in five graduates are finishing their Education to Careers (ETC) program of study by taking multiple ETC classes and additional non-core graduation requirements. Many students are also taking what could be characterized as an "elective heavy" senior year. With most seniors having completed their three required math and science courses by eleventh grade, the most common courses in senior year are electives in both core (social studies and English) subjects and non-core (music, art, and physical education) subjects, a schedule that fits the stereotype of seniors choosing to "coast to graduation." This means that the majority of CPS seniors are not going beyond the basic graduation requirements and taking AP courses, a fourth year of math, or, as we will see in this chapter, a schedule that signals a strong senior year. It also means, as we will see in Chapter 4, that many students' senior year course load is dominated by classes that students describe as largely unchallenging.

In this chapter, we conclude, however, that the lack of advanced coursetaking in CPS is driven primarily by the norms and practices of high schools rather than student choice. Across the district, the highest achieving students in CPS are nearly universally enrolled in an academically strong senior year. At the other extreme, CPS seniors with the lowest achievement who are the most vulnerable in the transition to college or work are the least likely to take an academically focused senior year. In between these two groups are students who enter senior year with test scores and grades that should make them eligible to attend a four-year college, and high school educators are making very different decisions across schools about what courses these students should take. The most important implication of this lack of consensus is that what students take senior year—whether their coursetaking demonstrates a "rigorous" schedule or simply the completing graduation requirements—largely depends upon which high school they attend.

The combination of senior year coursetaking being stratified by achievement as well as across high schools means that African American and Latino students in Chicago are much less likely than white/other ethnic and Asian American students to be participating in a senior year that appears to be preparing them to be competitive in college admissions. In this chapter, we develop these findings by identifying common coursetaking patterns in twelfth grade, describing how these coursetaking patterns differ by race/ethnicity and achievement and looking across students and schools to identify the central "drivers" that explain those coursetaking patterns.

Senior Year in CPS

As students move into senior year, there is a dramatic shift in the academic emphasis of students' course schedules, with fewer core courses (especially in math and science). From freshman to junior year, CPS graduation requirements mean that, at least on paper, there is little variation across students and schools in coursetaking in the major subjects. Some juniors may take honors or Advanced Placement (AP) courses, but usually in the same subject area as their classmates. For the most part, ninth graders take Algebra I, tenth graders take Geometry, and eleventh graders take Algebra II/Trigonometry. In senior year, by contrast, there is only one core graduation requirement: English IV. Thus schools and students are allowed a range of choices that results in a wide variation in what students take.

The shift from core to non-core classes and the lack of commonality in coursetaking in twelfth grade can be illustrated by comparing the frequency of participation in specific courses between eleventh and twelfth grade (see Figures 4 and 5 on p. 30). Juniors and seniors in CPS are all scheduled for seven full class periods. Over 80 percent of students in the 2009 graduating cohort took five core academic classes out of their seven total possible courses in eleventh grade. Ninety-one percent of CPS

How We Define Senior Year Courses

Core Course
An English, math, science, social studies, or world language course

On-Level Core Course
A core course that a student should not have taken prior to twelfth grade. For English, an on-level course would contain advanced content (AP or IB), English IV, or an English elective course. Similarly, a student is defined as taking an on-level math course only if the math course taken contains advanced content (AP or IB) or is higher than the level of Algebra II/Trigonometry. This can include Statistics, Pre-Calculus, Calculus, and College Algebra. Because there is no required sequence for science, we count any science course other than Biology or Earth/Environmental Science as an "on-level" course. However, we also made school-year specific adjustments for those high schools, in certain years, that have abnormal science sequences (e.g., most seniors take Earth/Space Science). For social science, an on-level course would be a social science course other than U.S. History and World Studies. All world language courses are considered to be on-level.

Makeup Course
A course that a senior should have taken prior to senior year. For English, a make-up course includes English I, English II, or English III. For math, a make-up course would be Algebra, Geometry, or Advanced Algebra and Trigonometry. Because there is no required sequence for science, we count any Biology or Earth/Environmental Science as a make-up course. However, we also made school-year specific adjustments for those high schools, in certain years, that have abnormal science sequences (e.g., most seniors take Earth/Space Science). For social science, U.S. History and World Studies are considered make-up courses. We do not distinguish world languages courses as make-up courses because CPS high school transcripts vary on whether they indicate the level of students' world language classes and because many CPS students take more than one language in their high school career. We did not want to assume the first level of that additional language as a make-up course.

Fourth-Year Math
A math course that is above the level of Algebra II/Trigonometry. This includes Statistics, Pre-Calculus, Calculus, and College Algebra. CPS students are required to take three math courses to graduate (Algebra, Geometry, and Algebra II and Trigonometry) and can opt to take an additional math course their senior year.

Vocational Course
A career or vocationally oriented course, such as Computer Software Applications, Culinary Arts, Accounting, or Small Business Ownership.

juniors took a science class; and at least 80 percent took math, English, world language, and social studies classes.

In contrast, a required English IV course and a social studies elective are the only common experiences that describe the twelfth grade curriculum.[28] Over 90 percent of seniors take English IV and 79 percent of seniors take at least one social studies course. More than one-quarter of students take two or more social studies courses, opting to use at least one of their required electives for an additional social studies course. The list of social studies electives in CPS is quite long. Students can take a range of history courses (e.g., African American History or Latin American History) or take a course in the social sciences (e.g., Economics, Psychology, or Sociology). Social studies courses are also the most commonly taken AP courses.

The clear shift away from science and math courses and towards art, music, and physical education is illustrated in **Figures 4 and 5**. Only slightly more than half of seniors take a science course and the same proportion takes math. The proportion of students taking art, music, and physical education increases significantly for seniors.

Finally, a significant difference between junior and senior years is that many seniors enrolled in multiple periods of vocational coursework, largely representing students who were enrolled in what CPS at the time called the Education to Careers (ETC) program. The percentage of students taking ETC is similar in eleventh and twelfth grade, but the number of vocational credits those students take increases in twelfth grade.

HOW WE DEFINE SENIOR YEAR COURSES... CONTINUED

Electives

Courses in core or non-core subject areas that are not specifically named in the graduation requirements (e.g., African American Literature, Art II, Journalism), but can be used to fulfill the required three electives. In addition, we refer to social studies classes that are not World Studies or U.S. History as electives, even though some students take these courses to fulfill the graduation requirement of three years of social studies.

How Do We Count Courses that Fall into More Than One Category?

Courses that fall into more than one category (e.g., AP Calculus is a core course, an advanced math course, and an AP course) are counted in all three categories. That is, in the case of the AP math course, the student is recorded as having taken a fourth year of math and at least one AP course, and the course counts as one core course in our measure of four or more core classes.

Why Do We Count the Percentage of Students Taking Four or More Core Courses?

Throughout this chapter, we report the percentage of students who are taking fourth-year math, AP courses, and a total of four or more on-level core subjects. We do this to align our research findings with those of other studies of coursework in high schools. Perhaps the most well-known study in this area is Clifford Adelman's *Answers in the Tool Box* (1999). Adelman drew on transcript data from the U.S. Department of Education's high school longitudinal studies to examine the link between a student's high school GPA, achievement test scores, and high school coursework and the likelihood of college graduation. Adelman created a measure of the academic intensity of a students' high school curriculum that used the total number of Carnegie units students take in major subjects (English, math, foreign language, social studies/history, and computer science); whether students took an AP course; and whether students took an advanced math course.

Adelman and others count the total number of Carnegie units completed in high school in core subjects but do not look specifically at senior year. To adapt this approach to senior year, we used the count of four or more core courses. Students have room for seven courses their senior year. A student who takes three core subjects (e.g., an English course, a social studies elective, and one more major subject) is taking less than half of their courses as core courses. Thus, we chose the cutoff as four or more core courses to identify students who are going beyond the modal pattern of coursetaking and whose transcripts could be characterized as academically focused.

FIGURE 4

The overwhelming majority of juniors take courses in each core subject area

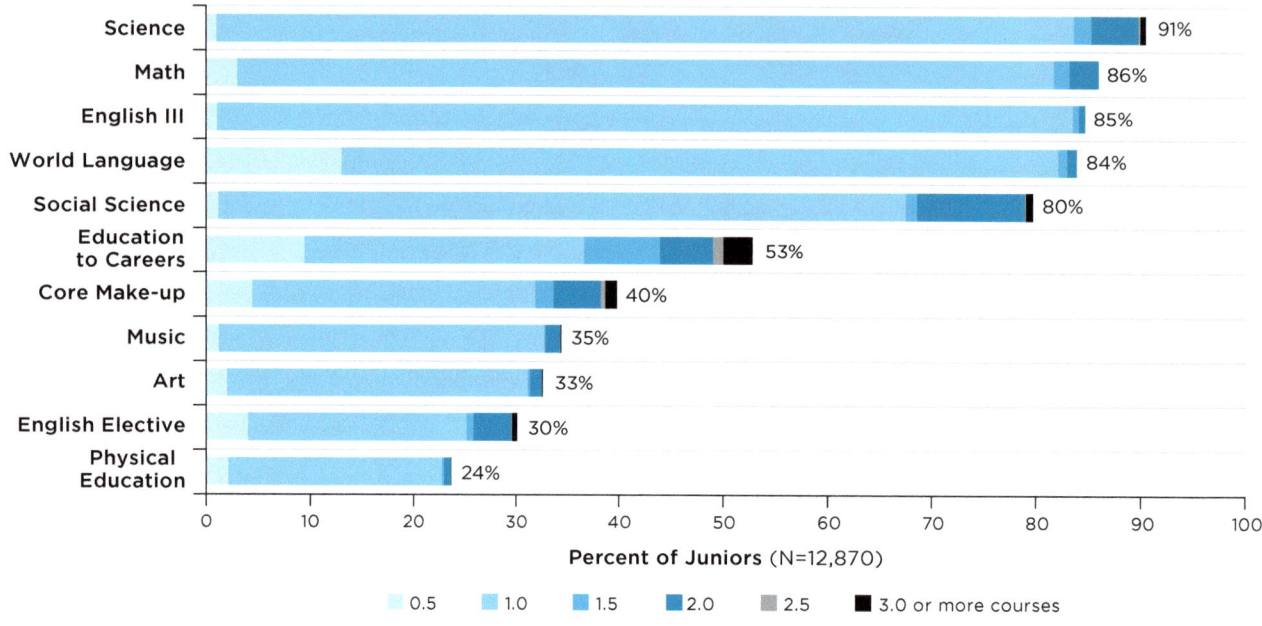

Note: Students included in the figure are those who graduated from CPS and were in the eleventh grade in 2008 and twelfth grade in 2009. The sample does not include students who were enrolled in special education or in alternative or charter high schools. This sample excludes students who took fewer than four courses when enrolled.

FIGURE 5

In 2009, seniors were less likely to take courses in core subject areas, particularly in math or science, than in their junior year

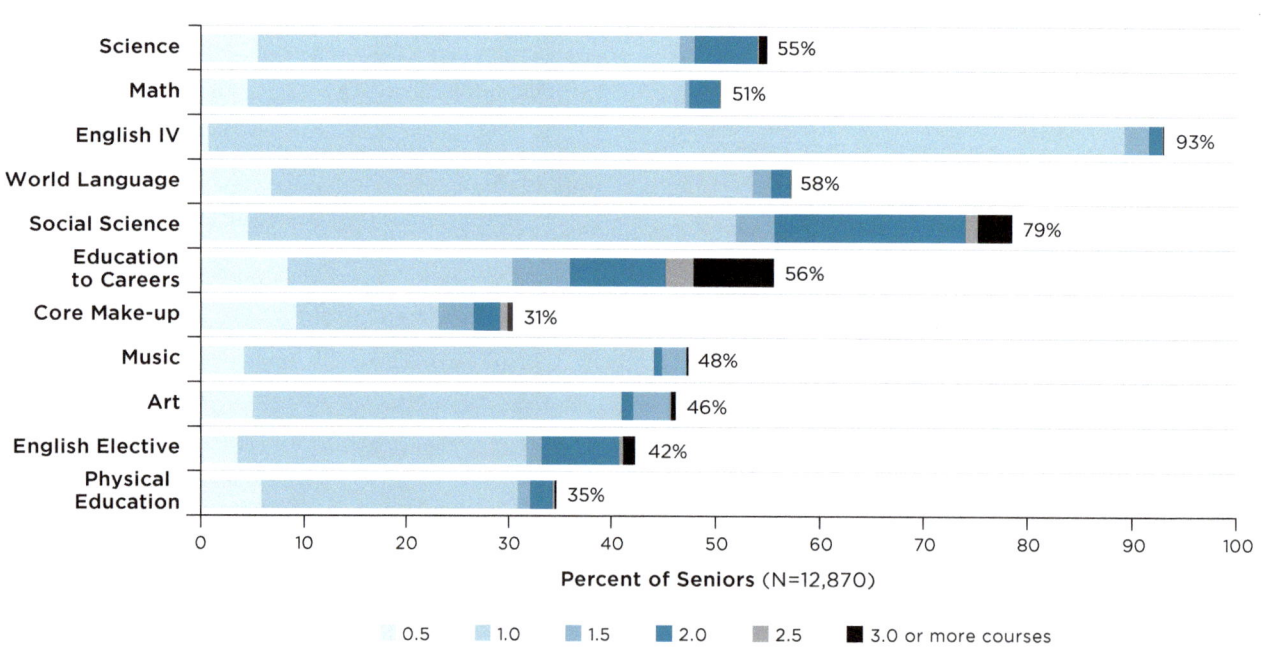

Note: Students included in the figure are those who graduated from CPS and were in the 11th grade in 2008 and 12th grade in 2009. The sample does not include students who were enrolled in special education or in alternative or charter high schools. This sample excludes students who took fewer than four courses when enrolled.

For example, approximately one-fourth of the 2009 graduating class took two or more periods of ETC in their senior year, compared to 16 percent of this cohort in eleventh grade.

Moving from Participation in Individual Courses to a Course Schedule

Comparing the percentage of students who took specific types of courses in eleventh and twelfth grade presents a sharp contrast in the academic focus of junior versus senior year. This descriptive comparison does not provide a picture of how these courses are coming together for students to make up a senior's course schedule. There are two reasons for looking at course schedules rather than simply looking at participation in individual courses. First, looking at a students' full schedule allows us to examine the extent to which the set of courses that students are commonly taking meets the bar of a "strong" academic schedule. Second, looking at students' course schedules also allow us to consider what factors explain this shift in academic focus for different groups of students.

A common interpretation of the lack of participation in twelfth grade in math, science, and more advanced courses is that students are choosing to "coast to graduation." An alternative explanation is that the need to finish graduation and program requirements constrains students' options. For example, some efforts to reform ninth grade, such as requiring double periods of reading or Algebra, have pushed non-core elective requirements (e.g., art, music, and physical education) into later grades. In addition, students who participate in Education to Careers (ETC) need to complete both their graduation requirements and their program requirements, which requires multiple periods of vocational coursework in both junior and senior years.

Resolving these two interpretations—whether the current state of senior year stems from a lack of requirements or an overabundance of requirements that place students in a position of scrambling to graduate—is important because these interpretations have very different policy implications. How best to remedy low rates of participation in math and science courses would depend on whether seniors were precluded from taking math and science because they needed to complete other graduation requirements or whether seniors could take a fourth year of math and science but opt not to. Thus, we can get a much better picture of the nature of these problems and the dynamics that may be shaping coursework patterns by looking at a students' entire course schedule.

Latent Class Analysis (LCA)

In order to look at patterns in coursework, we employed a statistical technique called Latent Class Analysis (LCA) that uses commonalities in the types of courses students took to identify common patterns or groups (see Appendix D). Using data from 2006 to 2009, this analysis identified five distinct patterns of coursework that we characterize as: (1) *Making Up Courses,* (2) *Vocationally Focused,* (3) *Elective Heavy,* (4) *Core Concentrators,* and (5) *Advanced Placement* (see Appendix D for averages of courses taken by each group). The first three groups, which together make up 58 percent of seniors, are students whose course schedules would suggest that they are not going beyond the graduation requirements (see Figure 6).

Making Up Courses

Given very high failure and dropout rates, there is a concern that many students in CPS are barely persisting to graduation and need to use senior year to make up credits. Indeed, a large number of seniors need to make up core credits during senior year. For most of these students, make-up courses do not represent a significant constraint on their schedule. Though 31 percent of CPS seniors take make-up courses in their senior year (see Figure 5 on p. 30), approximately 10 percent need to make up only one semester of a core course and 14 percent need to make up only one full year of a course. This means that about 8 percent of students have schedules that are seriously constrained by make-up courses.

When we grouped students by common course-taking patterns, unsurprisingly, we find this small but important group distinguished by taking multiple make-up courses. We characterize this group as *Making Up Courses.* On average, these students retook almost two full year courses that they had previously failed (see Figure 7). These students also had above average

FIGURE 6

Almost one-third of CPS seniors take an elective heavy senior year

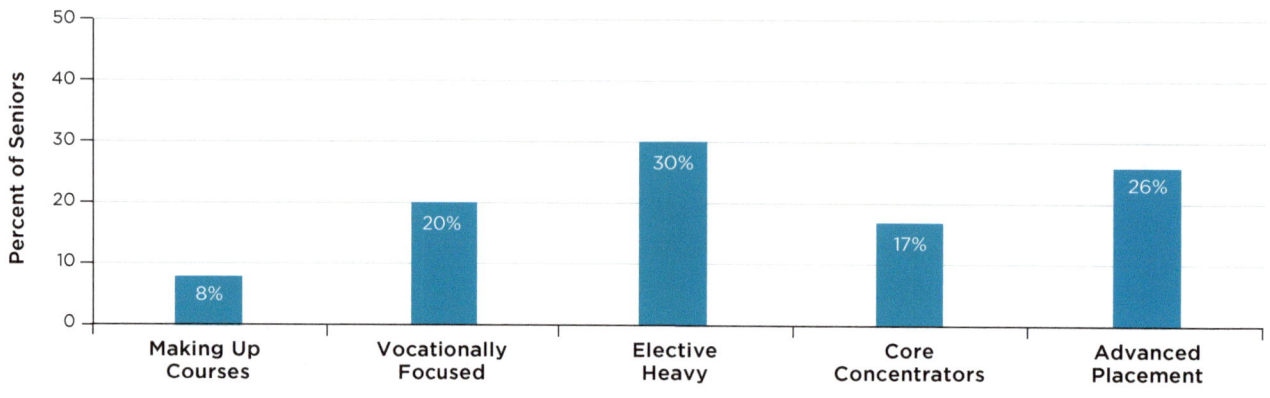

Making Up Courses	8%
Vocationally Focused	20%
Elective Heavy	30%
Core Concentrators	17%
Advanced Placement	26%

Note: Students included in these figures are those who graduated in 2006–09 (N=50,567). The sample does not include students who were enrolled in special education or in alternative or charter high schools. This sample excludes students who took fewer than four courses when enrolled.

FIGURE 7

Sample Transcript 1: Making Up Courses Group

Period	Class
1	British Literature (English III)
2	World Literature (English IV)
3	Creative Writing (English Elective)
4	History Chicago Architecture (Social Science Elective)
5	Fall: Computer Software App (ETC)
	Spring: Earth/Space Science
6	Fall: Physical Education
	Spring: Advanced Algebra w/Trig
7	Studio Drawing and Painting I (Art)

▪ Make up classes

FOR THIS GROUP:

19% Take 4 or More Core Classes

20% Take Math

22% Take One or More AP*

* 48% of students taking AP take AP Spanish.

Note: Students in this group take on average 1.87 make-up core courses; 1.55 Art, Music, and PE courses; and .5 ETC courses—accounting for over half of their credits. Total credits taken for this group = 6.79.

participation in non-core elective courses (art, music, and physical education). Thus, the *Making Up Courses* group consisted largely of students who were using their senior year to make up the courses they needed, finishing graduation requirements, and taking enough credits to qualify for graduation—without those credits necessarily being intended to prepare them academically for college.

Vocationally Focused

A second and much larger group of students—approximately 20 percent of CPS graduates—are students whose course schedules we characterized as *Vocationally Focused*. These are students whose schedules were primarily distinguished by their enrollment in two or more ETC courses (see *Changes in Vocational Programming in CPS* and Figure 8). *Vocationally Focused* students also took many non-core subject courses (art, music, and physical education). Indeed for this group, ETC, music, art, and physical education classes comprised almost half of their schedule. Students in this group took, on average, fewer than three core academic classes in their senior year, including their required English IV class. Only 21 percent of these students took a fourth-year math class.

Changes in Vocational Programming in CPS

Throughout this report, we discuss the implications of vocational programs on seniors' coursetaking options and their senior year experiences. However, our analysis of Education to Careers (ETC) courses predates major changes to the ETC program over the last three years. On January 4, 2010, Mayor Richard M. Daley announced the restructuring of CPS Career and Technical Education (CTE) programs. This restructuring was part of a long-term strategic plan to overhaul what was formerly known as the Education to Careers (ETC) program. There were five broad components in the long-term strategic plan, centered around a goal of driving higher rates of student access and success in college and employment: (1) ensuring rigor and relevance by aligning CTE with industry needs and standards, (2) increasing workplace exposure by expanding business partnerships, (3) creating seamless pathways to postsecondary by strengthening college partnerships, (4) improving student access to CTE programs, and (5) creating data infrastructures to measure and promote progress and success. Thus, it is important to note that experiences of students in ETC prior to this restructuring and remodeling may be quite different from the experiences of students in CTE today.

A major impetus for revamping the ETC program was that it was believed that ETC courses were disjointed in topic, weak in skills taught, and not tied to current industry needs. To address these criticisms, CPS has moved the CTE program to a Career Academy approach in which small learning communities—organized around themes like business, health care, and construction—are developed in large high schools in partnership with local employers. Career Academies have existed for decades, and many have been found by MDRC to be positive models for youth-focused interventions.[c] As part of the Career Academy approach, CPS is restructuring CTE such that almost 300 non-standardized career programs in more than 60 high schools—many of which were supported by only one teacher per high school—are being collapsed into 100-plus College and Career Academies (CCA) at 40-plus CPS high schools over five to seven years.

The experiences of current CTE students also may differ from experiences of students in our analysis because CPS has taken major steps to improve students' opportunities for work-related experiences outside of the classroom. In early 2011, CPS modified its Cooperative Education program (also known as work-study program). As of academic year 2011-2012, high schools can choose to offer one of two course options to seniors participating in a CTE program: (1) CTE Advanced Training Course (i.e., in-class senior-level CTE course), or (2) Cooperative Education (Co-op). Co-op is a yearlong program in which students learn advanced CTE skills both in the classroom and at a local worksite. CTE's modifications to the Co-op program aim to improve student placement and monitoring, potentially addressing concerns brought up in Chapter 4. Strategies to improve student placement include setting minimum hours worked, developing clear job placement guidelines, and clarifying teacher responsibilities in terms of worksite monitoring and student evaluation.

Finally, our findings on ETC coursetaking may differ post-reform because the students who enrolled in ETC programs in the past are not necessarily those who are served by CTE programs today. First, CPS established citywide boundaries, thereby making CTE a program of choice. Now, a student who wants to be in a specific CCA program outside his/her neighborhood can apply to enroll in that program. Also, and perhaps more importantly, in an effort to attract top students into these CTE programs, College and Career Academies now give preference in enrollment to students with above-average test scores (stanine 5+). This change in population may have important implications for the outcomes of high-achieving students who currently are in CTE and for the senior year options for students with weak academic qualifications who are no longer in the program.

Many aspects of the long-term strategic plan for CTE address the challenges of the former ETC program. However, we are unsure whether these changes will have real impacts for students; this outcome will not be known for several more years. However, these changes suggest that CPS is taking a serious step to improve options for Chicago youth who enter vocational programs and/or join the workforce directly after high school.

Chapter 2 | Making Sense of Senior Year in the Chicago Public Schools

FIGURE 8

Sample Transcript 2: Vocationally Focused Group

Period	Class
1	World Literature (English IV)
2	Contemporary American History (Social Science Elective)
	Psychology (Social Science Elective)
3	Culinary Arts (ETC)
4	Culinary Arts (ETC)
5	Culinary Arts (ETC)
6	Art I
7	Fitness Wellness (PE/Health)

■ Vocational Classes

FOR THIS GROUP:

22% Take 4 or More Core Classes

21% Take Math

12% Take One or More AP

Note: Students in this group take on average 6.9 total classes in their senior year. They enroll in 2.6 ETC courses; 1.1 Art, Music, and/or PE courses; and 0.2 make-up courses. As a result, students take less than three (2.8) credits in core subjects in their senior year.

Elective Heavy

The most common pattern of coursetaking in twelfth grade was a schedule comprised predominantly of elective courses in both core and non-core subject areas (**see Figure 9**). We characterized this course schedule as Elective Heavy, because these seniors' schedules are filled with social studies and English electives, as well as non-core electives (art, music, vocational courses, and /or physical education). Very few of these students took an AP course, and less than one-third (30 percent) took a fourth-year math class.

Core Concentrators

The final two groups demonstrate, in different ways, seniors who went beyond the graduation requirements (**see Figures 10 and 11**) and took a more academically focused year. Senior year for students we classify as *Core Concentrators* looks very different from that of the *Elective Heavy* group. As seen in Sample Transcript 4, *Core Concentrators* filled their senior year with academic subjects, taking on average 5.5 of 7 total credits in the four core subject areas (English, math, science, social studies, and/or world language). While these students enrolled in a very academically focused senior year, less than one-fourth took an AP course (**see Figure 10**).

Advanced Placement

Our final group, which we term the *Advanced Placement* group, was distinguished by a high level of participation in AP courses in their senior year. On average, students in this group took almost two AP courses, and approximately two-thirds took a fourth-year math class. This is an important group of students, representing the one-quarter of CPS graduates who had participated in a set of courses that would clearly signal to colleges that they were preparing for college.

Summary of LCA Groups

When we look across students' full schedules, we would categorize almost 60 percent of students as not taking an academically focused senior year. We could describe the first three groups (*Making Up Courses, Vocationally Focused,* or *Elective Heavy*) as using senior year to finish requirements needed for graduation. Though specific coursetaking patterns were different for each group, all three were similar in that neither AP nor fourth-year math was a significant part of their senior year. All three groups participated heavily in both core and non-core electives.

Ostensibly, there is little wrong with taking an Elective Heavy senior year. Social studies electives may be an important introduction to college level work, and art and music could be important subjects that give students an experience that is too often

FIGURE 9

Sample Transcript 3: Elective Heavy Group

Period	Class
1	World Literature (English IV)
2	Drama (English Elective)
3	Urban Studies (Social Science Elective)
4	Spanish (World Language)
5	Computer Software App (ETC)
6	Beginning Mixed Chorus (Music)
7	Physical Education (PE)

■ Elective Classes

FOR THIS GROUP:

65% Take 4 or More Core Classes

30% Take Math

8% Take One or More AP

Note: Students in this group take on average 2.0 art, music, and/or PE courses; and 0.5 ETC courses. The rest of their senior year tends to be comprised of their required English IV class, social studies, English electives, and world language.

FIGURE 10

Sample Transcript 4: Core Concentrators Group

Period	Class
1	World Literature (English IV)
2	Radio/TV Broadcasting (English Elective)
3	Modern World History (Social Science Elective)
4	Physics (Science)
5	Probability and Statistics (Math)
6	Spanish (World Language)
7	Studio Sculpture (Art)

■ Core Classes

FOR THIS GROUP:

100% Take 4 or More Core Classes

66% Take Math

22% Take One or More AP

Note: Students in this group take on average 7 classes in their senior year, 5.5 of which are in core subjects. Students in this group are likely to take an English class, nearly 2.5 courses in social sciences and English electives. This group takes, on average, close to 1.5 credits of math and science. Less than one-quarter, however, take an AP class.

FIGURE 11

Sample Transcript 5: Advanced Placement Group

Period	Class
1	Journalism (English Elective)
2	AP English Lit and Comp (English IV)
3	AP U.S. Government (Social Science Elective)
4	Law (Social Science Elective)
5	Forensic Science (Science)
6	AP Statistics (Math)
7	Photography (Art)

■ AP Classes

FOR THIS GROUP:

85% Take 4 or More Core Classes

67% Take Math

98% Take One or More AP*

Note: Students in this group take on average 6.7 courses in their senior year. These students, on average, take 4.6 courses in core subjects. Of those core subjects, the average student in this group takes almost 2 (1.96) AP courses. These students are also very likely to take math and sciences courses. On average 1.6 of their total credits are made up of math or science courses, including AP. *See Appendix D for more information on latent class analysis.

missing in education. However, there are two potential reasons to be concerned about this concentration in electives. First, if there are students in this group who are applying to four-year colleges, not taking math, science, or AP courses may matter for college access. This is a question we will address in the next chapter. Second, as we will see in Chapter 4, what on paper looks like an interesting and fun senior year too often resulted in a year where little work was assigned and students were in unchallenging classes.

In examining elective coursetaking, an important question is whether students are taking non-core electives as optional classes or taking them in order to fulfill requirements. **Table 4** presents the percentage of students who took art, music, both art and music, or physical education in their senior year. Table 4 then breaks down that proportion by students who took the course as required or optional. Across the identified groups of students, with only minor exceptions, roughly one-third of seniors are taking fine arts electives as required courses. For some seniors, however, these electives constitute a double constraint. For instance, although roughly the same percentage of students in the *Making Up Courses* and the *Elective Heavy* groups took an art or music elective as a required course senior year (roughly 36 percent), students in the *Making Up Courses* group were effectively more constrained because so much of their schedules was already comprised of make-up courses. Similarly, students in the *Vocationally Focused* group took required fine arts courses on top of at least two vocational courses, crowding out academically focused coursework. By contrast, physical education courses taken senior year are virtually always taken voluntarily across all groups. Few seniors were in fact required to take physical education, though many did. For example, nearly half of students in the *Elective Heavy* group voluntarily took physical education during their senior year.

TABLE 4

Forty-three percent of seniors need to complete at least one fine arts class to fulfill a graduation requirement

Group	Required or Optional?	EITHER Art OR Music	BOTH Art AND Music	Physical Education
All Students	Proportion Taking Course	48%	17%	31%
	Took Course as Required	34%	9%	2%
	Took Course as Option	14%	8%	29%
Making Up Courses	Proportion Taking Course	47%	18%	41%
	Took Course as Required	37%	12%	11%
	Took Course as Option	10%	6%	30%
Vocationally Focused	Proportion Taking Course	45%	13%	27%
	Took Course as Required	39%	10%	1%
	Took Course as Option	6%	3%	26%
Elective Heavy	Proportion Taking Course	53%	28%	48%
	Took Course as Required	36%	13%	4%
	Took Course as Option	17%	15%	44%
Core Concentrators	Proportion Taking Course	38%	1%	19%
	Took Course as Required	25%	1%	1%
	Took Course as Option	13%	0%	18%
Advanced Placement	Proportion Taking Course	51%	15%	21%
	Took Course as Required	35%	7%	1%
	Took Course as Option	16%	8%	20%

Note: This table represents graduates from the classes of 2006-09 who were categorized in our LCA analysis. How to read the BOTH Art AND Music column: In instances where students took BOTH Art AND Music courses as a requirement, they took both courses as required. In instances where students took BOTH Art AND Music as an option, students took both courses but either one or both courses were optional.

Distribution by Qualifications for College

An important question is: To what extent are the students in the *Advanced Placement* group just the highest achieving students in CPS who are attending selective enrollment high schools? One reading of these coursetaking groups is that senior year becomes the grade in which students are being sorted by achievement.

It is hard to evaluate the potential importance and implications of these coursetaking patterns without knowing the characteristics of students who are taking different sets of courses. Are AP and fourth-year math reserved for only the highest achieving students, in which case the focus of the discussion should be on the extent to which other students might benefit? Or are students with the same qualifications having very different experiences, in which case the focus should be on understanding what is driving those differences in experiences and whether they matter?

Our approach to addressing these questions is to look at the composition of each coursetaking group by students' college qualifications at the end of eleventh grade. All CPS students take the ACT test in eleventh grade. This means that, at the beginning of senior year, we can get an early indication of whether students would likely be admitted to a four-year college and the selectivity level of colleges that would be most likely to accept them (see *Identifying College Access...*). We group students in five college access categories: access to (1) *two-year college only*, (2) *nonselective four-year college*, (3) *somewhat selective four-year college*, (4) *selective four-year college*, and (5) *very selective four-year college*. Students who have access to at least somewhat selective colleges are likely eligible to attend the majority of public universities in Illinois.

As you would expect given these coursetaking groups, the lowest achieving CPS students (those students who have such low GPAs and ACT scores that they likely only would have access to open

---

Identifying College Access Based on Students' Likelihood of Acceptance at Colleges with Different Selectivity Ratings and College Qualifications (2005 Cohort)

Throughout our work in the From High School to the Future series, we characterize students' academic qualifications using a rubric that identifies the level and selectivity of colleges (two-year versus four-year colleges, and the Barron's selectivity rankings of four-year colleges) a student would likely have access to given their GPA, coursework, and ACT scores. Because all CPS juniors take the ACT as part of the Prairie State Achievement Exam in the eleventh grade, we can get an early indication of the selectivity of colleges that students can gain admission to on the basis of their ACT scores and cumulative GPA at the end of their junior year.[D] The college access rubric identifies cutoffs for each "qualification category" using a multivariate analysis that models the likelihood of four-year college enrollment[E] of CPS students into colleges of various selectivity levels and the modal college attendance patterns of CPS students with different GPA and ACT combinations in prior cohorts (see Appendix E for more information on how we calculate the access categories). We used five categories for this report.

College Access Category	Example of Most Frequent Colleges Among CPS Graduates
Very Selective	University of Illinois at Urbana-Champaign, Northwestern University
Selective	DePaul University, Loyola University
Somewhat Selective	University of Illinois at Chicago, Northern Illinois University
Nonselective	Northeastern Illinois University
Two-Year Only*	City of Chicago Colleges

* Because all high school graduates have the option of attending a two-year college, we categorized graduates with ACT scores and GPAs that fall even below the level necessary for likely admittance to a nonselective four-year college as being limited to attending a two-year college.

enrollment two-year and nonselective colleges) are overrepresented in the group that is making up courses and the group that is elective heavy. Almost 60 percent of the students in our *Making Up Courses* group entered senior year with very weak qualifications (**see Figure 7**). At the other extreme, students who enter senior year with very high GPAs and ACT scores (those with access to very selective college) are concentrated in the *Advanced Placement* and *Core Concentrators* groups (**see Figures 10 and 11**). But what is surprising is that students who enter senior year with ACT scores and GPAs that would suggest that they would be qualified to attend a somewhat selective or selective four-year college are represented in each of these coursetaking groups (**see Figure 12**).

To restate, students with the qualifications to access a somewhat selective college are on track to enroll in the majority of four-year public universities in Illinois. This group comprises 31 percent of the CPS graduating class. Eleventh graders who enter senior year eligible to attend a somewhat selective four-year college are equally represented in the *Elective Heavy, Vocationally Focused,* and *Advanced Placement* groups.

In the introduction to this chapter, we noted that there is little agreement on what students should take senior year. This lack of consensus is best manifested by the fact that students with access to somewhat selective and selective colleges are represented in every one of our coursetaking groups. The result is that there is no modal coursetaking pattern for students who enter senior year likely qualified to attend a four-year college. **Figure 13** looks more closely at the distribution of coursetaking groups for students with access to a somewhat selective college. Among students who start senior year with grades and ACT scores that would likely qualify them for admission to a four-year college, 25 percent are taking courses that place them in our *Advanced Placement* group, 22 percent are taking a *Vocationally Focused* senior year, and 29 percent are taking an *Elective Heavy* senior year. If coursetaking in senior year is associated with college enrollment and retention, then these differences in what students with access to somewhat selective and selective colleges take in senior year may have very real implications for their college access and performance. The same concern arises for students with access to selective colleges. Forty-seven percent of students who come into senior year with access to selective colleges are taking an academically challenging senior year, falling into our *Advanced Placement* group. Yet, at the same time, more than one-third are not taking a college preparatory curriculum with or without AP.

Coursetaking Across Schools Among Students with Access to Somewhat Selective and Selective Four-Year Colleges

Why are students with similar qualifications having such disparate experiences? The central explanation is that they attend different high schools. **Figures 14, 15, and 16** describe the proportion of seniors who enter senior year with access to somewhat selective and selective colleges who take (1) four or more core classes, (2) a fourth-year math course, and (3) one or more AP courses (see *How To Read Figures 14, 15, and 16,* p.40).

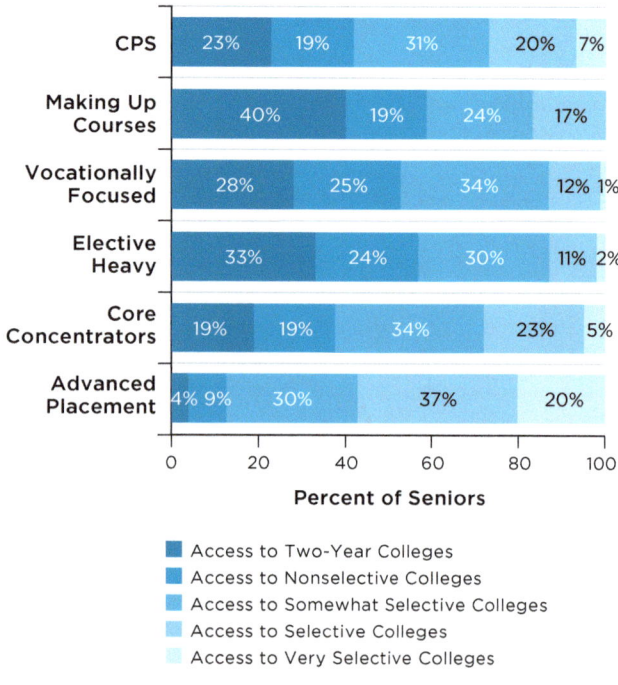

FIGURE 12

Students' junior qualifications differ by coursetaking group

Note: Students included in these figures are those who graduated in 2006–09 (N=50,053). Cumulative GPAs from their junior year were not available for 514 students to calculate their access to college. The sample does not include students who were enrolled in special education or in alternative or charter high schools. The sample does not include students who took fewer than four courses when enrolled during senior year.

FIGURE 13

Students who enter senior year qualified for a somewhat selective college have no dominant pattern of coursetaking in senior year

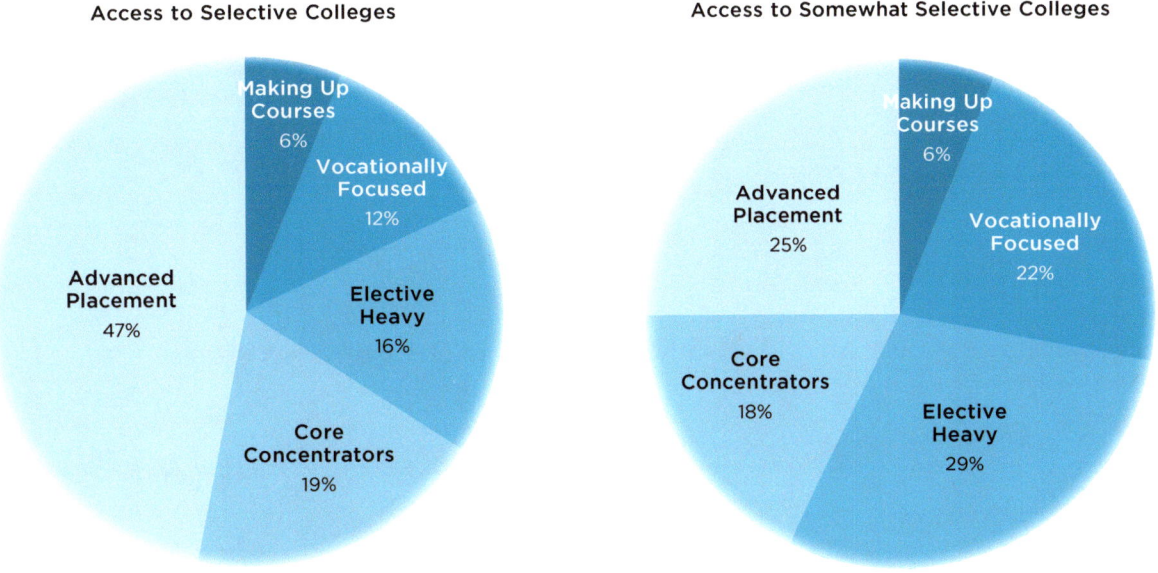

Note: Students included in these figures are those who graduated in 2006–09 (N=50,053). Cumulative GPAs from their junior year were not available for 514 students to calculate their access to college. The sample does not include students who were enrolled in special education or in alternative or charter high schools. The sample does not include students who took fewer than four courses when enrolled.

Schools are ordered from lowest to highest based on the coursetaking of their seniors with access to somewhat selective colleges.

Strikingly, the percentage of students with access to somewhat selective colleges who take four or more core courses ranges from less than 10 to 100 percent. In the bottom quarter of high schools, less than half of these students take four or more core courses; whereas, in the top quarter of high school schools, over 80 percent take four or more core classes. Even more variation is observed in the percentage of students with these qualifications who take a fourth-year math course (**see Figure 15**). In the top quarter of schools, two-thirds of students with access to a somewhat selective college took a fourth-year math course; while in the bottom quarter of schools, less than one-third of similarly qualified students took math during their senior year. A similar pattern occurs for AP coursetaking (**see Figure 16**).

These differences in coursetaking among similarly qualified students are best illustrated by comparing schools that have similar student bodies. At North-Grand High School, for example, 89 percent of seniors with access to a somewhat selective college take four or more core classes in their senior year compared to 50 percent at Kelvyn Park. The percentage of seniors taking one or more AP courses also differs with 55 percent of North-Grand graduates with these qualifications taking at least on AP class compared to 42 percent of Kelvyn Park graduates.

These two schools share attendance boundaries and are both neighborhood high schools serving similar populations of students. In fact, North-Grand High School was opened to relieve overcrowding at Kelvyn Park.

Do these differences in school practice and norms matter for access to and performance in college? This is a critical question and one we turn to in the next chapter. What it does mean, however, is that which high school students attend matters in shaping whether students will take an academically focused senior year.

How To Read Figures 14, 15, and 16

On the x-axis is a listing of each CPS high school in our analysis (order of schools changes from graph to graph). On the y-axis is the percentage of seniors in each high school (from 2003 to 2009) who take four core courses, fourth-year math, or at least one AP course.

The squares represent the percent of seniors with access to a selective four-year college in the high school who take four core courses/fourth-year math/at least one AP course.

The triangles represent the percent of seniors with access to a somewhat selective four-year college in the high school who take four core courses/fourth-year math/at least one AP course.

FIGURE 14

Participation in four or more core courses varies widely across high schools, even among similarly qualified students

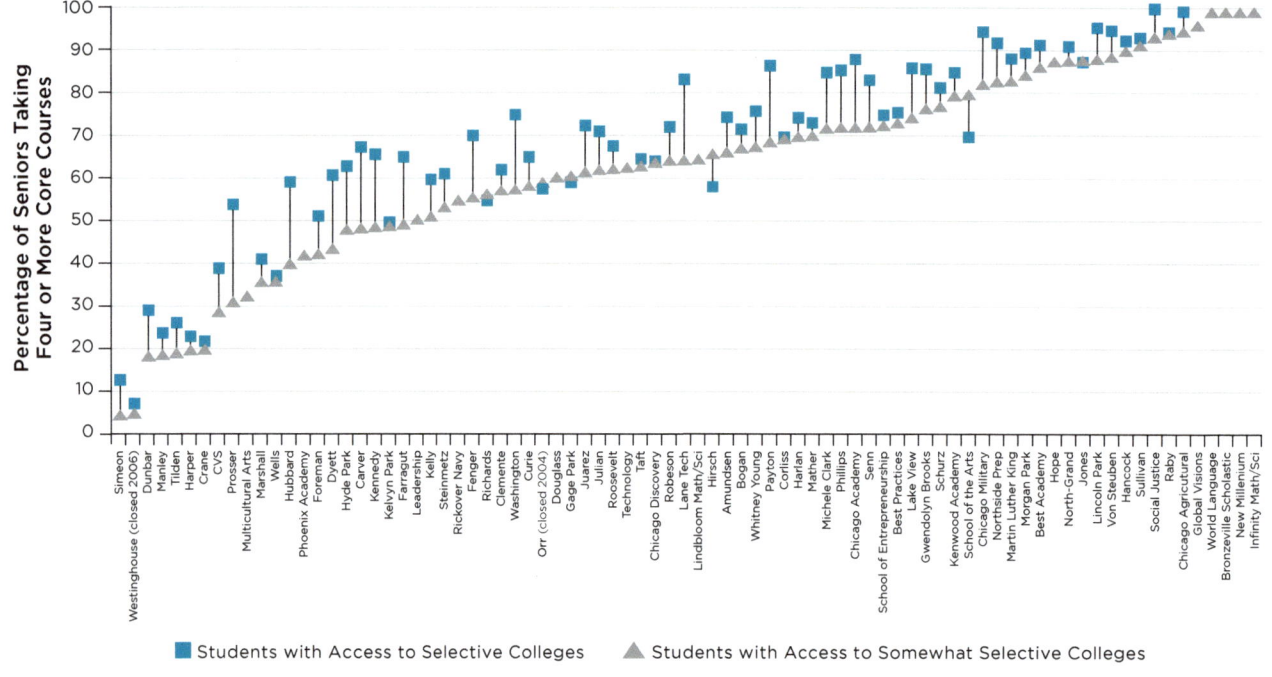

Note: Numbers in this table come from 2003–09 CPS graduates who were not enrolled in special education and not in alternative or charter high schools. Data points were only included if school had 15 or more students in a given category.

FIGURE 15

Participation in advanced math courses varies widely across high schools, even among similarly qualified students

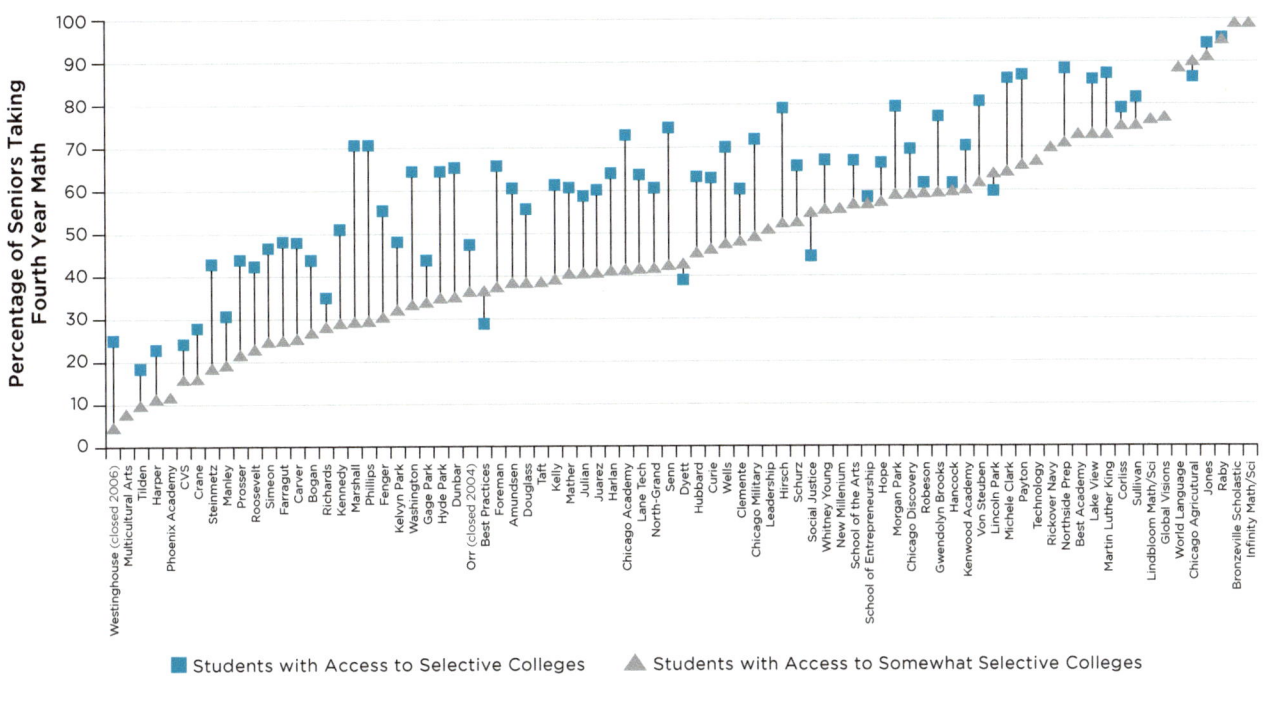

Note: Numbers in this table come from 2003-09 CPS graduates who were not enrolled in special education and not in alternative or charter high schools. Data points were only included if school had 15 or more students in a given category.

FIGURE 16

Participation in AP coursework varies widely across high schools, even among similarly qualified students

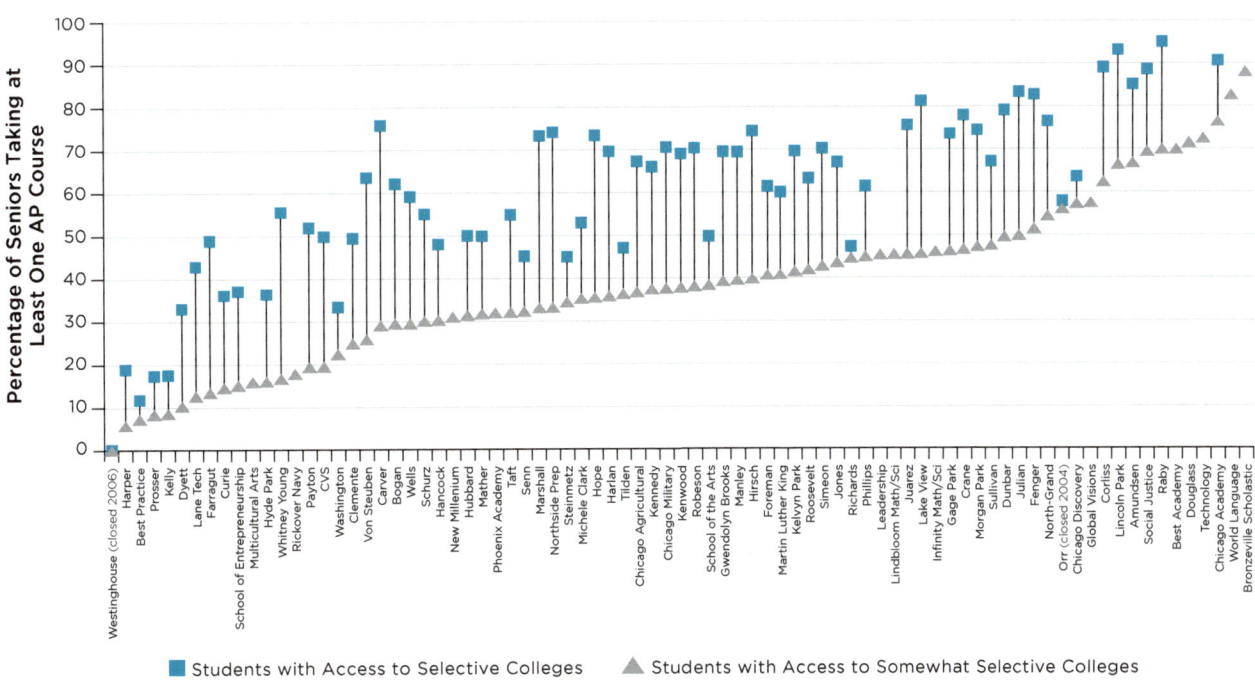

Note: Numbers in this table come from 2003-09 CPS graduates who were not enrolled in special education and not in alternative or charter high schools. Data points were only included if school had 15 or more students in a given category.

Chapter 2 | Making Sense of Senior Year in the Chicago Public Schools

The Bottom Line: Senior Year Is Stratified by Achievement and Race/Ethnicity

In the previous section, we noted that it was not surprising that the lowest performing CPS students are concentrated in the *Making Up Courses* groups and the highest achieving CPS students are concentrated in the *Advanced Placement* group. What this means, however, is that there is a clear pattern that is somewhat paradoxical—the more academically vulnerable a student may be in the transition to college and work, the less likely s/he is to take an academically focused senior year. To summarize these patterns, **Table 5** shows the percentage of students across levels of college access who are taking core classes, fourth-year math, and AP courses.

What is clear is that there is little consensus for what students of differing qualifications should be taking senior year. This lack of consensus is most dramatically seen in the variation we observed in coursetaking among those seniors who are minimally college eligible—meaning they are likely to be offered admission into a four-year somewhat selective college. Students with access to somewhat selective colleges are entering their senior year on track for entrance into the majority of public universities in Illinois. Yet, 40 percent of these students take fewer than four core classes in their senior year, over half (57 percent) do not take a fourth year of math, and less than one-third take an AP course. Even among students with access to selective colleges, such as DePaul University, one-third do not take a fourth year of math and one-third do not take an AP course, likely because these students are attending high schools where students with these qualifications are not taking AP courses and a fourth year of math.

These disparate coursetaking patterns among seniors who may be qualified to attend a four-year somewhat selective or selective college stand in contrast to the commonality in coursetaking patterns among students with access to very selective colleges. Ninety-two percent of the most highly qualified CPS students take four or more core classes (with 80 percent taking a fourth year of math as one of those core classes) and 85 percent take an AP class (with 60 percent taking two or more AP classes).

Finally, in Chapter 1 we found that, while nationally racial and ethnic gaps in coursetaking through eleventh grade have narrowed considerably, it is in students' participation in advanced coursework where racial and ethnic gaps are widening. This same pattern occurs in Chicago. The combination of wide variation in school practice around senior year coursetaking and the fact that coursetaking is differentiated by students'

TABLE 5

Senior year coursetaking varies widely by students' junior qualifications

	Percent Taking Four or More Core Courses	Percent Taking Fourth-Year Math	Percent Taking One or More AP Courses	Percent Taking Two or More Vocational Courses	Percent Taking a Make-Up Core Course
Access to a Two-Year College (N=22,141)	44%	15%	7%	33%	46%
Access to a Non-Selective Four-Year Colleges (N=17,295)	51%	27%	17%	35%	29%
Access to a Somewhat Selective Four-Year Colleges (N=27,237)	60%	43%	33%	32%	23%
Access to a Selective Four-Year Colleges (N=17,100)	75%	64%	66%	21%	22%
Access to a Very Selective Four-Year Colleges (N=5,339)	92%	80%	85%	6%	9%

Note: Numbers in this table come from 2003-09 CPS graduates (N=89,112) who were not enrolled in special education and not in alternative or charter high schools. The sample does not include students who took fewer than four courses in their senior year.

TABLE 6

Senior year coursetaking is unevenly distributed by race/ethnicity

	Percent Taking Four or More Core Courses	Percent Taking Fourth-Year Math	Percent Taking One or More AP Courses	Percent Taking Two or More Vocational Courses
All CPS (N=90,041*)	59%	39%	30%	30%
African American (N=42,162)	54%	34%	25%	37%
Latino (N=30,672)	58%	36%	29%	25%
White (N=11,264)	70%	47%	43%	18%
Asian American (N=5,792)	77%	68%	57%	14%

Note: Numbers in this table come from 2003–09 CPS graduates (N=90,041) who were not enrolled in special education and not in alternative or charter high schools. The sample does not include students who took fewer than four courses in their senior year.

*Some ethnic groups were excluded from this N due to the small numbers of students in those groups.

academic qualifications means that senior year in CPS has become differentiated by race and ethnicity. As seen in **Table 6**, African American students are least likely to take an academically focused senior year. Only slightly more than half of African American graduates take four or more core courses in their senior year, about one-third (34 percent) take a fourth-year math class, and only one-fourth take at least one AP course. Participation rates are only slighter higher for Latino seniors.

Summary: Making Sense of Senior Year

The conclusion we come to in this chapter is that what students take senior year is driven less by decisions that students are making than by decisions that their high schools are making. There is little agreement in CPS on what courses students who want to attend a four-year college should actually take to get ready for this important academic transition. This group raises two questions that we follow up on in the next two chapters. First, to what extent do differences in coursetaking across schools matter for students' access to and enrollment in four-year colleges and more selective colleges? Second, to what extent does the lack of participation in advanced coursework shape students' experience senior year?

What is not straightforward is what should be happening senior year for students who enter twelfth grade with very low GPAs and ACT scores. These are the students we characterize as only having access to a two-year college or a nonselective four-year college. At present, they are the least likely to be taking an academically focused senior year. These students also face many constraints. They spend a large proportion of their senior year making up courses and finishing courses required for graduation. Thus among seniors, they currently face the most constraints adding advanced coursework. As shown in the following insert, these students are also very unlikely to make a successful transition from high school to either work or schooling. Because of this, we included this special discussion of the unique set of challenges these students face.

CHAPTER 2 SUPPLEMENT

Not in College, Not Working, and Out of Options

A Closer Look at the Characteristics and Post-Graduation Outcomes for Seniors with Low Qualifications

In 2012, high school graduates with low test scores and low GPAs are in deep trouble. While students with poor academic records at the end of high school have always faced limited college options, this was less of a problem in the past. The majority of high school graduates traditionally found employment immediately after high school, with workplace readiness skills often developed through employment during high school. In the current economy, such avenues to employment have been largely cut off for these young adults whose college options remain extremely limited. As a result, these graduates are primarily out of school, out of work, and out of options.

This section investigates the post-graduation outcomes of the large group of CPS graduates who fit this profile: those who have access only to either nonselective four-year colleges (whom we describe as having very limited college access) or to open enrollment two-year colleges (whom we call marginal high school graduates). We consider the postsecondary outcomes of three cohorts of these students (graduates of 2003-05) and add further analysis on their employment. In light of the current recession, we use national data to consider how youth employment prospects have changed in recent years. The breadth and complexity of the problems facing these students makes it easy to declare that this is not a "senior year" issue. This is true. In the long run, it is critical to ensure that all CPS students enter senior year with higher grades and test scores and greater college access. In the short run, however, these very low-achieving students and their post-graduation prospects must be part of an immediate, critical discussion of senior year and of what needs to happen both in high school and in the postsecondary sector to ensure that vulnerable students are not left behind.

Characteristics and Post-Secondary Status Nine Months after Graduation

Perhaps the most daunting challenge in this report is posed by the 25 percent of seniors who graduate from CPS with such low ACT scores and GPAs that they would likely only be eligible to attend a two-year college. Another 20 percent of CPS graduates have such low ACT scores and GPAs that they would have difficulty gaining admission to most public state universities in Illinois. Together, these two groups of students represent nearly half of all CPS graduates. **Table 7** describes the demographic characteristics and college qualifications of these two groups of students. Strikingly, graduates of CPS with access only to two-year colleges are disproportionately male, African American, and old-for-grade relative to their classmates. Their average ACT score of 14.2 places them in the bottom 10 percent of students nationally. An average GPA of 1.51, moreover, means that these students have passed their classes with Cs and Ds and barely made it to graduation. Students with access to nonselective four-year colleges look somewhat more demographically similar to system averages and are slightly higher achieving, though they still face very poor college prospects.

What do these vulnerable students do in the year after graduation? As part of its postsecondary tracking systems, CPS collects employment records from the Illinois Department of Employment Security.[29] CCSR obtained employment data for the CPS graduating classes of 2003, 2004, and 2005. Thus, for these three cohorts, we were able to examine both college and work outcomes from October 1 through April 1 in the year after high school graduation (two quarters). Among CPS graduates with the lowest qualifications, more than one-third (37 percent) were neither working nor in college in the fall following high school graduation (see Figure 17).[30, 31] When these students did find employment, they were substantially underemployed. We can gauge the extent

TABLE 7

Demographic and achievement characteristics of CPS graduates with limited college options

2003-05 Cohorts	Marginal High School Graduates (Not Eligible to Attend a Four-Year College)	Very Limited College Access (Eligible for Only Non-Selective Four-Year Colleges)	CPS Average
Percent of CPS Graduates	25%	20%	100%
Average ACT	14.2	15.7	17.5
Unweighted GPA	1.51	2.10	2.36
Race/Ethnicity			
African American	58%	52%	46%
Latino	34%	36%	34%
White	6%	9%	13%
Asian American	2%	3%	7%
Concentration of Poverty in CPS Graduates' Neighborhoods	.338	.263	.237
Male	52%	42%	41%
Old for Grade	22%	14%	14%

Note: This table represents students from the graduating classes of 2003-2005. Concentration of poverty is taken from the 2000 census data. Higher values represent higher concentrations of poverty.

of underemployment by comparing the earnings of a graduate to the earnings that graduate would have if she or he worked full time at the minimum wage. The median earnings of this group of graduates who worked but were not in college was $3,824, equal to 67 percent of a full-time minimum wage job.[32] Thus, these young adults were either working less than full time or working intermittently in this six-month period. Underemployment was most pronounced for African American graduates. African American males who finished high school with very low ACT scores and GPAs and who worked at some point during the six months after high school graduation had earnings equal to 56 percent of a full-time minimum wage job (**see Figure 18**).

Finally, in the fall after high school, approximately one-third of graduates with access only to two-year colleges were enrolled in college—predominantly in two-year colleges. Tracking these enrolled students, we find that, of those students who enroll in two-year schools, only 55 percent were still enrolled two years later and less than 5 percent had earned a degree. Similarly, students who enrolled in a four-year college had a 55 percent likelihood of being enrolled in school two years later. For students with access to nonselective colleges, the average persistence two years out is 63 percent at four-year colleges and 65 percent at two-year colleges.

Nationally, the Percentage of High School Graduates Not In College Who Are Working Has Fallen Precipitously in the Last 10 Years. These outcomes are not encouraging, but the prospects of young high school graduates has become even more dismal in the current recession. Though we do not have current employment data for CPS students, the employment outcomes nationally for students who graduate from high school and do not go to college have declined dramatically over the past 10 years. The Bureau of Labor Statistics (BLS) tracks the employment and school enrollment status of recent high school graduates in the annual October Current Population Survey. From 2000 to 2010, an analysis of BLS data done for this report by the Economic Policy Institute shows that the percentage of high school graduates not in college who are employed in the fall after high school graduation has declined from 75 to 60 percent (**see Figure 19**).

Employment outcomes are much worse among African Americans who have recently graduated from high school and do not go to college. In 2011, only 49 percent of African American recent high school graduates who did not go to college found jobs by the fall after graduation, compared to 64 percent of white and 58 percent of Latino recent graduates. Strikingly, this analysis also shows that the gap between African American and white graduates has always been significant.

Chapter 2 | Making Sense of Senior Year in the Chicago Public Schools

CHAPTER 2 SUPPLEMENT CONTINUED

FIGURE 17

CPS marginal high school graduates were most often not in college or employed in the fall after graduation

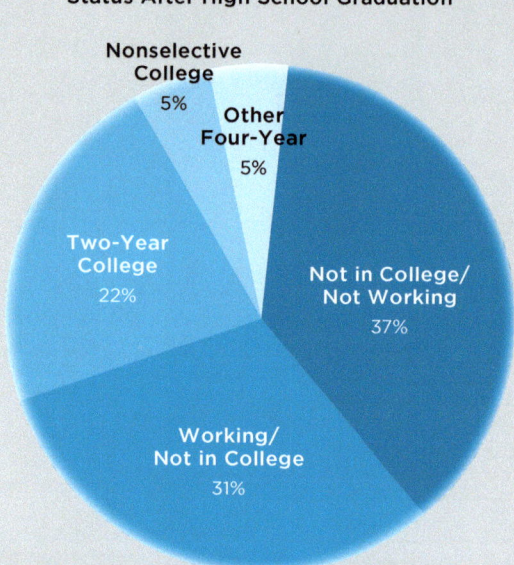

Status After High School Graduation

- Nonselective College: 5%
- Other Four-Year: 5%
- Two-Year College: 22%
- Not in College/Not Working: 37%
- Working/Not in College: 31%

Earnings Outcomes

2003-05 Cohorts N=10,253	Median Earnings Over 6 Months	% of FTE 2004 Minimum Wage
No College or Work	$52	0%
Work Only	$3,824	67%
Two-Year	$3,365	59%
Non-Selective College	$3,182	56%
Other Four-Year College	$1,610	28%

Note: % FTE is the percent of what a worker at minimum wage would make if they worked full time. If a person was working full time (40 hours/week or 1,040 hours over six months) at the 2004 minimum wage rate ($5.50), s/he would have earned $5,720. So a student who earned $3,824 over six months at a minimum wage job would have worked 695 hours (4,376/5.50) which is 695/1040 = 67% of a full-time job. Earnings data is collected by the Illinois Department of Employment and Security. Earnings are measured for a six-month period starting the October after a student graduates.

FIGURE 18

The 31 percent of CPS marginal high school graduates who were employed and not in college in the year after graduation were substantially underemployed

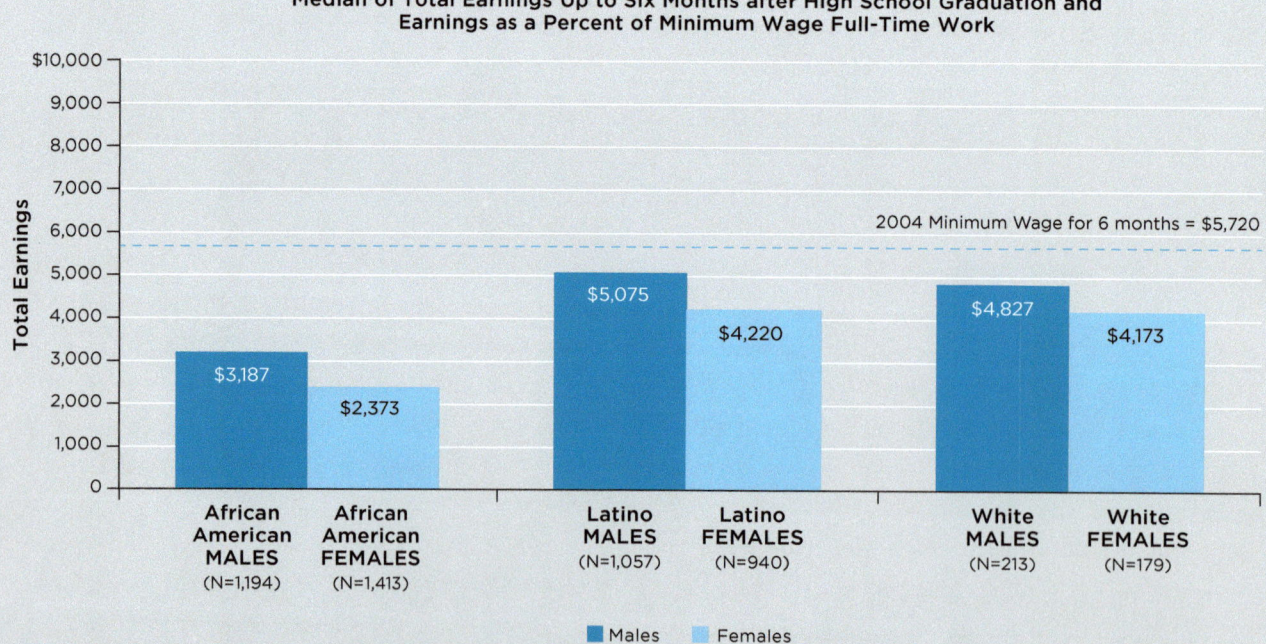

Median of Total Earnings Up to Six Months after High School Graduation and Earnings as a Percent of Minimum Wage Full-Time Work

- African American MALES (N=1,194): $3,187
- African American FEMALES (N=1,413): $2,373
- Latino MALES (N=1,057): $5,075
- Latino FEMALES (N=940): $4,220
- White MALES (N=213): $4,827
- White FEMALES (N=179): $4,173

2004 Minimum Wage for 6 months = $5,720

Note: This figure shows students from the graduating cohorts 2003-2005 who had access to a nonselective four-year college or a two-year college (N=17,710). The sample in this figure does not include students who were in special education, alternative high schools, or charter high schools. Students were categorized as "working" if they accumulated at least $100 in earning over two quarters. Data on earnings come from IDES information.

What Should Be the Purpose of Senior Year for Students with Weak Skills and Poor Grades?

For seniors with such low qualifications for college, the central question is: What should be the goals of senior year? At present, students with very low qualifications are the least likely to take an academically oriented senior year, in large part because many of these students need senior year to complete basic graduation requirements. Nearly half of these students (46 percent) were taking make-up courses their senior year, and almost two-thirds needed music and art credits to graduate.

The question of how high schools can facilitate a more effective transition for students who are just making it to graduation is particularly challenging for two reasons. First, there are very few options available for these students, making it difficult to know what an effective approach would look like. A recent Harvard University report by the *Pathways to Prosperity Project* argued that the United States must develop a broader set of options that mix employment and academic training and add at least one more year of education. As the report concludes:

> ...the message of college for all places far too much emphasis on a single pathway to success; attending and graduation from a four year college after completing an academic program of study in high school...It is long past time that we broaden the range of high-quality pathways that we offer to our young people beginning in high schools.[33]

But at present, high schools do not have those pathways available; few training and employment supports are offered to students who do not go to college.

Second, the constellation of problems facing these low-achieving CPS graduates is compounded by the fact that few of these students work in high school. Historically, for many youth, employment during high school played a critical role in developing work readiness skills and creating pathways to adult employment. Over the last 10 years, however, the employment rates of high school students across race/ethnicity have been cut in half (**see Figure 20**). In 2010, only 9 percent of Latino and 8 percent of African American high school students were employed.

FIGURE 19

Over the past 11 years, the employment rate of high school graduates nationwide not in college has declined from over 76 percent in 2000 to 61 percent in 2011

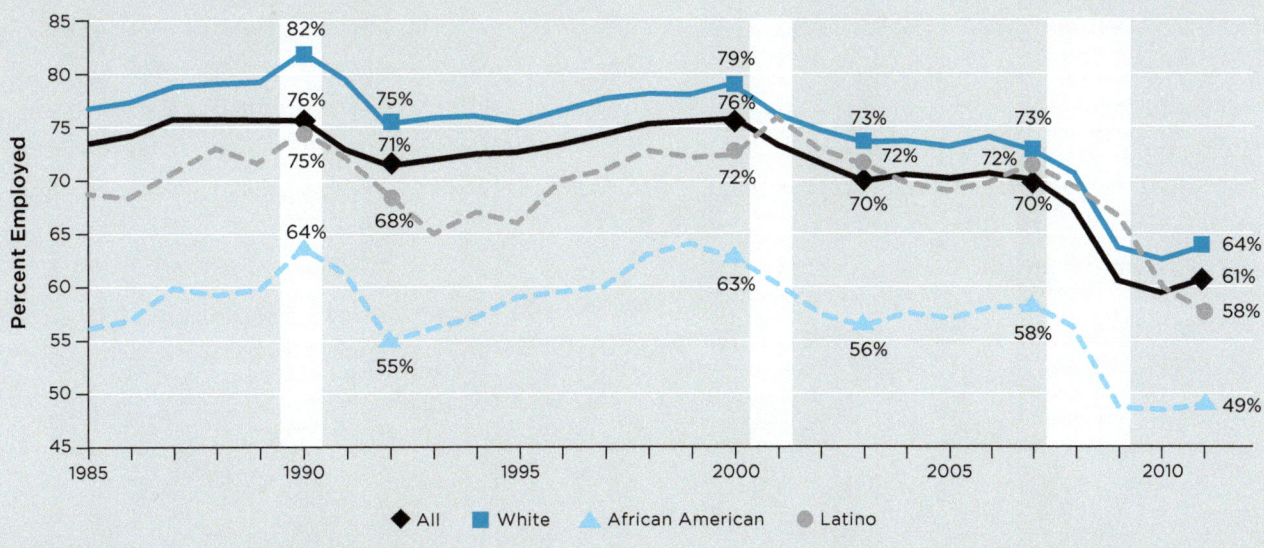

Source: EPI analysis of Bureau of Labor Statistics Current Population Survey data. Population is high school graduates never enrolled in further education. Recessions are highlighted.

CHAPTER 2 SUPPLEMENT CONTINUED

FIGURE 20

The percentage of students nationwide working while in high school declined precipitously from 2000 to 2010

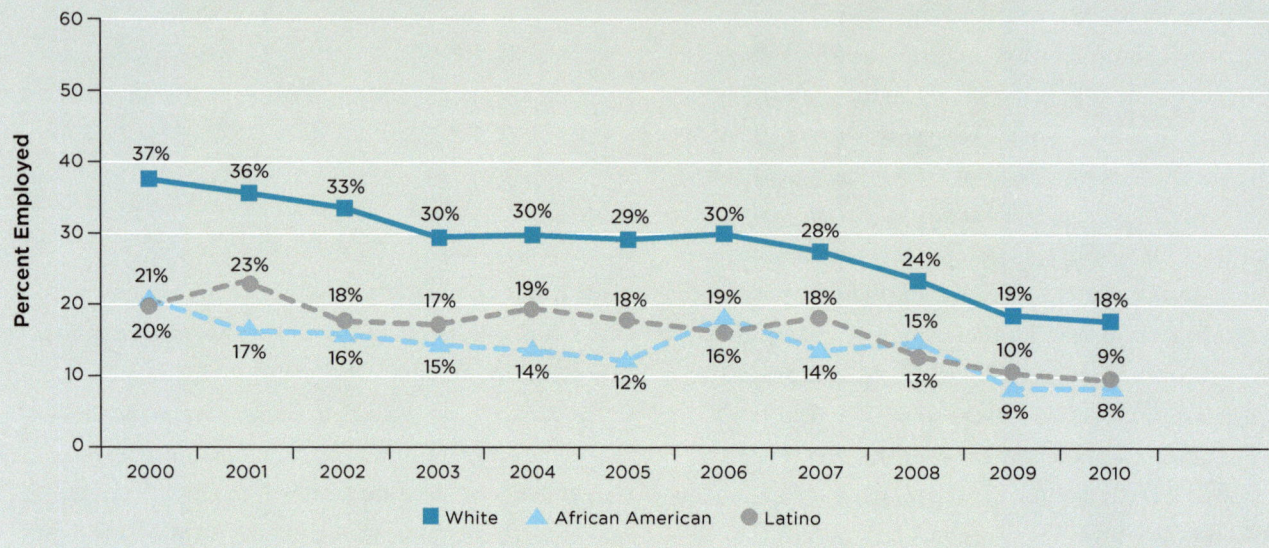

Source: http://www.childtrendsdatabank.org/?q=node/374 accessed on 5/4/2012.

Taking a closer look at the challenges facing these students in twelfth grade does not mean that the solution is to fix only twelfth grade. Senior year is far too late to intervene. During the senior year, teachers cannot make eligible for college a group of students who, after 11 years, are barely meeting graduation requirements. And clearly high schools cannot address these students' needs without the development of new postsecondary training and institutions.

At the same time, it is clear that high schools play an increasingly central role in the lives of urban youth. As we demonstrated in *Potholes on the Road to College*, first generation college students are especially dependent upon high schools for the information, experiences, and supports that allow them to translate aspirations and achievement into college access. The problems facing the lowest-achieving CPS graduates, outlined in this section, pose an equally significant challenge. Even 20 years ago, most high school graduates did not attend college and most students were not relying on their teachers to help them make an effective transition to the labor market. The fact that over 45 percent of CPS graduates essentially did not have the academic qualifications to attend a four-year college would not have sounded alarms in earlier times. Now the situation constitutes a call to action. Dramatic changes in the economy mean that youth who barely manage to graduate from high school and who lack work experience are increasingly dependent upon high schools and postsecondary training to help them develop skills and connect to the labor market.

CHAPTER 3

Getting In and Staying

Evaluating the Impact of Senior Year Coursetaking on College Access and Retention

If the new purpose of high schools is to be a "launching pad rather than a last stop destination," what does that mean for senior year? Throughout the *From High School to the Future* series, we have demonstrated the importance of senior year as a time when students must be supported in the process of college search and application. In this report, we add yet another task for senior year: ensuring that students take the courses that make them competitive in college admissions and prepared to succeed in postsecondary education.

A central theme in the last chapter is that we observe wide variation in coursetaking across high schools. With the exception of the highest achieving CPS students, there seems to be little common agreement on what courses students who are qualified to attend four-year colleges should actually take to prepare for this important academic transition. Differences in coursetaking across high schools were particularly pronounced for two groups: (1) those students who entered senior year with GPAs and ACT scores that make them positioned to attend somewhat selective colleges and (2) students with slightly higher qualifications who have access to selective four-year colleges (**see *Identifying College Access*… on p. 37**).

While this wide disparity in coursetaking across high schools among similarly qualified students is provocative and raises questions of equity, ultimately we need to know whether these differences actually matter. In this chapter, we focus on the question: To what extent are differences across high schools in the norms and practices around senior year coursetaking associated with whether students: (1) attend a four-year college, (2) attend a selective or very selective four-year college, and (3) persist in college once enrolled. Building on our analysis in Chapter 2, we look at three aspects of coursetaking that colleges may use to assess the rigor of a students' transcript and that previous research has used to measure the "academic intensity" of coursetaking: whether seniors take (1) four or more core courses, (2) a fourth-year math course, and (3) one or more AP courses. We focus our analysis on the college enrollment and persistence of the two groups of students where we observe significant variation in coursetaking—students positioned to enroll in somewhat selective and selective four-year colleges.

The questions we deal with in this chapter are relatively straightforward. Identifying the answers is far from straightforward because of what academics call selection issues. Simply, students who opt to take a fourth year of math will likely be different from their classmates in the same high school who do not in ways that would affect whether they go to college and what kind of college they go to. Thus, any differences in college enrollment will reflect both the effect of that fourth-year math course and the effect of differences in the attitudes, motivations, and supports of students who decide to sign up for a fourth-year math course and those who do not. We employ another approach in this chapter by using variation in coursetaking across high schools to simulate a matched sample.

The central findings are:

- Among students who enter senior year positioned to attend a *four-year somewhat selective college,*
  - Those who took an AP course were substantially more likely to enroll in a four-year college.
  - Those who took a fourth year of math were more likely to enroll in a four-year college.

- Among students who enter senior year positioned to attend a *selective college,* taking two or more AP courses is associated with a substantial increase in the odds of "matching" (e.g., enrolling in a selective or very selective college).

- After addressing selection, students who take AP courses their senior year, who take four core classes, and/or who take a fourth year of math are no more likely to persist in a four-year college than a matched comparison group.

In the conclusion to this chapter, we discuss possible interpretations of these findings in the context of the broader research findings on the impact of coursetaking on college performance.

Why Would Senior Year Coursetaking Matter, and What Has Prior Research Found?

Among the most-studied areas in educational research are: the high school curriculum, what courses students take, and who is in what curricular track. Even so, we are limited in the research evidence we can draw upon for this study for two reasons. First, we are focusing only on twelfth grade and are interested in isolating the effect of taking a specific course (AP or fourth-year math) or set of courses (four or more core classes, or one versus two or more AP) in senior year. Because much of prior research on coursetaking has focused on the question of whether engaging more students in a college preparatory curriculum is beneficial, it has evaluated sequences of courses students are engaged in over four years.[34] This is an important topic in education and one on which our CCSR colleagues have done seminal research.[35] This research, however, does not help us understand the particular effect of taking a fourth year of math over and above students' prior and concurrent coursework.

The second problem is more significant. Up until recently, researchers studying the effects of coursetaking primarily compared students who took more advanced courses to those who did not without addressing issue of selection effects.[36] There are numerous studies that demonstrate that students who take AP, advanced math courses, or more Carnegie units in major subjects in high school do better on an array of indices.[37] Much of this research, however, uses cross-sectional data and compares students who take a specific course or set of courses to those who do not. There is a problem with this approach. Even students with similar family background and prior school performance may differ in their (unmeasured) motivation and aspirations that would explain why one student would take a more challenging senior year. Indeed, colleges assert that this self selection is in fact important in admission decisions. As we saw in Chapter 1, college counselors and admissions materials explicitly state that they judge whether a student is motivated and/or academically ready by examining their coursetaking in twelfth grade, essentially asserting that a student who takes advanced courses senior year has more motivation than a classmate with the same ACT score and GPA who takes an easy senior year. The importance of selection, then, means that we are limited in the number of studies that we consider providing rigorous estimates of the effects of specific courses.

Access Versus Preparation Effects

There is an underlying tension in the question of whether taking an AP course or a fourth year of math would matter for college access and persistence: On the one hand, why wouldn't a student who takes advanced courses do better? On the other hand, after 11 years of education, why would one specific course or set of courses make a difference? To understand how the classes students take affect their college outcomes, we focus on two potential effects of senior year coursetaking: first, what courses students take may influence their college enrollment (an access effect); and second, what courses students take senior year may shape how academically ready students are for the transition to college level work (a preparation effect).

Access Effects

Colleges, as we noted above, state that they look at what students are taking senior year to evaluate motivation and preparation. Economists refer to this phenomenon as "signaling": Colleges rely on particular credentials—such as whether students go above and beyond the basic graduation requirements or participate in specific coursework (e.g., AP and advanced math)—as a signal of motivation or the quality of the high school attended. Signaling may be particularly important in shaping the effects of participation in AP courses because colleges are explicitly advantaging participation in AP courses in admissions. Thus, if taking AP courses or a fourth year of math functions as a signal, students who take these courses should be more competitive in the application process.

If colleges use coursework to judge a student's motivation and preparedness, so might teachers and counselors. Seniors who take advanced courses, particularly AP and fourth-year math, may also be more likely to enroll in a four-year college and more selective colleges because advanced courses give them access to more positive norms for college attendance, information, and supports.[38] Counselors and teachers may be more likely to target information and support towards those seniors who are labeling themselves or are being labeled as college bound by their participation in advanced coursework. In addition, students who are taking more academically advanced courses senior year may have access to greater information and college-going norms simply because they are around a more academically advanced peer group who are more likely to be applying to four-year and more selective colleges and are more likely to be engaged in the details of applying to college and for financial aid.[39]

Recent studies provide evidence that advanced coursetaking shapes college outcomes by increasing the likelihood that students will enroll in four-year colleges and more selective colleges.[40] Using data from Florida, Mark Long, Dylan Conger, and their colleagues (2012) find that participation in advanced coursework in any subject is associated with increases in the probability of enrollment in college, with the payoffs being larger for low-income students and students attending higher-poverty schools.

Two studies of the effects of expanding AP participation for predominantly low-income and minority students also find positive effects on college enrollment. Jackson (2007) and Roderick and Stoker (2010) compared changes in college enrollment over time in schools that were and were not expanding AP. Both studies found that AP expansion was associated with increases in the proportion of students who enroll in a four-year college. In a follow-up dissertation, Stoker (2010) looked at the effect of taking two or more AP courses and similarly concluded that even after addressing selection, seniors who took two or more AP courses were very likely to attend a four-year college and attend a selective or very selective college.

Effects on College Readiness

Senior year coursetaking could also shape college outcomes by increasing students' academic preparation, which would allow them to do better once enrolled in college. Inversely students who do not take a rigorous senior year may be poorly prepared to succeed in college courses. These are two quite different sets of concerns. For higher-achieving high school students, the question is whether senior year is academic and developmentally preparing students for changes in the academic demands that they will experience as they move into college classrooms.

However, for more academically vulnerable high school students, taking a less academically focused senior year may increase their risk of being placed into remedial college courses as freshmen. The high proportion of first-year college students placed in remedial non-credit bearing courses is a critical issue in higher education. Of entering first-year undergraduate students, almost 40 percent at four-year public institutions, and 26 percent in four-year private colleges, are placed in at least one remedial course.[41] African American (45 percent) and Latino (43 percent) first-year college students are much more likely than white (31 percent) students to be placed in at least one remedial course.[42] Most CPS seniors who have access to nonselective and somewhat selective colleges attend public four-year universities. At a minimum, a senior year lacking in serious academic coursework may place these students at high risk of remediation. Math is the most common subject area in which students are deemed not ready for college.[43] Students who do not take a fourth year of math enter college having been off task for over a year. Simply avoiding remedial education is not a very high bar to guide students about what courses may matter for shaping college performance, but it is a particularly important concern for CPS students.

Beyond just keeping students "on-task," however, senior year courses may play an important role in shaping college readiness (e.g., performance in credit bearing college classes).[44] The AP program, in particular, advertises AP courses to students as a way to "acquire the skills and habits you'll need to be successful in college…improve your writing skills, sharpen your problem-solving abilities, and develop time management skills, discipline, and study habits."[45]

The conclusion on math is clear: studies with rigorous methods find that students who take higher level math courses are less likely to be placed in remedial education, are more likely to receive higher grades in college, and are more likely to persist and graduate from college. The findings on higher level math are remarkably consistent, regardless of whether you look at advanced math as early as tenth grade or the highest level of math taken at the end of high school.[46] Math coursetaking has also been linked to later earnings, primarily through its effect on raising the likelihood of college enrollment and completion.[47]

There is, however, little evidence that students who take AP courses do better in college unless they pass the examination. Our reading of the existing research evidence on AP courses may seem surprising given the ubiquity of the AP program. Over the past two decades, the AP program was transformed as students and high schools began to use AP as a means of increasing college preparedness and gaining advantage in college admissions. In 2002, the National Research Council conducted a review of the AP and International Baccalaureate (IB) programs and concluded that there was little evidence on which to base an evaluation of this use of AP courses. The review issued a call for more rigorous research and, since then, several studies have investigated whether AP participation is associated with improved college performance.[48]

Although researchers have consistently found that students who take AP have higher college grades; are more likely to persist in college; and are more likely to graduate, even after adjusting for measured differences in demographic characteristics and prior school performance, these effects do not hold up in more rigorous analysis once these researchers control for both selection into AP coursework and students' overall coursetaking patterns.[49] In fact, there is little rigorous evidence that just taking an AP course leads to better college grades, increased college persistence, or a higher college graduation rate. ***The Summary of Critical Studies...* Box** summarizes the results of several of these studies.

One complication is the consistent finding that passing the AP exam and/or students' AP exam score is associated with higher performance in college.[50] It is unclear, however, how to interpret this finding. There are several reasons that students who take an AP course and pass the exam may do better than their classmates who take the course but not the exam, or do not take AP at all. First, this may mean that mastering the material in AP courses benefits students once in college. Second, it may mean that students who master the material in any of their classes do better—students who pass AP exams may do better than those who do not because passing the exam is another indicator that they are simply better students and would do better in college regardless of the content in AP. And, third, it could mean that subject matter exams are better predictors of college performance than generalized exams like the ACT and SAT.

To summarize, there are no comparable studies that look solely at senior year, but we can draw on research evidence on the effects of advanced coursetaking more generally to postulate what we might find looking only at senior year in an urban school system. There is some evidence that AP participation has a positive influence on college enrollment for urban low-income and minority students, but there is no strong evidence that participation in AP is associated with improvement in college performance and persistence once in college. There is also strong evidence that students who take advanced math have more positive college and post-college outcomes. This would suggest that CPS students might expect increased college access as a result of taking AP but it is unclear whether there is any benefit in college performance and persistence. It might also suggest that taking a fourth year of math would have a positive effect on persistence. The question is: Do these findings hold in Chicago?

The answer to this question depends upon what characteristics of coursetaking are driving the research results. If it is a high score on AP exams rather than taking AP courses that matters, then we would expect that CPS students would get few benefits from taking AP courses. Only 35 percent of CPS students who take an AP exam receive a passing score. Passing rates are particularly dismal for African American CPS students (13 percent), and are much lower for Latino students (21 percent) if we exclude Latino students' scores on the AP world language exams.[51] If the effects of taking math are driven by the importance of not taking a year off from math, low-income

Summary of Critical Studies of Effects of Advanced Placement and Fourth-Year Math

Willingham and Morris (1986)
Four years later: A longitudinal study of Advanced Placement students in college. New York: College Board Publications.

This College Board study was one of the first to look at the impact of AP coursetaking on college performance. This study was conducted on nine college campuses and used self-reported AP participation and exam performance, as well as propensity score matching, to construct an appropriate comparison group, equivalent on the basis of high school performance and scores on admissions rankings. While students who took an AP course and scored a three or higher on the exam outperformed the matched counterparts in their course performance and likelihood of graduation, students who took AP but did not pass the exams did no better than similar students who did not take AP.

Geiser and Santelices (2004)
The role of Advanced Placement and honors courses in college admissions. Berkeley: Center for Studies in Higher Education, University of California Berkeley.

This study used data from the University of California at Berkeley to examine the extent to which advanced coursework impacted college outcomes. The authors found that AP and honors coursework in high school was not associated with an increase in the likelihood of persistence in the first or second year of college; student achievement (unweighted high school GPA, SAT scores), family background (parental education), and high school quality (average test scores of the student's high school) were accounted for. A student's AP examination score, however, was positively associated with course performance across college majors.

Dougherty, Mellor, and Jian (2006a)
The relationship between advanced placement and college graduation. Austin: The National Center for Educational Accountability. The University of Texas at Austin.

This study found that not addressing student selection in AP courses would lead to the conclusion that students who take AP courses do much better. After addressing selection, however, there is no evidence that taking AP courses is associated with college graduation.

Doughtery, Mellor, and Jian (2005)
Orange juice or orange drink? Ensuring that "advanced courses" live up to their labels. National Center for Educational Accountability.

This study examined the effect of AP participation and AP test scores on the likelihood of graduating from a Texas public university, separately assessing the outcomes of students who: (1) took an AP course but did not take the exam, (2) took the exam but did not pass, and (3) took an AP exam and passed. Controlling for pre-high school test scores, high school GPA, and high school characteristics, Doughtery and his colleagues found that each of the AP groups outperformed students who had not taken an AP course in high school. But they went on to conclude that many of these positive effects can be attributed to the fact that AP participants were a select group who would have done better in college regardless of their AP course participation.

At the high school level, the percentage of students taking but not passing AP exams was not associated with higher average college graduation rates for Latino and white students, although some positive effects were found for African American students. The study did, however, find a positive effect of AP exam performance. The percentage of students in a high school who passed the AP exam was associated with an increase in the likelihood of graduating from college after adjusting for average pre-high school (eighth grade) test scores, the demographic characteristics of the student body, and the average level of non-AP advanced coursetaking in the school. This could mean that AP courses do not proffer benefits unless students demonstrate mastery of the material. The average AP test scores of a high school, however, could also serve as a proxy variable for the overall quality of that school.

Klopfenstein and Thomas (2006)
The link between Advanced Placement experience and early college success.

Again using Texas data, this study found a positive association between the number of AP courses a student took in high school and GPA and retention in the first year of college. The effects were most dramatic for African American and Hispanic students. Klopfenstein and Thomas conclude, however, that much of this positive association reflects the fact that students who took AP courses simultaneously

SUMMARY OF CRITICAL STUDIES... *CONTINUED*

enrolled in higher level math and science courses, which was associated with better performance in college.

Jackson (2009)
"A little now for a lot later." *Journal of Human Resources 45:3* 591-639. Madison: University of Wisconsin Press.

This study evaluated the impact of the Advanced Placement Incentive Program (APIP), a privately funded program in Dallas, Texas, that combined enhanced professional development and support for teachers in implementing pre-AP and AP curriculum with monetary incentives for teachers and students for passing exams.[F] Jackson compared changes in student performance between schools that adopted the program and schools that had not adopted the program, adjusting for the general demographic characteristics of schools and school effects. Over several cohorts, APIP schools saw substantial increases over and above comparison schools in the proportion of students with high scores on college entrance exams and the proportion who attended college in Texas. Though it is difficult to tell in this case which changes in school or student practices were responsible for the improvements, Jackson's qualitative data suggest that the AP incentive program may have led to improvements in counseling, both in terms of recruiting students for AP and in supporting students in college search.

Roderick and Stoker (2010)
"Bringing rigor to the study of rigor: Evaluating the efficacy of Advanced Placement as a strategy for increasing college preparation in urban schools" in Judith Meece and Jacquelynne Eccles. *Handbook of Research on Schools, Schooling and Human Development.* New York: Routledge. 216-234.

Against the backdrop of rapid but uneven expansion of AP offerings in the Chicago Public Schools, this study uses an approach similar to Jackson (2007), comparing differences in college enrollment over time at schools that did and did not invest in AP coursework. The study included substantial controls for student background, student performance, and high school characteristics. The change in the odds of a student attending a four-year college was nearly 30 percent higher in the group of schools that invested heavily in expanding AP than in schools with little change in AP enrollment. There was also a positive but not statistically significant impact on the odds of a student attending a selective or very selective four-year college.

Long, Iatarola, and Conger (2009)
Explaining gaps in readiness for college-level math: The role of high school courses. American Education Finance Association.

Using data from Florida's public postsecondary institutions, Long, Iatarola, and Conger examined the relationship between the highest level of math taken in high school and placement in remedial math at a public four-year university. Differences among students in the highest math course taken explained approximately one-third of the difference in remedial placement between black, Hispanic, and white students, and explained over three-quarters of the lower placement rates of Asian Americans.

---

and racial/ethnic minority students might garner the greatest benefits because they are much more likely than more advantaged youth to be deemed in need of remediation in math. Alternatively, if the benefits associated with math coursetaking is driven by the effects of taking advanced math, particularly Calculus and Pre-Calculus, then Chicago students would benefit less because CPS students when enrolled in a fourth-year math courses are more likely to be enrolled in Statistics and College Algebra than Calculus and Pre-Calculus.

Looking at the Effect of Senior Year Coursetaking in Chicago

In many ways, the Chicago Public Schools offers the ideal opportunity to study the effects of senior year coursetaking. First, all CPS juniors take the ACT exam as part of Illinois' state testing system. This allows us to assess students' qualifications by the end of eleventh grade. Second, as we saw in Chapter 2, because most CPS students have taken quite similar courses from ninth to eleventh grade, we can focus on differences in coursetaking in one year among students who had similar experiences up until twelfth grade. Finally, the fact that coursetaking senior year varies so dramatically across high schools means that we

FIGURE 21

In CPS, what courses seniors take can vary by what side of a street they live on

Twelfth Grade Coursetaking Among Graduates with Access to Somewhat Selective Four-Year Colleges

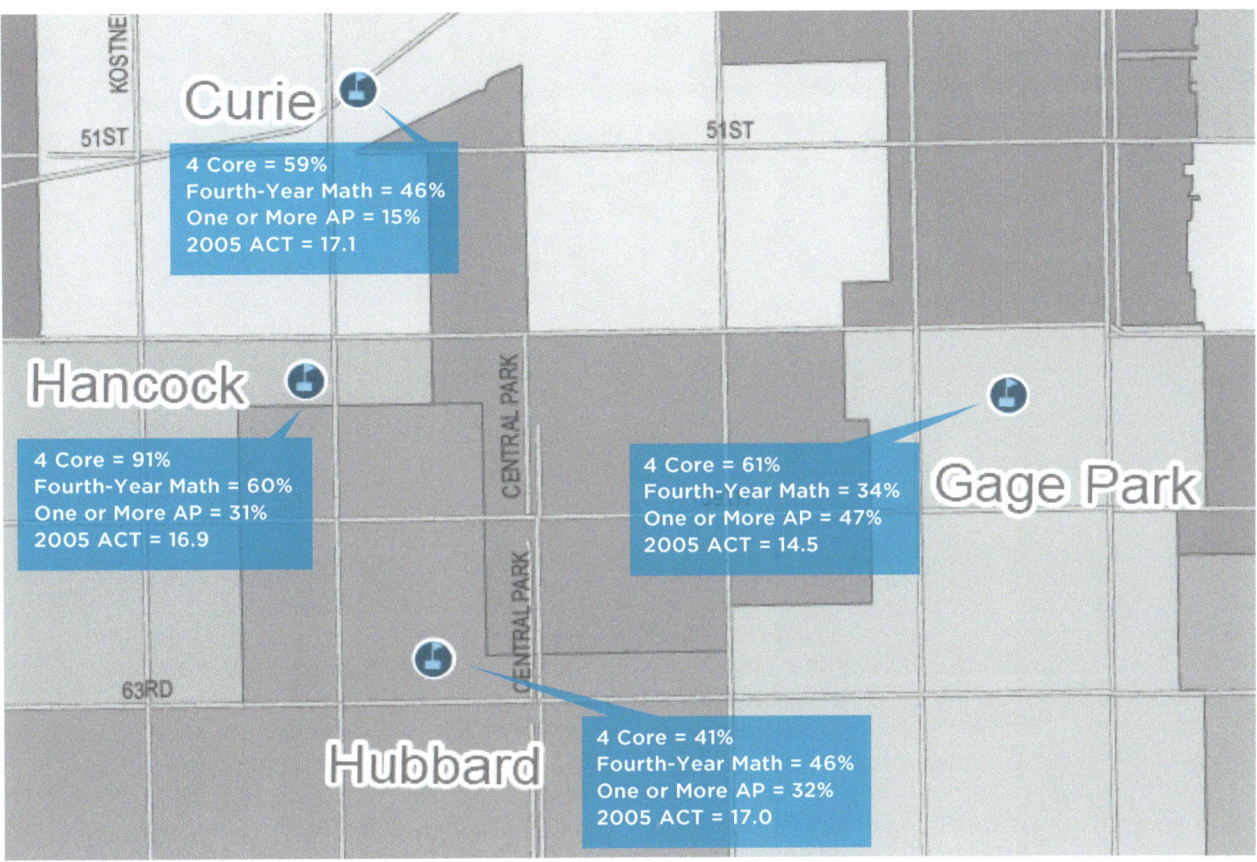

Note: For each school we report the percentage of graduates 2003 to 2007 taking at least on AP course, a fourth year mathematics and/or four or more core courses among those graduates who entered twelfth grade on-track to a somewhat selective college. The ACT score represents the composite ACT score for all graduates from the schools in 2005.

might be able to identify students in different schools that look similar in terms of their qualifications and experiences up until eleventh grade but differ in twelfth grade simply because of the school they attend.

This approach only makes sense if there are schools that look alike in terms of their student population and achievement prior to twelfth grade but differ in what courses their student take senior year. What is a potential problem for CPS is a particular advantage for this study. There are many schools that have quite similar student bodies and performance through junior year but who have widely divergent senior year coursetaking patterns, particularly among students with access to somewhat and selective colleges. This administrative variation is best illustrated by comparing the course-taking of students with similar qualifications at the end of junior year in geographically adjacent schools.

Figure 21 compares the percentage of twelfth graders with access to somewhat selective colleges who took one or more AP courses, a fourth year of math and/or four or more core classes in four schools that share attendance boundaries (Curie, Gage Park, Hancock, and Hubbard). In just these four schools, the percentage of similarly qualified students who took four or more core courses senior year ranges from 91 to 41 percent; the percent taking AP courses range from a low of 15 percent to a high of 47 percent.

The case of these four adjacent schools is meant to illustrate the extent to which there is variation in coursetaking in senior year across CPS high schools that serve similar student bodies, even in the same neighborhoods. **Figure 22** looks at this phenomenon across the city. Each point on this figure represents a high school's average ACT score and the percent of

FIGURE 22

Even among high schools with similar average ACT scores, the percentage of students with access to somewhat selective colleges taking at least one AP course varies substantially

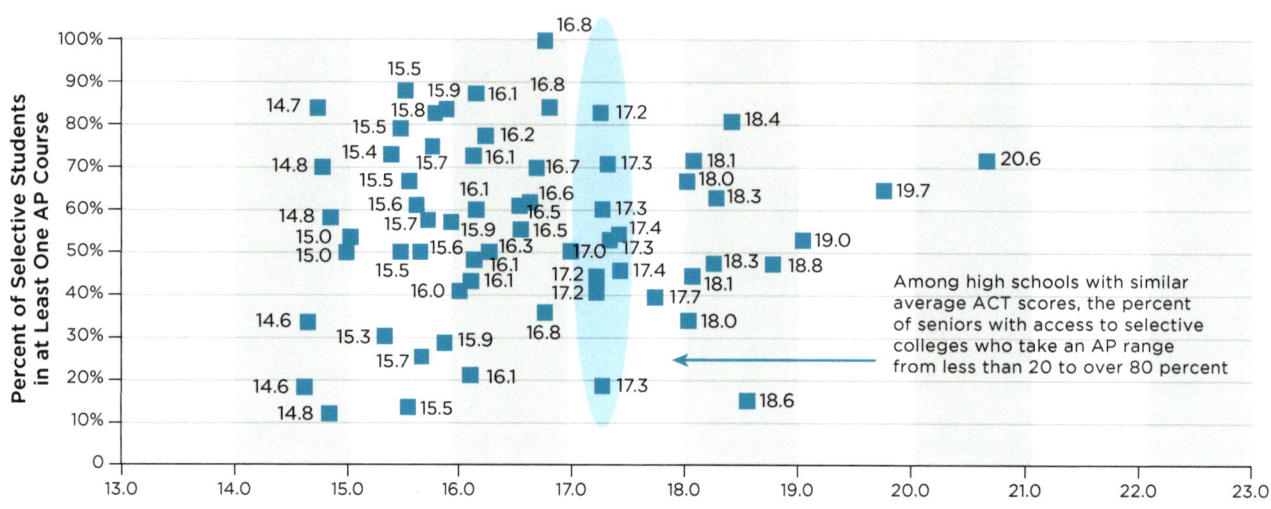

Our Approach to Matching Students and Addressing Selection

Our general approach to matching students and constructing a control group is relatively easy to understand. To illustrate, we use the example of estimating the effect of taking a fourth year of math on the odds of enrolling in a four-year college for students who would have access to a somewhat selective college. The analysis has three separate steps. First, we start with students who have access to a somewhat selective college in schools in the top quartile of participation in fourth-year math. For each student in those high schools with a high participation rate, we predict the probability of taking advanced math given a student's demographic characteristics, prior math coursetaking, ACT math scores, and junior year cumulative unweighted core GPA. By the end of eleventh grade, we should be able to estimate with a high degree of accuracy which students would be the most likely to take a fourth year of math in schools that have high participation rates in math. They would be the students with higher ACT scores, particularly in math; with good grades in math prior to twelfth grade; with no failures in math; and who took honors math courses in previous years.

Second, we turn to students who attend those schools in the lowest quartile of math coursetaking for this group of students. Using our results from Step 1, we simulate the probability that these students would have taken a fourth year of math if they had been enrolled in the higher quartile schools. By including high school characteristics, we can match students in the top and bottom quartile of high schools in terms of both their prior school performance and the achievement level of their high school. Finally, using this matched sample, we estimate the association between taking a fourth-year math course and three different outcomes: (1) enrolling in a four-year college, (2) enrolling in a selective or very selective college among four-year college-goers, and (3) persisting in a four-year college for two years (see *College Enrollment and Retention...* on p. 59 and Appendix B). We call this the simulated control group analysis. **Appendix F** describes our methodology in detail.

We limit our analysis in this chapter to students who entered senior year with qualifications to attend somewhat selective and selective four-year colleges. Our approach to addressing selection only works if students with similar qualifications attend different high schools and vary in their coursetaking across those high schools. In the previous chapter, we found that there was very little variation in the coursetaking of CPS students with the highest qualifications (students with access to very selective colleges). These students are also concentrated in a small number of schools where there is little variation in coursetaking. The same problem occurs for students with very low test scores and grades. Because the effects of coursework might be different for students with different qualifications, we estimate effects separately by whether students have access to a somewhat selective four-year college or a selective four-year college.

seniors with access to a somewhat selective college taking at least one AP course. Looking closely at the figure, there are four schools with an average ACT score of 17.3, yet in one school 70 percent of students eligible for a somewhat selective college take at least one AP course while on the other end of the spectrum, only 18 percent of students with the same qualifications take AP. This case is not unique; across the range of average ACT scores, there is large variation in the rates of AP taking. This means that we can identify and compare high schools that look quite similar in terms of their student bodies but that differ in which courses students with similar qualifications take during senior year.

Using Variation Across High Schools to Identify the Effects of Coursetaking Senior Year

This variation across high schools in coursetaking among students with similar access levels provides a unique opportunity to isolate the effects of taking specific courses or sets of courses because it suggests that we can find students with similar achievement levels who attend schools that have comparable student performance yet differ in their senior year coursework because of the school they attend.

Estimating the Effects of Senior Year Coursework

As we discussed earlier, cross-sectional research generally finds a positive association between senior year coursetaking and college outcomes even when adjusting for differences in the qualifications and background of students. These effects do not hold up in more rigorous analysis once researchers use methods that adjust for student selection. We find that same pattern. To illustrate, **Tables 8 and 9** compare the results of two models, estimates where we do not control for selection and our estimates from simulating a control group to address selection. For each outcome, the first column presents the estimated effects we would find if we just

TABLE 8

Taking AP courses and a fourth year of math significantly increases the probability that CPS students positioned to enroll in somewhat selective colleges will enroll in a four-year college.

Not Addressing Selection Leads to Overestimates of the Benefits of Coursetaking

		Enrolling in a Four-Year College		Enrolling in a Selective or Very Selective College Among Four-Year College Goers		Persisting for Two Years Within a Four-Year College	
		Predicted Probability		Predicted Probability		Predicted Probability	
		No Selection Controls	With Selection Controls	No Selection Controls	With Selection Controls	No Selection Controls	With Selection Controls
Advanced Placement (AP)	No AP	42.0	41.8	14.0	13.8	61.0	61.2
	One AP	50.5	50.4	17.8	15.8	65.1	54.0
	Two or More AP	54.0	51.0	21.1	14.3	77.2	52.7
Effect (Difference From No AP)	One AP	8.5**	8.5**	3.8*	Not Sig	5.1*	Not Sig
	Two or More AP	12.0**	9.1**	7.1**	Not Sig	16.2**	Not Sig
Fourth-Year Math	No Math	42.0	40.5	13.0	13.1	55	55.4
	Math	46.6	44.7	15.3	16.2	56.7	55.8
Effect of Math		4.6*	4.1**	Not Sig	Not Sig	1.7*	Not Sig
Four or More Core Classes	< Four Core Classes	44.0	43.7	10.0	9.7	55.0	55.1
	Four or More Core Classes	46.3	44.8	12.3	14.9	58.4	55.8
Effect of Four Core Classes		2.3*	Not Sig	Not Sig	5.2**	3.5*	Not Sig

Note: * = significance of 0.1 and ** = significance of 0.5

TABLE 9

Taking two or more AP courses significantly increases the probability that CPS students positioned to enroll in selective colleges will enroll in a very selective college.

Not Addressing Selection Leads to Overestimates of the Benefits of Coursetaking

		Enrolling in a Four-Year College		Enrolling in a Selective or Very Selective College Among Four-Year College Goers		Persisting for Two Years Within a Four-Year College	
		Predicted Probability		Predicted Probability		Predicted Probability	
		No Selection Controls	With Selection Controls	No Selection Controls	With Selection Controls	No Selection Controls	With Selection Controls
Advanced Placement (AP)	No AP	67.0	66.6	33.0	33.0	70.0	70.3
	One AP	72.8	71.7	41.2	36.4	73.8	68.3
	Two or More AP	77.5	71.2	53.0	51.7	77.2	77.2
Effect (Difference From No AP)	One AP	5.8**	Not Sig	8.2**	Not Sig	3.8**	Not Sig
	Two or More AP	10.5**	Not Sig	20.0**	18.7**	7.2**	Not Sig
Fourth-Year Math	No Math	60.9	61.1	35.0	35.5	71.0	73.5
	Math	67.9	62.0	35.8	38.7	75.1	72.1
Effect of Math		7.0**	Not Sig	Not Sig	Not Sig	Not Sig	Not Sig
Four or More Core Classes	< Four Core Classes	69.0	69.8	35.0	35.3	72.0	71.2
	Four or More Core Classes	73.8	71.9	38.3	36.9	69.0	72.3
Effect of Four Core Classes		4.8**	Not Sig	3.3**	Not Sig	Not Sig	Not Sig

Note: * = significance of 0.1 and ** = significance of 0.5

compared students who do and do not take specific courses (no selection controls). This is a traditional multivariate analysis that estimates a student's likelihood of enrolling in a four-year college, enrolling in a selective college and persisting in college for two years on the basis of their senior year coursework, junior year cumulative GPA, ACT score, and demographics. The second column presents results from our simulated propensity analysis (with selection controls) where estimates are based on comparing the college outcomes of matched students in different schools.

The differences in these two sets of estimates are stark. The results in **Table 8** would suggest that, without addressing selection, what courses students take in twelfth grade has important effects on college enrollment and persistence—even increasing the odds that a student with access to a somewhat selective college would "overmatch" and enroll in a selective four-year college. Most of these differences in college enrollment and persistence appear to be driven by the fact that, within schools, the students who take more advanced courses during their senior year are those who would likely have better college outcomes regardless of participation in specific courses.

The results of our simulated propensity analysis (with selection controls) are quite different. Students with access to somewhat selective colleges are those who at the end of junior year we predict would be competitive in gaining admission to the majority of four-year public colleges in Illinois. Among these students, taking one or more AP courses is associated with a significant increase in the probability of attending a four-year college. The effect of taking AP classes is substantively important. Taking an AP course was associated with an almost 20 percent (the 8.5 percent effect of taking an AP course divided by the baseline 42 percent probability of enrolling in a four-year college) increase in the predicted probability of enrolling in a four-year college among those CPS seniors in our matched sample with access to somewhat selective

College Enrollment and Retention Among CPS Students with Access to Somewhat Selective and Selective Colleges from 2003–07

In this chapter, we examine the college enrollment and persistence of CPS graduating classes of 2003 through 2007. The 2007 graduating class is the most recent cohort for whom we can estimate the likelihood of making an immediate transition to college and staying two years. We restrict our analysis to CPS students who are not in special education or alternative high schools and who entered senior year with the ACT scores and GPAs that would suggest that they would have access to: (1) somewhat selective four-year colleges, and (2) selective colleges. These are the two groups where we observe wide variation in coursetaking within and across schools.

Figures 23 and 24 present the college outcomes of CPS students from these cohorts among graduates with access to somewhat selective colleges (qualified for a four-year college) and graduates with access to selective colleges. Students in **Figure 23** represent 30 percent of CPS graduating classes in these years. Students in **Figure 24** represent 19 percent of CPS graduating classes in these years.

Among CPS students who are qualified to attend a four-year college, 43 percent enrolled in a four-year college in the year after graduation. These students largely attended nonselective and somewhat selective colleges (36 percent). We counted a student as retained in college for two years if s/he remained continuously enrolled in any four-year college for two years after graduation. As seen in **Figure 23**, overall only 60 percent of graduates with access to a somewhat selective college enrolled in a four-year college in the fall after graduation and were continuously enrolled in any college for two years.

Figure 24 shows the same outcomes for students who have access to selective colleges. The majority (66 percent) of students who are more qualified to attend four-year colleges (access to a selective four-year college) enrolled in a four-year college in the year after graduation. Less than one-third, however, enrolled in a selective or very selective college. Once in college, more qualified students had significantly better retention. Overall, three-quarters of more qualified students who enrolled in a four-year college were continuously enrolled for two years after graduation. While this is substantially better than our students with access to somewhat selective colleges, it still means that only half (0.66* 0.76 = 0.50) of CPS students who have access to selective colleges go to a four-year college and stay in college for two years, and only 24 percent enrolled in a selective or very selective college (a match college) and stayed for two years.

FIGURE 23

Seniors with access to somewhat selective colleges (CPS Graduates 2003–2007)

College Enrollment

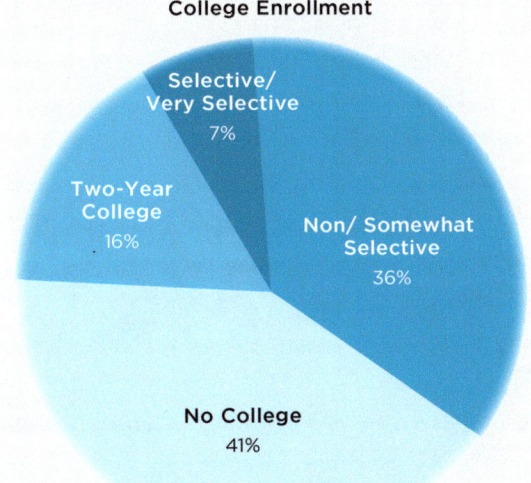

- Selective/Very Selective 7%
- Two-Year College 16%
- Non/Somewhat Selective 36%
- No College 41%

College Enrollment and Persistence at Four-Year Colleges

	Retention Rate of College Goers
Overall	60%
Non and Somewhat Selective Colleges	58%
Selective/Very Selective Colleges	71%

Note: This figure represents 18,983 CPS graduates between 2003–07 with access to somewhat selective colleges.

Chapter 3 | Getting In and Staying

COLLEGE ENROLLMENT AND RETENTION... *CONTINUED*

FIGURE 24

Seniors with access to selective colleges (CPS Graduates 2003–07)

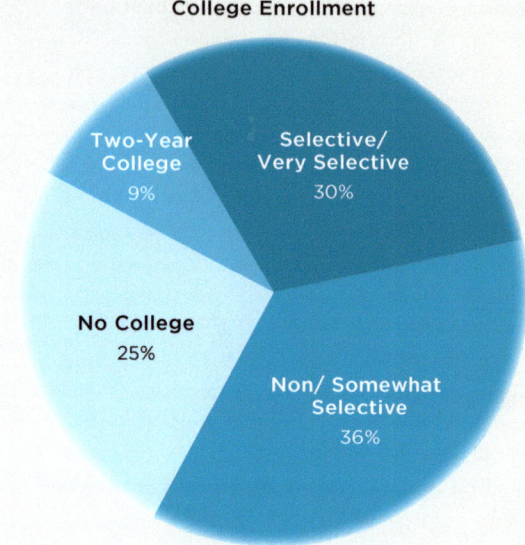

College Enrollment
- Selective/Very Selective: 30%
- Non/Somewhat Selective: 36%
- No College: 25%
- Two-Year College: 9%

College Enrollment and Persistence at Four-Year Colleges

	Retention Rate of College Goers
Overall	76%
Non and Somewhat Selective Colleges	72%
Selective/Very Selective Colleges	80%

Note: This figure represents 18,983 CPS graduates between 2003–07 with access to selective colleges.

---

colleges.[52] The estimated effect of taking two AP courses is about the same as the estimated effect of taking only one AP course senior year. This suggests that for students with access to a somewhat selective college, it is having an AP experience—not the number of AP courses—that matters. Taking a fourth year of math is also associated with a smaller, but statistically significant, effect increase in the probability of these students enrolling in a four-year college.

Table 9 presents the same set of results for students with access to selective colleges. After addressing selection, students who are positioned to attend a four-year college and who take two or more AP courses are substantially more likely to enroll in a selective or very selective college than similarly qualified students who take one or no AP class.[53]

Among these more highly qualified students, taking one AP class has no greater effect than not taking any. But the predicted effect of taking two or more AP courses on the probability of a student with access to a selective college enrolling in a selective or very selective college is quite large. We estimate that, among these higher achieving seniors, taking two or more AP courses is associated with a 19 percentage point increase in the probability of enrolling in a selective or very selective college. This translates into a 60 percent increase in the probability of a college match or overmatch. Importantly, our estimates of the effect of taking AP courses on these students' college enrollment vary little between the two models (with and without selection controls), suggesting that these findings are robust.

The general pattern of results, as seen in **Tables 8 and 9**, is that coursework, particularly participation in AP courses, matters for college enrollment at the margin. For students who have access to somewhat selective colleges AP increases the likelihood of enrolling in a four-year college. However, for this group of students AP does not have a significant impact on attending a selective or very selective four-year college, which is unsurprising given their ACT scores and eleventh grade cumulative GPA. Among those students who are qualified to attend selective four-year colleges, taking multiple AP courses is strongly correlated with enrollment in a selective or very selective four-year college. AP does not, however, increase the likelihood of attending a four-year college among this second group—partly because these students already are overqualified for most colleges.

Finally, for both groups, we find that coursetaking has no direct effect on persistence within four-year colleges. It is important to recognize, however, that while there are no direct effects of coursework, AP in particular does have an indirect effect on college retention because participation in AP is associated with enrolling in a four-year college and, among more highly qualified students, entering a selective college. Thus, AP indirectly leads to increases in the probability of persisting in college for two years. That is, taking an AP course is associated with improvement in college graduation, not because students who take AP do better once enrolled but because a student's likelihood of enrollment increases substantially.

Summary

This chapter is focused on whether there is evidence that the differences we observe in students' coursetaking across high schools shape their college access and performance. The central finding is that senior year coursetaking makes it more likely that students will attend colleges that they are qualified to attend. Taking AP courses and a fourth year of math makes it more likely that students who have GPAs and ACT scores at the end of eleventh grade that position them to enroll in a somewhat selective four-year college will enroll in a four-year college. Taking two or more AP courses makes it more likely that students who have GPAs and ACT scores at the end of eleventh grade that position them to enroll in a selective college will enroll in a selective four-year college. In some ways, these findings are not surprising. The most obvious interpretation is that senior year coursework is advantaging students in college admissions. In Chapter 1, we found that colleges explicitly state that they use students' coursetaking senior year as a signal of a students' motivation and academic preparation, often conflating AP with rigor and college preparedness. That interpretation is supported by the fact that we find that it is taking one AP course and a fourth year of math that matters for enrollment in somewhat selective colleges, and it is taking two or more AP courses that matters for more selective colleges. CPS students who are more qualified and competing for slots in selective institutions in Chicago, such as DePaul or Loyola, are competing against students from other school systems who most often have multiple AP courses over multiple years.

Yet another interpretation is that students who take AP and a more college preparatory senior year may also garner more support in their college search and application process from their high school. Using CCSR data, Stoker (2010) found that CPS students who take two or more AP courses in their junior and senior years report greater levels of information and support in college planning and application. Even after matching students on their demographic characteristics, prior coursetaking, and school performance (ACT scores and GPAs), seniors who have taken two or more AP courses before graduation reported higher levels of support from teachers and counselors in filling out applications, applying for scholarships and financial aid and making decisions about colleges.[54] These students were also more likely to report that their peers valued academic achievement. Importantly, Stoker did not find differences in reports of parental involvement and expectations for college attendance. The lack of a difference in parental support between students in the AP and matched control group suggests then that the differences students reported in guidance and support for college planning from teachers and counselors reflects differences in these students' experiences in school.

It also is not surprising that we did not find that AP courses alone led to greater college persistence within four-year colleges once we accounted for student selection. This is consistent with previous research and the very low passing rates of AP exams for students in Chicago. As with our positive findings on the effects of AP on college enrollment, there are several alternative interpretations of what is driving the lack of effects of AP on college performance. The first is simply that AP is oversold and does not increase college readiness for any student, especially students who have low probabilities of passing the exam. A second interpretation, however, is that one or two AP courses may help a student in particular subjects (e.g., AP English will assist in developing college ready skills in English) but that we cannot expect one AP course to have effects across disciplines and effects on overall persistence. Sadler (2010), in a study of the effects of honors and AP science coursework on performance in college science, found that students who took AP reported higher science grades. This study did not address selection, but it does suggest that AP could have positive effects that are not picked up when AP is being judged by a student's overall performance across her/his classes. And yet a third connected interpretation is that two-year retention in college is not an appropriate measure with which to evaluate the effect of AP. Unfortunately, we do not have access to CPS students' transcripts once in college; thus we cannot examine whether CPS students who take AP do better in their courses, are placed in higher level courses, or are less likely to be placed in remediation—all potentially important effects.

Where we do diverge from prior research findings is that we do not find evidence that taking a fourth year of math shapes college retention. Again, we are using a rather blunt outcome—second year persistence within a four-year college. The most direct effect of students taking a fourth year of math might be on college grades and remediation rates outcomes that we were not able to study.[55] Just as important may be the difference in the kinds of math students are taking. Many CPS students who take a fourth year of math do not take advanced math (e.g., Pre-Calculus and Calculus), which might dilute benefits.

At the beginning of this chapter, we argued that coursework in senior year must accomplish two objectives. First, students need to be competitive in college admissions; and second, they need to be well prepared academically for college. Senior year coursework may benefit students through shaping college access and enrollment. But just adding a fourth year of math or an AP course, or ensuring that students take an academically focused senior year, does not appear to offer a magic bullet for college readiness. What would a senior year that is preparing students for college look like and how would that differ across students? In the next chapter, we turn to this final question by using a qualitative lens to look within and across courses.

CHAPTER 4

The Sum of Its Parts

A Qualitative Look at Senior Year

In the previous chapters, we have characterized students' senior year solely on the basis of course titles. Examining the specific courses a student takes is one way to assess the quality of a senior's academic experience, but which courses students take should not be the only consideration in assessing the quality of senior year. It is equally important to consider the quality of those courses, as previous research has shown. For example, Elaine Allensworth and other CCSR colleagues have rigorously evaluated the impact of CPS's 1997 policy change "college prep for all," which ended remedial coursework and raised graduation requirements. Their analysis found that, despite the dramatic changes in coursetaking that occurred under this policy, there was little evidence of substantial improvements in student learning, college enrollment, or college retention. In short, changing the courses students took did not lead to a different educational experience—most students completed the new curriculum with grades of Cs and Ds.[56] They conclude:

> As long as students are minimally engaged in their courses and attend school irregularly, policymakers should not expect substantial improvements in learning…. Real improvements in learning will require states and districts to develop strategies that get students excited about learning, attending class regularly, and working hard in their courses.[57]

This conclusion—that simply moving students into different courses does not guarantee greater learning—suggests that we look beyond course titles to examine students' experiences in these classes. To what extent are students experiencing senior year as challenging? To what extent do students portray senior year as a time when they are working hard and learning? And, are seniors' classes engaging them in developing the academic behaviors they will need to meet new academic demands? In this chapter, we turn to the students themselves to explore these questions.

The Chicago Postsecondary Transition Project is unique in that we were able to combine large-scale quantitative analysis of successive cohorts of CPS graduates with an in-depth qualitative longitudinal study. From 2005 to 2008, CCSR researchers followed 105 juniors in three CPS high schools through eleventh and twelfth grade and through the second fall after high school graduation. The goal of the study was to understand students' experiences in both preparing for and making the transition to college. In three different schools, we recruited students from an International Baccalaureate classroom (**see *The International Baccalaureate Programme...* on p. 64**), an AP/honors classroom, and two regular English classrooms (**see Appendix A** for further details of the qualitative study). Students were interviewed three times during senior year; we asked about their experiences in specific classes, as well as their overall senior year experience. In this chapter, we draw on these student interviews to address two sets of questions:

1. Do students describe senior year as a challenging experience? Do their reports differ by their level of qualifications for college (test scores and GPAs), or by their coursetaking patterns?
2. Are there specific types of courses or groups of courses that emerge as more or less challenging from the students' perspective? What makes these courses or groups of courses challenging or unchallenging?

Given the coursetaking patterns we describe in Chapter 2, it may not be surprising that nearly three-quarters of the students in our longitudinal study who were not in the IB program described senior year as unchallenging. Students portrayed senior year as easier than previous grades, described specific classes in which little work was required, and often felt like they had learned so little in senior year that they might just as well have skipped it. What is most surprising is that students who took a more academically focused curriculum and enrolled in AP and/or a fourth year of math were not any more likely to experience a challenging senior year, even though AP courses themselves stood out to students as challenging experiences in which they felt they were working hard and learning a lot.

The findings in this chapter are at first confusing. On the one hand, the classes that students take matter. Those who take AP classes, on average, describe these classes as much more challenging than their other courses. However, in determining challenge, we find that what happened in other classes often mattered more than taking one or two advanced courses. The central problem was not one that taking one or even two advanced courses could solve; even when taking these advanced courses, students often had the majority of their time in senior year allocated to courses that were rated as particularly unchallenging—social studies and English electives; vocational, fine arts, and physical education classes. Looking at senior year from the students' perspective moves the conversation away from which courses students should take to the broader question of what set of academic experiences students should be engaged in if they are to be college ready.

This chapter is organized into four sections. The first section describes our approach to coding the level of challenge in students' courses and across their senior year schedule. Second, we present our summary categorization of whether seniors were coded as having a low-, medium-, or high-challenge senior year. We also examine how students' reports of challenge differed by their academic qualifications and the types of courses they took senior year. The third section looks more closely at the challenge of specific courses, how the challenge differed by subject area, and how the distribution of students' time across classes in these subject areas shapes their overall experience senior year. Finally, the last section looks more deeply within courses to identify the common themes that distinguish high- versus low-challenge classes.

The International Baccalaureate Programme in the Chicago Public Schools

The experiences of students in the International Baccalaureate Diploma Programme (IBDP) have been featured throughout the *From High School to the Future* series of reports, and our qualitative analysis of senior year once again highlights this group of students as having a very distinctive educational experience within their high schools.

The IBDP program is a two-year, internationally recognized, college-preparatory curriculum used in secondary schools across the world. Beginning with the long-standing IB program at Lincoln Park High School and expanding to an additional 13 high schools in 1997, CPS has been at the forefront of a movement to use IB as a means of creating college-preparatory programming for high-achieving students in comprehensive urban high schools. Students participating in these programs complete IB coursework in eleventh and twelfth grades, often completing a two-year sequence of the same courses with the same teachers. Much of the IB coursework in senior year is geared towards completing a diverse and rigorous set of assessments. Requirements include written work for each class; timed exams; extensive lab reports; oral presentations; and the Extended Essay, which is a 4,000-word essay that is intended to be the capstone of a student's learning in IB.

In this report, IB students' accounts of their senior year coursework stood out as substantially different from the experiences of their peers—even from those who were taking a large number of advanced courses. Though the case study of Nadia provides an example of what senior year was like for IB students in our qualitative study, the bulk of this chapter focuses on the experiences of students not enrolled in IB. More information on IB students in CPS can be found in the report *Making Hard Work Pay Off*, as well as in *Working to My Potential*, a working paper specifically about the experiences and outcomes of graduates of CPS's IB programs.

Looking at Challenge in Senior Year From a Student's Perspective

Beyond course titles, what would it mean to assess the challenge of senior year? The goal of senior year, regardless of students' qualifications for college, should be the same: to engage students in a course of study that gives them exposure to the content, skills, and experiences they need to make a successful postsecondary transition. We would expect that a challenging senior year would include individual classes that push students to master new levels of content and build the academic skills they will need to succeed in the transition after high school. We would also hope that the sum of those experiences would be demanding as well, and that students would describe their overall senior year experience as one that pushed them to develop new skills, new strategies to meet challenges, and a broader sense of themselves as learners across courses.

What might this look like? Nadia **(see Nadia: A** *Case Study* **on p. 66)**, a student in our longitudinal study, had a senior year that illustrates how students used both their experience within and across classes to assess the "challenge" of their senior year and how much they learned. Nadia was a student enrolled in a selective International Baccalaureate program in a neighborhood high school. Nadia described her senior year as a distinctly challenging experience that was the culmination of her four years of work, requiring her to synthesize much of what she had already learned in high school and push herself to achieve new heights. As Nadia explained, each of her individual classes represented a different kind of challenge for her. Her English class did not appear to demand a lot of work but did present her with new analytic demands. By contrast, Nadia felt that mastering the concepts in Chemistry had become easier over time, even though it had always been her most difficult subject. Math required a great deal of effort, but the class felt manageable because the teacher had clear expectations. Other classes were less challenging but very engaging for Nadia, leading her to feel that, by the end of senior year, she had dramatically increased her capacities as a student. She said she learned, above all else, *"how to think."*

Most students in our study did not have Nadia's experience in twelfth grade. They described their senior year as a time of minimal work and coasting to graduation—the least challenging year of high school and sometimes a waste of time. Gregory **(see Gregory: A** *Case Study* **on p. 68)** describes a far more typical student experience of senior year. His case study demonstrates how filling senior year with electives—even electives in core subject areas like English and the social sciences—can result in a low-challenge experience. Though Gregory's grades and ACT scores at the end of his junior only afforded him access to nonselective colleges, his success on the football team helped make college eligibility a priority for him. Gregory's goal was to focus on his grades, and he signed up for electives—African American History, Law, and Creative Writing—to explicitly have an easier senior year. What he had not bargained for was a senior year that he described as *"a waste of time"* or his frustration with classes where it seemed as if literally nothing happened.

Our Approach to Assessing the Level of Challenge in Senior Year for CPS Students

How common were these experiences? And what contributed to these students' assessments that they were not challenged in senior year? In order to answer these questions, we drew on our detailed interviews with students in senior year to code students' perceptions of the challenge of their individual classes and their senior year overall. Of the 105 students we interviewed, we coded the cases of the 93 for whom we had sufficient data about senior year coursework. These students attended three different high schools, taking a wide variety of senior year schedules. To code challenge, we drew on questions from interviews at three different time points in senior year that asked students about their experience in particular classes, as well as their experience across their classes, giving us a sense of how they assessed their senior years overall. Each class a student described was given a code of high-, medium-, or low-challenge, as was each student's description of senior year overall.

Students like Nadia who described a challenging senior year reported that they had to work harder senior year than they did in previous years of high school. They typically described classes that required them to work hard to do well, and could identify

NADIA: A CASE STUDY
The Culmination of Four Years of IB

In seeking out examples of a senior year experience that students believed to be highly challenging, a step up in difficulty from previous years, and good preparation for the academic demands of college, the only examples to be found were among students in the International Baccalaureate program. Though not all students who participated in the IB program felt the same way about their senior year, the IB program was the only place where we found a consistently high level of challenge across multiple classes.

Nadia had such an experience in her senior year in IB. Nadia was a talented and dedicated student throughout high school. Even without considering her advanced coursework in IB, Nadia finished her junior year with a B average in her classes and a 24 on the ACT, which put her solidly on track to gain admittance to a very selective college. Like all students who planned to complete the IB program, Nadia had almost no choice in what classes she would take her senior year. She was automatically enrolled in a course schedule that included Advanced Chemistry, an advanced math class, and a fourth year of French, in addition to courses in English, social studies, humanities, and art. Nadia had experienced high school as being harder every year, and she did not expect senior year to be any exception:

> "I've heard from this year's senior IB students that senior year is going to go by even faster, because that's when all the work is really going to start—especially all of the IB tests we have to take. I just hope I'm able to handle it and not get too over-stressed."

Nadia had a full course schedule her senior year. She began class at 7 a.m. with Theory of Knowledge, the philosophy-based class that is common across all IB programs, and also went to Advanced Chemistry, World Literature, History of the Americas, and Math Studies before lunch. After lunch, she attended Visual Arts and then French, finishing her classes at 2:15 p.m. but frequently staying after school to complete ROTC responsibilities.

Senior year did not fall short of Nadia's expectations, and she consistently mentioned the requirements of the IB program—preparing for a series of exams in May and writing a series of papers that would be sent to the IB program as a part of her profile—as being a primary source of challenge. At the very beginning of senior year, Nadia was asked if she was having any fun and replied:

> "Uh, no. It's really a lot of work. We've got all the IB tests coming up, and we have to write all these papers that they turn in somewhere in Europe. Everyone else [in the school] is taking it easy, having fun, like senior year is fun…All my friends in regular classes, they don't have to do anything, it's so easy…but I have all this work I have to do."

Nadia found nearly all of her classes to be challenging, though she describes the elements of that challenge differently across classes. Her English class, for example, did not require her to spend a great deal of time on homework. But the tasks she was asked to accomplish were difficult and new to her, especially as they related to literary analysis:

"I was used to writing [one] way from last year, and then this year, when we had to critically analyze a book, I thought I was going to be right, but I was completely wrong. I turned in my journal, and it was Fs on every sheet. I was like oh my gosh, I thought this was good, you know…. She's really expecting way more than what we're doing."

By comparison, Nadia thought her math teacher guided the class in such a way that it made the work seem easy, although she also reported working for two hours per night on the problem sets that were assigned. She describes:

"It's not that easy, but I like the teacher. I really understand. She's pretty dedicated. She offers a lot of help and really goes like the extra mile. She stays after school if we need help…[Math is] harder this year, but I think that's good. It's helping me way more than last year. I mean, she kind of does give a lot of homework, I think, but it's practice and I need it anyway."

Nadia also described her Chemistry class as being challenging, stating that it took three hours per night to complete her homework. However, she also found herself to be a more capable student in that subject in senior year than she had been in junior year. Much to her surprise, she found the class to be more engaging:

"My most interesting class I think is Chemistry. It was one of my worst last year, but now I'm starting to like it. I don't know what happened, but it started out with a topic that I understood, and it got me more encouraged and motivated. Now, I understand how to deal with it, so I'm starting to have more fun with it."

Not all of Nadia's classes required hours and hours of weekly homework, but they all presented her with some kind of challenge. Even her classes that she did not mention as being particularly challenging provided new ways of thinking for Nadia. She discussed how much she appreciated learning about Latin American history in her history class, and also singled out her Theory of Knowledge class and her art class as helping to introduce her to new ideas:

"My Theory of Knowledge is all about trying to make you think, but actually in my art class, we have to do this art book—it's more like history about art. I got interested in the whole surrealism thing, so I'm studying that right now."

Though one might assume that these "new ideas" classes were more engaging to Nadia than her classes that required more work, Nadia seemed equally engaged in all of her classes. In fact, Nadia said that she was really never bored in class because the content of her coursework was interesting to her, her teachers made class engaging, and many of her classes put a great deal of responsibility on the students themselves to answer questions and generate discussions.

Overall Nadia felt that her senior year was harder than previous years in high school. She discussed at great length the requirements for her IB program and the volume of work she was expected to accomplish. More importantly, though, Nadia's senior year felt like a new kind of learning that would provide a link between high school and college. Senior year was a culminating experience for her, requiring her to synthesize much of what she had already learned in high school and push herself to achieve new heights:

"I think I'm just learning how to think better. Looking back, before we had to memorize, memorize like dates and all these things. Now, it's more about thinking and analyzing and taking facts that you don't have to memorize—you just see them in books—and then coming up with ideas. We spend so much more time talking, discussing things, and writing that I'm learning how to think better."

GREGORY: A CASE STUDY

Getting What You Ask For: The Easy Senior Year

It was a commonly held belief among the students we interviewed that senior year was supposed to be easy. When they finished eleventh grade, a year that included intensive preparation for the ACT exam as well as the highest-level math and science courses most students would take, they knew what awaited them the next fall: a few required courses in core subject areas and a lot of electives. Sure, it was an option to take math, science, and AP courses, but what was the incentive?

Many students weighed the pros and cons of taking advanced coursework in senior year and came to the same conclusion: why do the extra work and risk the poor grade in an advanced class when you could just finish the graduation requirements, enroll in some interesting electives, and take it easy senior year? Why take Pre-Calculus when you could take History of Chicago? Why Physics instead of Sociology?

Gregory, a talented athlete with a chance to be awarded a college athletic scholarship, was one of the many students we interviewed who chose English and social studies electives over math or science classes. For Gregory, academics and athletics were inextricably linked. His coach had a stated goal that every senior on the team would win an athletic scholarship. He urged all players to give their best effort to the team in hopes of translating athletic success into college scholarship dollars —for themselves and their peers.

Gregory entered senior year focused on grades, athletics, and college. His biggest goal for senior year was very concrete: to *"get my GPA up so I can go to college."* Gregory was very familiar with NCAA eligibility requirements and knew that a C average and a composite score of 18 on the ACT only barely met minimum eligibility requirements. Gregory felt his odds would be better if he were able to bring his GPA up to a 2.5, believing that *"grades are more important now than I thought they were going to be..."*

Gregory's focus on boosting his GPA guided his course selection for senior year. He knew which classes he had to take in order to graduate, including making up a semester of a previously failed math class, and he chose to take elective classes that he expected would be fairly easy. He expected senior year to be *"more laid back...basically, I have all my credits so I probably only need a couple of more credits to graduate and that's why I'm taking more electives....Those classes ain't gonna be hard."*

Gregory intentionally chose a senior year that he thought would provide him minimal challenge and thus maximize his chances of getting higher grades to raise his GPA. From the very beginning of senior year, that strategy appeared to be a success. Like many students in the study, Gregory's senior year was dominated by electives, especially in the subjects of English and social studies. Switching some courses at the semester, Gregory took a total of 10 classes during senior year— not one of them appeared either to capture his interest or to require him to work hard or learn new skills.

Outside of his required English IV course (World Literature), Gregory described his classes as *"easy"* and *"boring."* He sat through many class discussions where only a few students participated; he spent hour after hour in African American History simply copying down notes off of material from an overhead projector; he was able to complete all of his homework for the day during his lunch period; he insisted *"nothing happens"* in several of his classes. When asked what he was doing in Creative Writing, Gregory challenged his interviewer to do a classroom observation of the class to document what was happening:

> S: Nothin'.
> I: Nothing? Really? You don't write at all?
> S: If you wanna come look at the class, like you did last year, you can come in the class and come look. Cause we ain't do anything.... [the teacher] talks. But in a way...she doesn't do a good job of teaching....She just do nothin'.

Gregory's History of Chicago class, which could have been an exciting course that tapped into students' own family history and experiences in the city, turned out to be another wasted 45 minutes of the day. He describes:

> "We don't do nothing in the History of Chicago...Never...We haven't had a class since like last Wednesday because my teacher—he's a cool teacher....he's just a laid back dude. He know we don't want to sit in the classroom and learn about the history of Chicago."

Describing his Financial Math Class, a social studies elective with a misleading title that was actually focused on such topics as budgeting and taxes, Gregory says, *"We got the easiest teacher I've ever had in my life. That's easy. I know I'll pass that one with an A."* These classes alone added up to almost half of the day, which was, to use Gregory's own word, *"wasted."*

It would be easy to assume that he was simply a disengaged student who was interested in athletics but not in the classroom. But the picture of Gregory as a student in senior year was quite different from what he described the previous year. Junior year required a fair amount of work, which he described as not terribly challenging but requiring several hours of homework per week. When describing his interest in his junior year courses, Gregory sounded like a different person. He was quite engaged in his Sociology and Economics classes, calling Economics his most challenging and most interesting class throughout high school. Specifically he enjoyed the teacher's "hands-on" approach to learning, which included a project about the stock market. He also enjoyed being pushed to think about and discuss different ideas in his Sociology class. He said, *"We got like a lot of open minds in my Sociology class so we have a lot of in-class discussions and we tend to run over the time."* As a result, he reflected on the possibility of pursuing a career in the social sciences:

> "I think that is what I'm going to major in... [either sociology or psychology]... I think I'm going to like Psychology because I kind of like Sociology and I'm taking that now and I'm taking Psychology next year."

Sadly, his Psychology class, like the rest of his courses during senior year, did not meet those expectations. He said little about the Psychology course in his interviews, but grouped it into the category of classes he felt were a waste of time.

Unfortunately, Gregory was by no means alone in his assessment that senior year had largely been a waste of time. What distinguished Gregory from other seniors in similar situations was how invested he remained in his course performance, dedicated to earning as many As and Bs as possible and boosting his GPA for college scholarship eligibility to the bitter end of the year. While many other students calculated that their elective courses were not required for graduation and seemed to almost completely disengage from school, Gregory was insistent that he not "catch senioritis."

When asked if he felt like he learned much senior year Gregory replied, *"Not at all."* Reflecting on high school, Gregory admitted that he should have been focused more on grades at the beginning of high school, especially once he started to think about his college athletic career. Still, he met his senior year goal, earning all As and Bs in his courses, which boosted his GPA sufficiently to be awarded his athletic scholarship. He expected college to be more serious than high school, given that he had to deal with *"too much playing"* in his high school classes. Gregory viewed college as a *"fresh start"* and was looking forward to being a college student.

multiple classes in which they felt they were learning skills and competencies that will be beneficial in the future. In comparison, students like Gregory, who had a low-challenge experience, generally described senior year as easier than previous years, described a number specific classes in which little work was required, and often felt like they had learned so little in senior year that they might just as well have skipped it entirely. Some students, coded as medium challenge, fell in between these two extremes, typically describing senior year as about the same level of challenge and requiring similar work effort to previous years of high school. (For a more detailed description of our qualitative sample and methodology, as well as examples of high, medium, and low challenge, (see Appendix A.)

Few Seniors Felt That They Were Challenged or Had Learned a Great Deal in Senior Year.

Most of the seniors in our study described their senior year as easier than previous years of high school and felt that they had learned little (see Figure 25). Our criteria for coding students as having a high-challenge senior year represent a fairly low bar, especially given that our qualitative sample was relatively high-achieving and took more advanced coursework than the average CPS senior. Among the 69 seniors in our sample who were not in the IB program, only nine students (13 percent) were categorized as having a high-challenge senior year, whereas 49 students (71 percent) were coded as having a low-challenge senior year.

FIGURE 25

Outside of the International Baccalaureate program, very few students experienced a challenging senior year

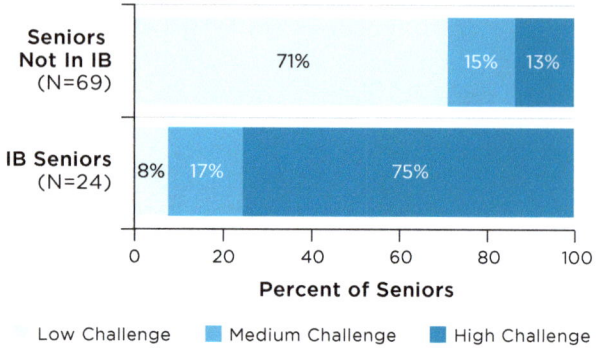

Even Students in Advanced Coursework Lacked Senior Year Challenge

Colleges, as noted in Chapter 1, use the "rigor" of a student's transcript to evaluate whether a student is motivated and has been exposed to challenging work. We would expect that students who took a more academically focused senior year (e.g., those who took four or more core courses and who enrolled in an AP and/or fourth-year math course) would be more likely to be challenged. We might also expect that students' level of challenge in senior year might be influenced by their level of achievement. In order to investigate these possible associations, we broke our sample into groups based on qualifications for college, then considered their level of advanced coursework in senior year, and finally assessed their level of senior year challenge. Surprisingly, none of these distinctions explain a general lack of challenge across our sample.

How to Read These Figures

Figures 26, 27, and 28 represent the coursetaking decisions and overall level of challenge experienced by each student in our study (excluding students in the IB program). The figures are read from top to bottom with each numbered column representing three outcomes for the same student.

For example, **Figure 26** shows the distribution of challenge and coursework for the most highly qualified non-IB students in our qualitative sample, a total of 17 students who had ACT scores and GPAs prior to senior year that would likely qualify them for admittance to a selective or very selective four-year college. These students are represented in dark blue in the top line of the figure. If we follow student number 12 through all three outcomes, we can see that this student took fewer than four core classes, did take an AP or math course, and ultimately did not experience a high-challenge senior year. Overall, while all but one of these students took an AP or math course, only about half took more than four core courses, and very few experienced a high-challenge senior year.

Figure 27 presents these same outcomes for the 25 students whose junior year ACT score and GPA would indicate they have access to a somewhat selective four-year college, and **Figure 28** shows results for the 27 seniors in our study with very low grades and ACT scores.

FIGURE 26

Even though many students with access to selective or very selective colleges took advanced coursework, few experienced a high-challenge senior year

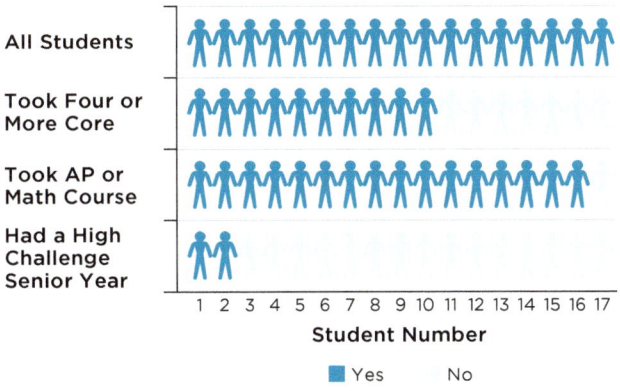

Note: Of the 15 students not coded as high-challenge, six experienced a medium level of challenge in senior year overall, and nine experienced low challenge.

FIGURE 27

Only about half of students with access to a somewhat selective college took advanced coursework and most experienced a low-challenge senior year

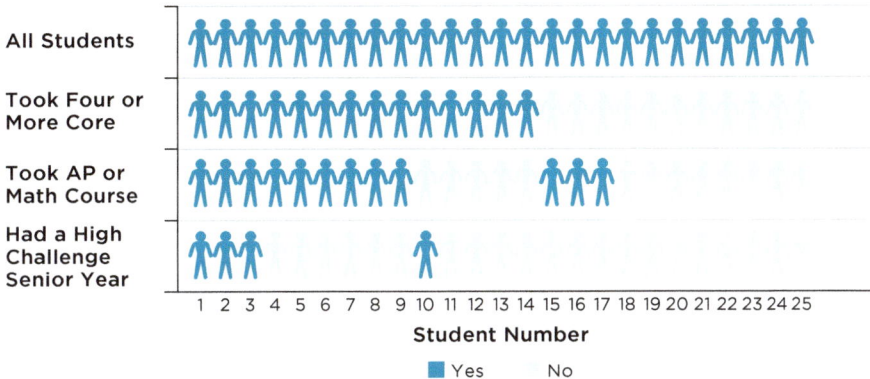

Note: Of the 21 students not coded as high-challenge, two experienced a medium level of challenge in senior year overall, and 19 experienced low challenge.

FIGURE 28

Some students with access to nonselective or two-year colleges took advanced coursework; very few experienced a challenging senior year

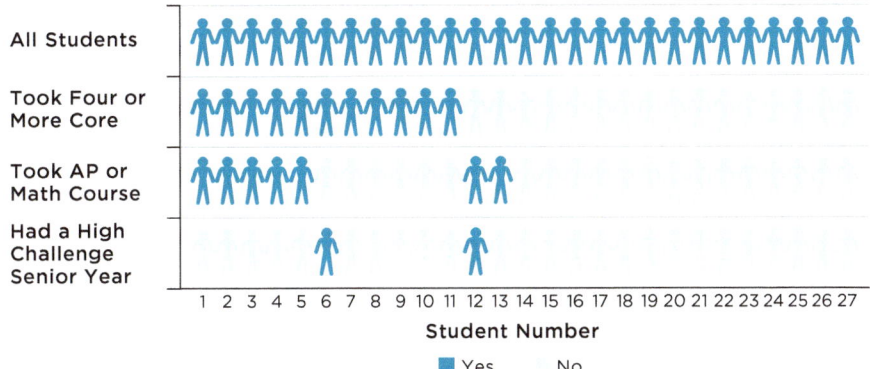

Note: Of the 25 students not coded as high-challenge, two experienced a medium level of challenge in senior year overall, and 23 experienced low challenge.

Almost all students in our study who had high grades and test scores and were not in IB took at least one AP or math course, and about half took four core courses in senior year (**see Figure 26**). Yet, only two of these students describe their senior year as high challenge. We see the same pattern among students with access to somewhat selective four-year colleges (**see Figure 27**). In the previous chapter, we noted that it was these students who enter senior year positioned to attend a somewhat selective four-year college for whom taking AP and senior year math makes the most significant difference in the likelihood of enrolling in a four-year college. However, in our qualitative sample, taking these same courses does not appear to shape a student's assessment of the academic challenge of their senior year. This pattern raises the question: Why are qualified students who are taking four or more core courses, as well as AP and math courses, not experiencing their senior year as challenging?

In addition, the seniors with the lowest eleventh grade GPAs and ACT scores (those with access only to two-year colleges or nonselective four-year colleges) were the least likely to have a challenging senior year (see Figure 28). These are the students who are the most academically at risk in the postsecondary transition. Yet they are the most likely to portray their senior year experience as less challenging than their prior years of high school—in which their classes were not difficult, they experienced minimal workload and minimal challenge, and they learned little.

AP Courses Are Challenging Even When Senior Year Is Not

Our analysis thus far indicates that taking more advanced courses and a more academically focused senior year does not ensure that students experience senior year as challenging. Many students who took AP and fourth-year math courses and appeared to be taking a challenging set of courses on paper did not actually experience senior year as challenging. One interpretation of this finding is that advanced courses, particularly AP courses in CPS, are falling short of their promise—suggesting that CPS students are taking AP courses that on paper look like they are rigorous when in actuality they are not. Another possible interpretation could be that AP courses are only a small part of a student's senior year, and would therefore only have a limited influence on a student's experience of the year overall. We can investigate these hypotheses directly by looking at descriptions of individual classes.

Once we group students' impressions of their classes into subject areas, it is clear that AP is not the problem (see Figure 29). While the vast majority of AP students described their senior year overall as being low challenge, AP courses stood out as dramatically more challenging than any other group of courses taken during senior year. In nearly all cases, AP classes were rated as medium to high challenge. Notably, the required English IV course was also perceived by students as being at least moderately challenging, though a smaller

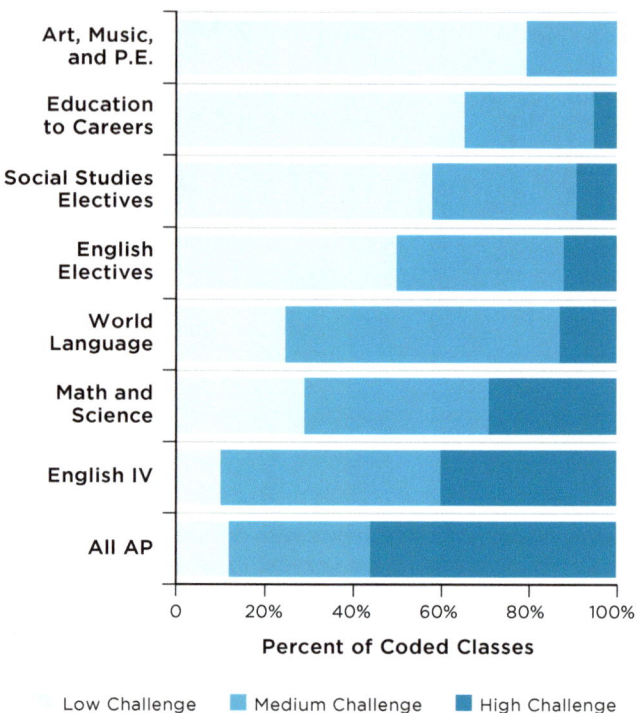

FIGURE 29

Students had more challenging experiences in AP and English IV classes, whereas electives were generally low challenge

proportion of English IV descriptions were characterized as highly challenging. Students' descriptions of their math and science courses were quite mixed, as were their impressions of world language courses.

Students' descriptions of their experiences in social studies and English electives contrast sharply with their descriptions of AP courses. In the majority of cases, English and social studies electives were coded as low challenge. In these courses, students reported that they did little work in and outside class, were not pushed academically, did not have to prepare for class, and learned little. Students only occasionally described a social studies or English elective as a high-challenge course.

Social studies and English electives, however, look challenging relative to arts, music, physical education, and ETC classes. It is of particular concern that nearly two-thirds of students' descriptions of their ETC classes were coded as unchallenging. Students completing ETC requirements took, on average, two periods of ETC during their senior year—with some students taking only one period of a class and two periods of work placement. Later in this chapter,

Categorizing and Coding Challenge Across Subjects and Levels

In order to summarize the level of challenge students experienced across different subject areas in senior year, we grouped classes into subject-specific categories—all AP classes, English IV, fourth-year math or science classes, world language classes, social science or English electives, ETC/vocational classes, or non-core elective courses (i.e., art, music, or physical education). If the student was taking two of the same kind of classes (e.g., two different social science electives), each of those classes is counted separately. If two students were talking about the same class (e.g., both students were in the same AP Psychology course) those two ratings are also counted separately. Figure 29 displays the ratings assigned to the various classes students described.

Students in our study took a variety of AP courses, with AP English being the most popular, followed by classes in the humanities and social sciences (e.g., Sociology, Psychology, Economics, and History). Across students, we coded instances of AP courses: 20 English courses; eight social studies/humanities courses (e.g., Economics, Psychology, U.S. History, and U.S. Government and Politics); and seven additional courses (e.g., Spanish, Biology; and Statistics.

Because of our small samples, we could not reliably differentiate between the challenge of AP courses across subjects. Also, it is important to note that while AP English was the common AP course taken by students in our sample, our summary of common themes across high-challenge AP and English classes includes descriptions of some courses from content areas other than English.

As seen in Figure 29, students often described their AP classes as being more challenging than other senior year classes and more challenging than similar classes taken in previous years of high school. They also thought their AP classes were teaching skills and competencies that would be beneficial in the future. The same general themes emerged in students' description of their English IV classes. All students in CPS are programmed into either AP English or English IV, and for many students it anchored senior year. We coded 48 students' descriptions of their English IV courses, and all but five of these students described the class as having a medium or high level of challenge (**see Figure 29**).

we will look in much greater detail at why ETC students felt little challenge.

One Challenging Course Does Not Constitute a Challenging Year

Our look at students' ratings of AP, English IV, math, and science courses suggests that, on balance, these courses were in fact relatively challenging for students. AP courses stand out in students' minds as particularly challenging; science and math courses appear more variable. Low levels of challenge in AP and other advanced courses cannot explain the overall low levels of challenge that students experienced in senior year. Even students who took multiple advanced courses still spent the majority of their time in courses that were rated as particularly unchallenging—including social studies and English electives; ETC; and art, music, and physical education classes. As we saw in Chapter 1, the most significant difference between junior and senior years is the fact that these core and non-core elective courses make up a much more significant portion of seniors' course schedules. Close to 80 percent of seniors take a social studies elective with many students taking two or more. And, particularly for students who in Chapter 2 we characterized as *Vocationally Focused* and *Making Up Courses*, senior year was dominated by their need to complete graduation requirements, including their non-core electives.

Whether due to graduation requirements or a student's own preference, the shift to social studies and English electives, as well as non-core electives in senior year, meant that students' transcripts were too often dominated by unchallenging courses. This finding is best illustrated by looking at the allocation of students' time between challenging and unchallenging courses during their senior year. **Figures 30 through 33** present examples of typical course schedules for students in our qualitative study. The schedules are color-coded to represent the average level of challenge experienced by all students in the study in that subject area. Course subjects fell into four categories: (1) AP and English IV courses, where the majority of classes were rated as highly challenging; (2) math, science, and world language courses, where classes were most often rated as medium but sometimes high challenge; (3) English and social studies electives, where the majority of classes were rated as low challenge; and (4) non-core electives, where virtually all classes were rated as low challenge. An accompanying pie chart represents the distribution of time students spend in the four categories.

Looking at seniors' class schedules can allow us to understand what proportion of a student's day is spent in low-challenge classes. **Figures 30 and 31**, for example, present two schedules that seem as if they would be representative of an academically challenging senior year. The first student took two AP courses, one English elective, one social studies elective, two non-core electives (art and physical education) and a world language. From the perspective of course titles, this schedule would be viewed as a rigorous senior year with two AP courses, more than five core classes and a science course. Two AP courses constituted about one-third of the student's day. Yet, the combination of two core electives, which on average are rated by students as low challenge, and two non-core electives meant that the majority of this student's schedule was spent in low- to very-low challenge courses.

Few seniors took such a rigorous schedule. The second student's schedule (**see Figure 31**) is even less challenging, in spite of the fact that it includes an AP class and an advanced math class. With one period of ETC and two periods of job placement, a student with this schedule would spend over half the day in extremely low-challenge courses.

The lack of challenge is even more striking for students who did not enroll in advanced coursework. **Figures 32 and 33** show typical schedules for students whom we characterized in Chapter 2 as *Vocationally Focused* and *Elective Heavy*. **Figure 32** shows a fairly common schedule for students completing the three-credit ETC sequence during senior year. The combination of three periods of ETC, classes which students reported as predominantly low challenge, and a non-core elective meant that over half of the day was spent in courses where students reported doing little work. This characterization of ETC programs might seem unfair. ETC programs are not intended to serve students in the same way as AP courses. And, while they may not be as academically rigorous, students might view these courses as engaging and beneficial in other ways. This was, unfortunately, not the case. We explore students' ETC experiences in greater depth later in this chapter.

Finally, we see how taking a course schedule loaded with electives results in a very unchallenging year for students. **Figure 33** shows a schedule that represents students whom we characterized as *Elective Heavy*, the most common coursetaking pattern senior year. As we showed in Chapter 2, a common schedule for students who are *Elective Heavy* includes, on average, almost two courses in art, music, and/or physical education; the required English course; an additional social studies and/or English elective; and perhaps a career education credit. This schedule results in more than two-thirds of a student's day being spent in classes where very few students report being challenged at all. All of the courses taken by this student, however, are required to meet graduation requirements, although in this specific case we do not know how many of these non-core electives the student actually needed to graduate. However, **Figure 33** makes abundantly clear that students taking an *Elective Heavy* schedule are unlikely to encounter a challenging class outside of their required English IV course.

We begin by examining the themes that emerge from students' perceptions of high-challenge AP and English IV classes. We then contrast those themes with those that emerge from students' descriptions of their low-challenge classes.

Common Themes in High-Challenge Classes

In our subject-specific analysis of challenge in students' courses, AP courses and English IV courses stood out as challenging to students. Given that many of the AP classes students completed were AP English courses, it is perhaps not surprising that similar themes emerged from both descriptions when we looked more deeply into students' accounts of what made those classes challenging. This section presents the results of a thematic analysis of both subject areas, noting distinctions and overlap when necessary.

Four major themes stood out in students' descriptions of challenging classes in their senior year. Students distinguished high- from low-challenge courses based

FIGURE 30

Even students who took two AP classes were often enrolled in multiple periods of electives, which were typically described as unchallenging

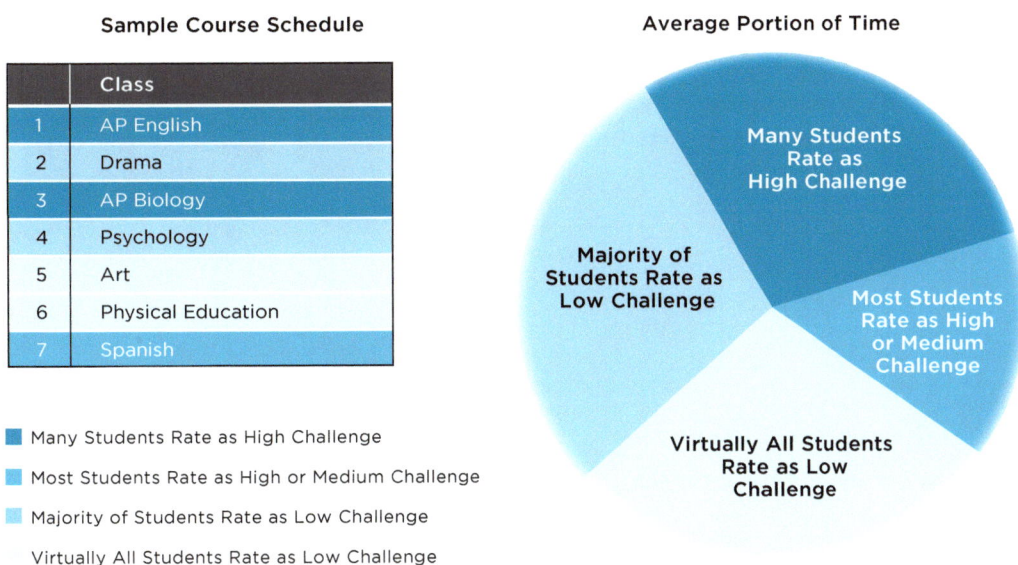

FIGURE 31

For students who completed the ETC program, even taking an AP and a math class does not amount to a challenging schedule

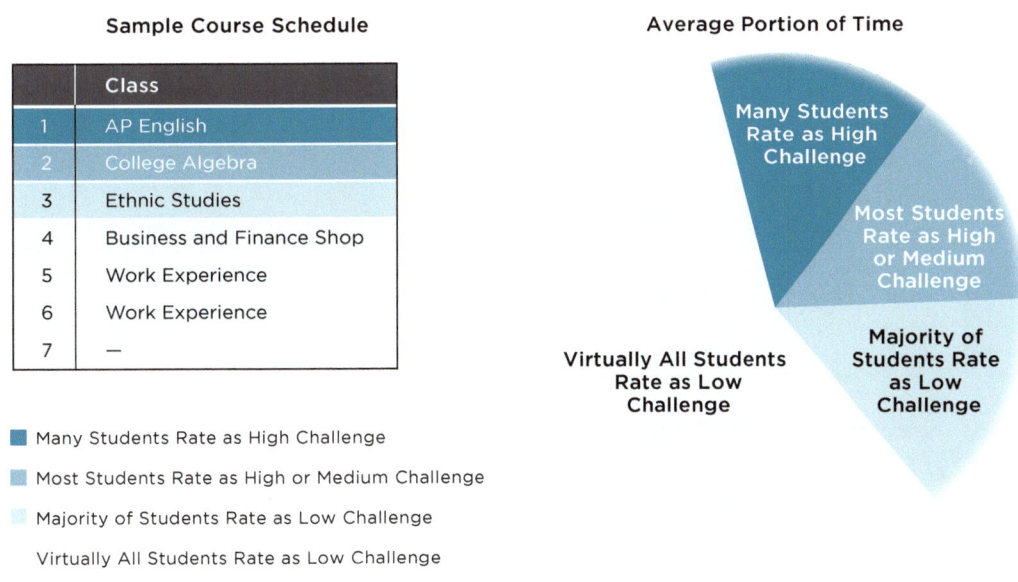

FIGURE 32

The typical senior year schedule for students leaving high school with low skill levels—filled with non-core electives and vocational courses—provided virtually no challenge

Sample Course Schedule

	Class
1	English IV
2	Journalism
3	Psychology
4	Physical Education
5	Construction
6	Construction
7	Construction

■ Many Students Rate as High Challenge
■ Most Students Rate as High or Medium Challenge
■ Majority of Students Rate as Low Challenge
  Virtually All Students Rate as Low Challenge

Average Portion of Time

- Many Students Rate as High Challenge
- Majority of Students Rate as Low Challenge
- Virtually All Students Rate as Low Challenge

FIGURE 33

Students who filled a senior year schedule with non-core electives were unlikely to encounter challenging classes

Sample Course Schedule

	Class
1	English IV
2	Law
3	Agriculture
4	Advanced Band
5	Physical Education
6	Studio Sculpture
7	—

■ Many Students Rate as High Challenge
■ Most Students Rate as High or Medium Challenge
■ Majority of Students Rate as Low Challenge
  Virtually All Students Rate as Low Challenge

Average Portion of Time

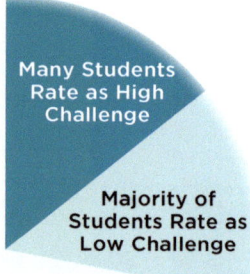

- Many Students Rate as High Challenge
- Majority of Students Rate as Low Challenge

Virtually All Students Rate as Low Challenge

UCHICAGO CCSR Research Report | The Challenge of Senior Year in Chicago Public Schools

on the extent to which: (1) the course developed and expected *academic behaviors* necessary to participate in challenging coursework; (2) students perceived that they were building a set of *academic skills* that they would need in college; (3) teachers held students to *higher academic standards* than what had been expected of them in the past; and (4) students needed to *work hard to succeed* in the course.

Academic Behaviors

The first characteristic that distinguished AP classes was that, often for the first time, students were expected to demonstrate positive academic behaviors. They were expected to come prepared to class. They were expected to complete homework and hand it in on time. In their own words, they could no longer "get away" with sloppy academic behaviors. Indeed, the accountability for maintaining positive academic behaviors was what most distinguished challenging AP classes from less-challenging AP classes, and it is also what most distinguished AP classes from non-AP English and social studies classes.

In talking about their AP courses, students emphasized that their teachers held higher expectations and, as a result, were helping them build important academic behaviors and habits. Students often described the effect of raised expectations in terms of what they could no longer *"get away with."* Halle, for example, experienced her AP English teacher's "no late work" policy the hard way, by trying to hand in a homework assignment five minutes late and being told five minutes was still late work. Halle, an honors student with strong qualifications for college, enrolled in two AP classes, which she found challenging, as well as a great number of electives, which she did not. At the end of the school year, Halle looked back on all of her senior year classes and explained, *"Out of every class that I have, that's the one I will not miss for anything. If I don't go to any other classes, I'll still go to AP English."* Other academic behaviors that students were held accountable for in AP included prompt and consistent attendance, time management, on-time completion of work, effective note-taking, the completion of long-term reading assignments on their own schedule, and participation in class discussions.

Most notably, AP classes stood out as classes where students had to prepare in advance—by reading or doing homework—in order to participate effectively in activities that took place during class time. Students would explain that in other classes, both prior to and during senior year, class time might be used to recap the previous night's reading for students who were not prepared, or to go over new information and start on the next day's homework. AP class time, in contrast, was used for analysis, projects, discussion, or other academic work that required students to have completed work in advance. Dani, an honors student, had always done well in her classes but thought her senior year AP-level English class was especially challenging. When asked if it's important to keep up with the reading, Dani, said yes, *"because the in-class essay will get you. If you don't read the book, you don't know how it ends, and you won't know how to go back and find examples. You need to read the book."*

Similarly, in describing high-challenge English IV classes, seniors described a level of accountability that reinforced positive work habits and academic behaviors. The specific habits and behaviors that students connected to English IV were somewhat different from those linked to AP courses. Whereas students in AP classes described a wide range of academic behaviors required to do well in class, students in regular- or honors-level English classes described a more limited range, focusing almost entirely on the necessity of completing day-to-day homework assignments, keeping up with the reading in order to pass quizzes on comprehension, having clear consequences for skipping class, and knowing that participating in class discussion was important for their grades. When asked whether it's important to prepare for her English class in advance, Inez, a student in a regular-level English class explained,

> "Yes, because if she gives you a story to read and you don't read it, the next morning, you'll be lost. We have a journal, and the journal topics come from what we read the night before, so when we do a group activity, you won't have any idea what they're talking about."

Though this might not seem to be a particularly high bar, this level of accountability for attendance, participation, and homework completion was often not present in students' other classes, as we will see in our description of senior year electives.

Learning Valuable Skills

The emphasis placed on academic behaviors led seniors to feel that they were getting ready for the academic demands of college courses. Particularly in AP courses, students asserted that they were learning valuable skills—including writing and analytic skills—which they saw as essential for success in college.

As noted above, the majority of AP classes we coded were AP English classes. Not surprisingly, a consistent theme in students' descriptions was the extent to which they felt that their writing had improved. In our final senior year interview, we asked students to look back on their high school careers and describe classes that they thought really prepared them for college or classes in which they felt like they had learned a great deal. Students' AP classes nearly always came up in these discussions, particularly around writing. Sabrina, who had an extremely disappointing senior year apart from a demanding AP English class, explained,

> "In my AP class, I think the writing has prepared me for freshman year English. At the end of last year, I know I wasn't ready to write 10-page papers."

Students' perception that AP classes were preparing them for college extended beyond writing. Students in AP classes frequently explained that they had to read texts for a deeper level of understanding than they had in the past. When we asked students at the very end of senior year to reflect on what they had learned in senior year that would be helpful for their academic futures, nearly all students in AP classes—even the ones who were not terribly excited about their AP classes—responded with an answer about skill-building in their AP classes.

While students in AP classes stressed experiences that they felt developed a broad array of new skills, including learning to think analytically, students in English IV classes primarily described experiences focused on improving their writing skills. English IV classes across the three high schools that participated in our study were strikingly similar. Students were reading many of the same works (e.g., *Hamlet, Oedipus, Things Fall Apart*) and also seemed to be doing similar assignments. At all three schools, students had to write a culminating paper that was intended to be significant in length, research based, and reflective of college-level writing standards. Students frequently referred to the assignment as the "senior paper." The assignment was a requirement for passing English IV; and, in many instances, it became the linchpin of students' senior year. As Norton, a student who struggled throughout high school but enjoyed his challenging English IV class senior year, describes: *"Reading the books, doing eight-, nine-page papers, that's getting us ready for college. So I'll be prepared."* Even students who were highly skeptical of the overall value of their senior year often identified the senior paper for English IV as something that provided them with valuable skills for the future.

Higher Standards

Connected to learning valuable skills, the academic standards set by their teachers for essay construction, literary analysis, content mastery, and precision in editing also stood out in AP classes. Again, as most AP courses in this analysis were English courses, students experienced this change in standards primarily around tasks relating to writing literary essays. For example, students in AP classes felt that they had gained a new understanding of what it meant to read a work of literature to understand concepts beyond fact and plot and get at an author's intent. As Javier, a student with a nearly straight-A average who was profiled in the *Potholes* report described,

> "In AP English, you have to think a lot. Like right now, we're analyzing poems, and it could be a four-line poem, but we have to take so much out of it that you could have more than four lines of notes for just a four line poem… we could talk about one line for fifteen minutes."

Students in AP courses also experienced significant challenge around the technical elements of writing, learning to fix their grammar, use proper MLA citation, use effective evidence, and make their writing clearer. Halle cheekily explains her frustration in having to reach new standards for effective communication in her papers:

> "My English teacher says that every time a writer writes something, they put it there for a specific reason. She keeps asking, 'Why is this comment there, why is that one?' And I'm like, 'I don't know! It's grammatically correct! What more do you want from me?'"

Many seniors, like Halle, were very aware of the differences in standards for work and connected it to skills development. For example, Omar, an honors student with a fairly challenging senior year course load, appreciated having to complete multiple revisions of his papers to meet his teachers' high standards:

> "My teachers used to say, 'Oh, your paper is great,' but this class is more intense. Now, I don't get a lot of positive feedback, but that's good, so I know how to improve. My teacher tells me exactly what I need to do to organize a paper."

Students in other challenging AP classes besides English also discussed learning to truly master the content of a textbook, which requires a new dedication to close reading.

Students in English IV similarly emphasized that a shift in expectations—particularly around organizing, crafting, and supporting written arguments with evidence—were moving them to a new level. For example, Vito, a student who had previously had a hard time finding value in his courses outside of his Construction and Architecture shop, described the tangible skills he was learning in his English class:

> "In World Literature, we're learning how to write a correct paper. We spend time every day learning how to write the perfect paper… In Freshman year, they'd be like one page long. Now they're teaching us to do more like three or four pages—and then in college, we'll do more like six. So they're trying to get us prepared."

Workload and Pace

Finally, the amount of work required in AP and English IV classes also distinguished them from less challenging classes. Students described how AP and English IV courses required them to read more and faster, to write more frequent and lengthier papers, and to manage a larger overall workload than other classes. Students nearly always described their AP classes as being harder than their other senior year classes, and in some cases, clearly identified the workload itself as the distinctive feature of their AP classes. Halle described her AP Economics class:

> "We got report cards yesterday… I got a D in AP Economics… After all the years I've been at [this school], I've never really had to work hard at anything… I could easily you know, read it, okay take some notes go get an A on the test, but this class is not like that… For you to excel, you have to be solely dedicated to it… You have to sleep, eat, and breathe economics."

For many other students, English IV stood out as the class in which they had to work the hardest—keeping up with the most homework, the most in-class activity, and the fastest pace of material. English IV was frequently the only class that required students to complete *any* work consistently. When asked which classes gave him homework, Chad, a student who often tried to avoid doing homework, said simply, *"World Literature gives you homework. She is **going** to give you homework."*

Describing the Low-Challenge Senior Year

English, AP, and math and science courses were predominantly rated as medium to high challenge (see Figure 29 on p. 72). In sharp contrast, students' description of their core electives (social studies and English electives), Education to Careers (ETC) courses and non-core electives (art, music, and physical education) were predominantly described as low challenge. One interpretation is that our focus on challenge is missing what is important about these courses. Social science and English electives could offer the opportunity for students to be exposed to new content and provide a transitional experience that introduce students, particularly in the social sciences, to the disciplines they will encounter on college campuses. While these are all potential benefits, unfortunately, the experience of the students in our qualitative study was unambiguous: in marked contrast to the description of their AP and English IV class, students described these classes as un-engaging, lacking concrete expectations for students, requiring little more than passive participation, and in the case of their ETC program, often devoid of content.

Electives: Rarely Challenging and Rarely Engaging

Electives are a hallmark of senior year. In the absence of AP, the course titles of fourth-year social science and English electives are enticing for many students. Journalism, Drama, Law, Film Studies, Latin American Studies, African American Studies, Ethnic Studies, Psychology, and Sociology all sound like fun and interesting classes to take. Not surprisingly, students expected these classes to be interesting and engaging. They were looking forward to the elective courses they chose themselves and were excited to learn about new subjects and topics.

Alita provides an example of how these classes can provide the backbone of a challenging and engaging senior year for students. In fact, Alita singles out her electives as the most important part of her senior year experience. (See *Alita: A Case Study* on p. 81.)

Unfortunately, for the most part, elective courses were not nearly as interesting or engaging as students had hoped—nor were they at all challenging. Students' descriptions of fine arts and physical education courses were overwhelmingly rated as low challenge; however, electives in core subject areas—English and social studies—were the most often rated as low challenge (see Figure 29 on p. 72). In contrast to the enforcing of academic behaviors, building of skills, setting of standards, and hard work required for high-challenge classes, students described elective courses as demanding none of this. Rather, they described courses that were dominated by "seat time," where little participation was required of students. Courses often focused largely on lecture and note-taking that students did not perceive as building academic skills or preparing them for college. Students virtually never described being held to higher academic standards in these courses or being pushed to learn new ways of thinking. Overall, these courses required little to no work.

Students were frank in their portrayal of electives, emphasizing that there was little accountability to be present in class and admitting that they often cut. When they did attend, students rarely described a need to prepare for class, and descriptions of these classes often sounded like a study hall or social time where games were played. For example, when Dorian, a student with very limited access to college and a Vocationally Focused senior year, was asked what his Contemporary American History class was like, he responded that most of the time students *"sit there and have free time."*

Often, students like Abel (see *Abel: A Case Study* on p. 84), who had access to a wide range of colleges and universities, described a lot of content coverage in their elective class and a great deal of note-taking, along with occasional tests and quizzes. Karla, a similarly highly qualified student with a concentration of electives, described her work in a social studies elective course as mostly note taking and class discussion. Karla expressed her frustration with the repetitive cycle of lecturing and note-taking required for that class by suggesting, *"I think we need more work...a project or something."* Similarly, Barbara, a student with weaker academic qualifications than Karla and Abel, nonetheless described her electives in similar terms, explaining that her psychology class had some

ALITA: A CASE STUDY

A Senior Year That Works Well

Much of this chapter focuses on the extent to which senior year was a disappointingly unchallenging year for students, with student after student describing courses that sounded interesting on paper but fell flat in practice. Add to that the several periods of vocational programming that many students took and even taking a challenging AP course was not enough to turn senior year into a rigorous, engaging, or even interesting learning experience. A few important exceptions did exist.

Alita, an honors student in the Education to Careers program, had a senior year that worked. The linchpin of Alita's senior year was the class her school called the "Senior Seminar." Students were required to apply for the Senior Seminar, which included an English class and a social studies class taught by two different teachers who often collaborated on lessons and projects. Alita was happy to be accepted into the seminar because she had heard that the class was very engaging and covered interesting topics. Even so, Alita did not expect to be overwhelmed by the workload, as she had already taken a demanding AP English class. In fact, she felt that senior year would be easier than previous years overall. Alita finished her junior year with an unweighted GPA of 2.5 and an ACT score of 18, putting her on track to attend a somewhat selective college or university. Alita planned to go to college and study 3-D animation.

Alita's senior year schedule started off at 8:30 a.m. with her Senior Seminar classes—first English, and then social studies. She then moved on to her electives of Film Study and Latin American History. After lunch, she was enrolled in three consecutive periods of shop, which in her case was Graphic Communication, before she left school at 3 p.m. Alita's schedule looked fairly typical of the students we interviewed in that it included a strong contingent of classes in the humanities and social studies, as well as a block of time dedicated to vocational coursework, but no math or science. What distinguished Alita from most of her peers with similar-looking schedules is how she experienced the challenge and engagement of these courses.

Alita found the two-credit Senior Seminar to be distinctly challenging, standing out in difficulty from other classes and from previous years. She felt that her English teacher was aggressively pushing them to build their writing skills, both in developing thoughts beyond the "five paragraph" style of paper writing, and also in strict attention to detail and editing.

> "[The paper] has to be more than five paragraphs—we write as much as we can about [a topic] without repeating ourselves… The paper should be three pages or four pages long. As long as it makes sense it's fine…She'll only make us do three [drafts], but if we want, we'll do another draft to make sure it's the way we want it to be and the way she would want it. And she'll help—she's been going over our papers and writing notes on them, so if I don't think my third draft really fits the notes too well, I'll go and change it and make a fourth draft."

Chapter 4 | The Sum of Its Parts

Though the workload in the social studies portion of the Senior Seminar was not as high as in the English portion, Alita appreciated the exposure to new concepts of philosophy and especially appreciated how those concepts related back to the works she was reading in English:

> "[The two different classes]—they're always related to each other somehow... we're learning about philosophy in [social studies], and then we relate it to "Oedipus," where Oedipus found how different philosophies think life is made up and [you can't] overrule fate... like, Oedipus, you know, he was trying to escape his fate, and so the chapter of the [philosophy] book we're reading now, it's about fate and how the philosophers explain that."

The electives Alita chose to take senior year—Film Studies and Latin American History—might not have been a great deal of work, but they were at minimum very engaging. Learning about lighting in Film Studies has helped her approach illustration differently:

> "We learn how like certain shading is used in movies and how lighting causes shadows, and in a drawing, it's the almost the same thing. It's a certain way like from the light coming through the window you have to make sure have your shading on the right side and on the right parts."

Alita's favorite class was her Latin American History class, where she had a transformational experience learning about history from a different perspective:

> "I learned a lot of different things in my history class—a different perspective on history, more from the Latin American side. [In other classes], they don't tell you everything...you don't know about the struggle that [the people] went through—like about how Puerto Rico became a commonwealth, and how...the people were in slavery, and they put African Americans down there, so that's how cultures are all mixed now...there are a lot of books on it and everything, but I didn't know. I started to read more and learn more about it, and it got more interesting."

Like all students in the Senior Seminar, Alita was also enrolled in the Education to Careers program. But contrary to the experiences of most students enrolled in ETC, Alita felt that the time she spent in shop class was used productively. The students designed and produced the school's yearbook, which Alita enjoyed. She also learned to use programs like Illustrator and Photoshop, which she felt would be useful for her future. All in all, Alita felt that her shop class was moving her forward on a path toward a career:

> "When I first chose this shop, I didn't know what graphic designing really was. I just wanted to get in there so I could learn to draw better. After I learned how to use the computer programs and everything, that really enhanced my interest in the 3-D animation. So that really got me into it more."

Contrary to what she had expected, Alita thought that senior year was harder than previous years of high school and also felt that she had learned a lot. More important for Alita, though, was how engaged she felt in her senior year classes:

> "The classes I'm taking now are actually classes I wanted to take. Like, I like learning about the history of Latin America and the Senior Seminar classes, they're really interesting—especially the social studies class. I like that class most."

discussion, *"but that wasn't too hard."* She had very little to say about her other electives, describing her Drama and Fitness & Wellness classes as *"just something to pass the time."*

The Education to Careers Program: Significantly Low Challenge for the Whole Afternoon

Fifty-six percent of CPS seniors take at least one vocational course in twelfth grade (see Figure 5 on p. 30). In addition, students who are completing multi-year vocational sequences often take two or more vocational credits—including both courses and credit for work experience—in senior year. Because all of the three high schools in our longitudinal study offered structured vocational programming, our qualitative sample provided a unique look into students' experiences in their third year of what was then called the Education to Careers program, which students simply called shop. (For more information on vocational programming in CPS, see *Changes in Vocational Programming in CPS* on p. 33.) Almost half of the students in our qualitative sample were completing at least two credits of vocational programming to finish the final year of the ETC program, which allowed us to code the descriptions of 35 students who described their experiences in the program in sufficient detail.[58] The nature and structure of vocational programming in CPS high schools varies significantly from school to school and continues to change over time. In the time since the students we interviewed were seniors in high school (2006), vocational education has undergone significant reforms designed to improve the quality of the program. Though it is important to keep in mind that this analysis is not an evaluation of current programming, we believe that these students' experiences in the ETC program can help to inform new initiatives.

Unfortunately, the vast majority of students in our study described their ETC courses as having low challenge (see Figure 29 on p. 72). There were four common themes in ETC students' descriptions of their experiences in the program that contributed to generally low levels of challenge in senior year: (1) Multiple periods of unstructured time; (2) minimal, easy, or off-task class activities or homework; (3) nearly universal inability to find appropriate work placements; and (4) the time investment in ETC leaving little room for challenging academic courses.

As illustrated by our sample course schedule, students typically had ETC courses for at least two consecutive periods (see Figure 31 on p. 75). Too often, students described this class time as unstructured and lacking even one full class period worth of work. Class time often resembled free time or study hall. Students would play games and described their classes as *"boring."* A typical description came from Shayla, a student with access to a somewhat selective college, who said of her Culinary & Hospitality course:

> "[It's] just boring. We ask [our teacher], and he just says it's up to us to know what to do, because he don't need no help cooking or anything, and I'm just sitting there, like, "Why do they do this to us sometimes?"... [we] just sit there sometimes for two whole periods."

Chad, a student in the same class, was a little more dramatic:

> "Half the time in [that class] I be sitting talking to the girls or something. It be boring, like you sit there and be like, you want to punch something, just to get excitement, kick the desk, it still be boring."

Similarly, Karla, also described above, said that in Information Technology: *"...we talk a lot. Most of the time is not about work...we get a lot of free time in there."*

In shop classes where students acknowledged doing some work, students frequently described projects and activities that were unrelated to the topic of their shop class. Some teachers used class time to prepare students for college by requiring them to do college searches, and a few teachers even brought in college representatives from technical schools. For example, Elvira, a student with access only to a two-year college, described how her Construction & Architecture class often became the place for college activities.: *"...we got to go to UIC... actually it was for my drafting class 'cause we went to the*

ABEL: A CASE STUDY

Vocational Programming and the Constrained Senior Year

Many students in our qualitative study were enrolled in the Education to Careers (ETC) program. Seniors completing an ETC program were under specific programmatic constraints: at least two periods per day would be filled with vocational classes, and many students would be required to find work placements to supplement their coursework.

These requirements left little time in seniors' schedules for academically focused coursework, and even students who chose to enroll in AP or advanced math classes were unlikely to find much challenge in their day.

Abel, a college-oriented student in the ETC program who planned to study engineering, finished his junior year having failed his English class and needing to make up the credit over the summer. Still, solid grades throughout high school earned him a 2.6 unweighted GPA in his core classes at the end of junior year. In addition, Abel scored an impressive 22 overall on the ACT, with even higher sub-scores in math and science. Abel insisted on signing up for College Algebra his senior year, because he had heard that students who took a year off of math were at a disadvantage in college—especially if they wanted to study engineering. After making up his English credit over the summer, Abel began his senior year on track to attend a selective college.

Abel entered senior year uncertain about what to expect. Junior year had seemed harder than previous years of high school, but he also felt he had learned more. Instead of its difficulty, however, the defining feature of Abel's senior year schedule turned out to be its brevity. Abel's day He began at 8 a.m. with his law class, followed by AP English, College Algebra, and finally his ETC class—Information Technology. His last class finished at noon, after which Abel was allowed to leave for work placement. Unfortunately, like nearly all students in his position, Abel struggled to find a job connected to his ETC class. He had very limited work experience and there did not appear to be anyone at the school tasked with helping him find a job, much less a job that was linked to his ETC curriculum. Ultimately, Abel failed both semesters of his Work Experience requirement his senior year.

Abel's AP English class stood out as the only source of challenge in his senior year. At first, he was reluctant to take the class, believing English to be his weakest subject. He began the year in a regular-level English class and, although the AP teacher continued to encourage him to switch sections and take AP, Abel remained apprehensive:

> "The [AP] teacher said there's still a chance to go with the AP, but ... [I think] I wouldn't do well in that class... because it's so advanced. You would need better grammar, to read more, and it's just more time-consuming... Supposedly there is way more homework than most classes, and it's way harder."

Abel acknowledged, however, that his English and reading skills needed improvement before college. When the school had to rearrange students' schedules to add more sections of English, he agreed to be switched to an

AP class. The course proved challenging, but not overwhelming. Compared to the writing required in previous classes, Abel's AP English class pushed him to write somewhat longer papers and to carefully craft a thesis rather than writing a summary. Although the workload wasn't unmanageable, Abel felt especially challenged by the close reading students were expected to do in order to understand and discuss texts like *Hamlet*, *The Glass Menagerie*, and *Death of a Salesman*:

> "[The teacher] expects us to do a reading log. That means we take notes personally from everything we're reading—at least one hour a day, on very specific things like why they use this metaphor and stuff like that. Plus, he gives other essays… At first, I didn't like doing all this work, because I was never good at English, but now, I guess it's helping me to get my GPA up."

Beyond AP English, Abel encountered little else that required him to work hard. His law class, which consisted of a great deal of note-taking, along with occasional tests and quizzes, was less interesting than previous years' social studies classes and he acknowledged that all the note-taking could get boring. College Algebra seemed more valuable, but Able also described it as *"more of the same thing"* he encountered in previous math classes: *"we had to do stuff that we did last year, because a lot of people will forget—and you need certain steps to do certain problems."*

Abel found his ETC class more interesting than in previous years. During sophomore and junior year, he was disappointed with his Information Technology classes feeling that he already knew much of what was covered. By senior year, however, he felt the class was more useful:

> "[Sophomore year], it was just typing, and I already know how to type fast, so that's not a challenge for me. Junior year, it was all pretty easy. And now we're getting into complicated stuff—the stuff that like really counts… like making webpages, how to get to the root of them, how to get the homepage and the childpages and all that."

Despite his interest, the work appeared to be fairly easy to complete, consisting primarily of following directions out of a textbook or off of a worksheet. The students in the class appeared to primarily teach the material to themselves:

> "[The instructions] are easy – all the steps are in bold. And you check what you're looking for, like, you gotta change a font, like how to change it and change a picture and stuff like that… There's really nothing to talk about. Before, we used to read the [instructions] out loud—everybody took turns reading it, but now, we read it to ourselves."

Overall, Abel was content with his senior year schedule. Although he did not describe senior year as challenging, he did feel that he was learning a lot, explaining, "even though I only have four classes, the classes are at a more advanced level." Despite failing both semesters of the Work Experience credit of his shop class, he was still glad he had taken ETC courses, believing that "it might help me with colleges I want to go to, because it's dealing with computers."

Though Abel was satisfied with his classes, he found little engaging or exciting about them, saying that he couldn't think of an example in any of his classes where he really enjoyed the subject matter or assignments.

drafting building over there and we took a tour." Most ETC classes characterized as medium challenge fell into this group of classes in which class time was used for college application or search. These activities did not, however, constitute engagement in course content.

In general, across ETC courses, almost no homework was assigned: there was minimal work assigned during class, and students did not report the work as difficult, resulting in several hours—almost one-third of the school day for some—where students were not pushed or challenged. For example, Monty, a student with access to a nonselective college, complained that while his class was involved in an activity, it was not related to learning construction and architecture. Rather, Monty's class was painting walls and hanging up drywall in the classrooms in the high school, but even that work tapered off by the end of the year, when he admitted,*"...truthfully, we're not even really doing any carpentry work or anything like that. We're basically doing GRPs [Guided Reading Practices]."*

Adding to unstructured class time, many students participated in the work experience program, which was largely unguided and unsupervised. Even if a student did not have to work on a given day, some still were able to leave school early. Students found the process of finding a job very difficult. Most students described an unorganized, unclear process; they were almost entirely on their own to find employment. Many were still searching for jobs well into the school year. Alberto, for example, a capable honors and AP student with access to selective colleges, described how, without a job, he simply sat around for a third period in his Business & Finance class:

> "Well right now some students from my class, they're working on like stores like JC Penney, as a sales clerk or at a restaurant, or newspaper, yeah...[I] just sit here [in class]. Stay with my friends....I don't go anywhere [to work]."

Alberto confirmed that he was assigned to a work placement for credit, and that he received a grade in the course, despite never having a job. Raquel, a similarly highly qualified student, simply left her Information Technology class, even though she did not have a job, citing a common frustration for students in finding appropriate work placements: *"[It's been] kind of hard [to find a job], because a lot of places ask you to be 18 already, and I'm not 18."*

Finally, when students did find jobs, they rarely had a job where the place of employment or individual job responsibilities related to their shop class. In all three fieldwork high schools, it seemed as though any job that a student found counted as an appropriate work placement. There were too many examples of this problem to truly do justice to students' frustrations with work experience in the scope of this chapter. As Montez explained, it was better to have any job than to be bored for three periods:

> "You gotta have...[a job] related to your shop. Some of [the students] do, and some of [the students] don't, but the teacher lets them get work release, because they figure, you had the class for 3 years, and for 3 periods—there isn't too, too much you can learn there. They only teach you so much."

It was clear from our interviews that even those students who wanted to take challenging work tended to be limited by their participation in ETC. Abel (**see *Abel: A Case Study* on p. 84**) demonstrates how ETC courses constrained course selection. Despite taking AP English and College Algebra, Abel's ETC requirements only allowed him to take three core classes senior year. Though Abel signed up for both a fourth year of math and an AP English course, he took only three core classes (and four classes total) senior year. He was finished with school by lunchtime and never reported finding a job that would count as work credit for his information technology program. Given his limited schedule, it is unsurprising that he did not describe senior year as being very challenging, despite finding AP English challenging.

Students' Final Assessment of Senior Year: "Real" Classes Versus "Blow-Off" Classes

Whether the root cause was a preponderance of non-core courses, the disappointment of English and social studies electives, or participation in the ETC program, the problem seemed to be the same for most of the students in our study: a schedule filled with these kinds of courses made for an easy, boring, often frustrating senior year. Even those students who excitedly described one or two classes they felt were challenging, engaging, and good preparation for the future then had to describe a larger number of classes where little if anything happened. In addition, some students were programmed to take fewer classes in senior year—or perceived that they were taking fewer classes if they were taking a double-block vocational course. When asked if he was learning a lot, Alberto, described above, explained *"no, not really. It's easy. This year's pretty easy...way easier [than last year]...last year, I had six classes. This year I only have four."* He summed up senior year as being *"laid back"* and *"way easier"* than his junior year. Jaime, a student with weaker academic qualifications, nonetheless had a similar explanation for senior year being unchallenging, noting that his individual classes were easy, he wasn't getting any homework, and his classes *"are probably...a lot easier to understand and everything than before."* But in addition, senior year was easy *"probably 'cause I have... less classes."*

What was clear in students' descriptions was that they distinguished between classes like English IV, AP courses, and many math, science and world language courses and electives, which students frequently referred to as *"not real classes."* The problem is that these *"not real classes"*—or *"blow-by", "no life,"* or *"nothing happens"* classes, all terms our students used to describe their electives—constituted a significant portion of many students' senior year schedules—much more so than they had in any other year of high school. For example, Kyle, who took a fourth year of science in addition to two other moderately challenging core classes, summarized how a combination of poor quality electives and vocational programming amounts to a *"blow off"* senior year.

"I got three real classes and the rest of them are blow by's. First period I have Spanish. Second period I got World Literature, and 3rd period I got Physics. The rest of my day is a blow off...4th period I got PE, 5th period band, and 7th period is just a work study class. My class is supposed to be with carpentry and architecture, and I have a job at a grocery store."

When asked why he thought senior year was easier than previous years, Franklin, an extremely ambitious young man profiled in the *Potholes* report, explains his belief that an easy senior year is a result of how his school schedules coursetaking over four years of high school:

"I believe it's that way because the way our school is set up. Each year you're losing classes. You start off freshman year with seven classes, excluding lunch. And as you go on you lose classes. This year I have maybe like four classes, so it's like of course it's going to be hard your first year, but as you go along you lose classes so that burden becomes lighter because you have less work to do so I mean it's not so much that it's easing up or it starts hard and ends hard it's just the amount of work that you're getting. You're not getting as much as you're used to."

Getting What You Asked For: The Senior Year Culture Problem

While many students in our study were extremely disappointed with their experience of senior year, many students were also, in a sense, victims of their own expectations for what senior year should be. In junior year, we asked students what they expected senior year to be like. Many students, reflecting what they had heard from older students, said that they expected senior year to be easy. As we has described, CPS graduation requirements gave students very little direction about what to take senior year, other than to finish up their requirements. This lack of direction for senior year was reflected in students' description of their expectations, and students did not appear to be thinking very carefully about what role senior year should play in their pursuit of postsecondary education. When asked why they chose to take some classes over others in senior year, some students reported that they knew it was important to maintain a good GPA to report on their college applications, so they decided to take classes where it would be relatively easy to maintain good grades.

Many students stated they chose AP courses because they felt that having an AP class on their transcripts, as well as the boost in their GPA for an AP class, would be an advantage in college admissions. Still other students reported taking classes because the content or skills learned in the class (e.g., Financial Math, College-Level Writing, Drafting) would be important for the post-secondary plans. Students also talked about signing up for classes because they looked interesting or because they knew they would enjoy the teacher, or because the class fulfilled a particular graduation requirement—for general graduation or sometimes for graduation from a particular program or track within their high school.

At the same time as students were stating that they meant to take classes that would be advantageous to their college plans, students also typically said that they expected senior year to be easy. There seemed to be a general cultural expectation that senior year should be a time to relax. Though this idea of preparing for college while taking an easy schedule seems inherently contradictory, this is not a contradiction that is clear to students. As Norton explained when asked why he chose not to take Pre-Calculus, *"I just want to breeze through my senior year and get ready for college."* One reason that students feel it makes sense to *"breeze through"* senior year could be that they receive very little guidance about what they should be doing senior year. Students in our sample typically did not speak to anyone about which courses to take in senior year. Only a handful of students reported talking with a counselor or a teacher about choosing their classes senior year. The most common topic of conversation was about whether to take a math class, and several students did report being urged by teachers to take AP classes. Finally, if students did interact with a counselor, it was most often in the form of a presentation to the whole class or occasionally because the student sought out a counselor to answer their questions. Overall, though there were sporadic examples of guidance, it did not appear to be the case that students were getting consistent or clear messages from the adults in their school about what classes to take senior year, what skills would be important for college, or how they should be making their decisions about coursework. Instead of receiving clear messages and strong expectations around the purpose of senior year, students experienced uncertainty across classes about the goals and objectives of individual courses or senior year as a whole. In short, they got what they asked for: a senior year that challenged them little.

Summary and Implications

Our analysis of the lack of challenge in individual courses and across senior year as a whole has a number of important implications for practice in high schools. First, the primary strategy that CPS has pursued in making senior year a college-preparatory experience is expanding access AP courses. Many of the highly qualified students in our sample enrolled in at least one AP course, in addition to whatever schedule was common for students at that school to take. Adding one or two AP courses or a fourth-year math course, however, does not ensure a challenging—much less culminating—senior year.

Unfortunately, the most common experience for students in our qualitative study was to take large numbers of electives, fewer than four core courses, and no AP or math class. ETC students, moreover, had a senior year dominated by a multiple-period block of unchallenging vocational classes. For these students, English IV often became a mainstay, presenting clear standards and goals for students' learning in their final year of high school instruction. Unfortunately, most other classes filling students' senior year schedules lacked this kind of focus. The coherent narrative that emerged in students' accounts of senior year coursework was one of minimal workload, low challenge, and generally lower expectations.

A sad reality that became clear over the course of our analysis was how difficult it was for students who wanted a challenging senior year to find it—and how frustrating and wasteful it felt even for students who expected an easy senior year. We hope in this chapter we have been able to convey these student voices. Students were surprisingly articulate about their feelings that senior year was not a year in which they had learned a lot, or had worked hard to prepare for college and careers, or in which teachers invested much time or effort. In a school system in which a sad number of students do not even make it to senior year, the fact that those students who persist to graduation are not provided with a senior year that give them the rationale, structure, and support for building the skills they will need in the future is more than disappointing.

CHAPTER 5

Interpretive Summary

The emphasis of the recovery will be largely on skilled jobs.... This recession, like the previous two, has intensified the underlying engine of economic change that has been evident at least since the 1980-81 recession. The industrial economy of the 20th century has slowly transformed itself into a new services economy that demands more education and different skills of its workers. (Carnevale, Smith & Strohl, 2010, p. 6)

In answer to the question *Why do you want to go to college?*, Armando, an International Baccalaureate student replied:

> "A good life, and I also want a good life for my parents, 'cause they work for me and they both work [hard] in factories. I want to get a good job, have a good life and if I don't get good grades, can't get into a good college. If I don't get into a college then I can't get a career; no career, no good paying job, no white picket fence."

Over the past several years, the term "college and career readiness," along with host of other combinations of these words, has become the mantra of educational reform in the United States. The Common Core State Standards (CCSS) promise that they will ensure that students "are able to succeed in entry-level, credit bearing academic college courses and in workforce training programs." [59] The goal of just about any educational program or district's plan is now to ensure that students are "college and career ready." While there is much uncertainty about what this nomenclature actually means in practice, the new emphasis on college-going is being driven by the very real recognition that educational attainment, particularly among low-income students, has been relatively flat for over a decade. Throughout the *From High School to the Future* series, we have grappled with two central questions. First, how do we bridge the gap between aspirations and a college degree for students like Armando? Second, what does the challenge posed by students like Armando mean for the work of high schools, the goals high schools set for their students, and the role that high school educators play in students' lives?

While we were working on this report, the United States entered a dramatic recession, which has both exacerbated and accelerated the deterioration of post-high school options for students who do not attend or complete college. The rules have been rewritten for high school students and their families: earning a high school diploma is no longer a secure pathway to economic stability. Given this economic reality, we now know that absent a dramatic shift in how urban high schools prepare students for college and careers, the new economy will leave many low-income graduates behind. If these trends continue, Bailey and Dynarski (2011) conclude that widening gaps in educational attainment will reinforce growing income inequality and seriously constrain economic mobility for low-income young adults. More than ever before, equipping students for college and postsecondary training will require high school educators to create higher levels of preparedness in their students.

Throughout the *From High School to the Future* series, our work has documented the barriers that graduates of CPS and their counterparts across the nation face in the pursuit of a college education. These roadblocks to college access have come in very concrete, technical forms (e.g., low grades and test scores, extremely limited family financial resources), but many can also be attributed to the less obvious but equally important lack of social capital experienced by students whose families and communities are unlikely to hold many college graduates: unfamiliarity with college options, confusion surrounding the financial aid process, or a lack of awareness of the steps necessary to apply to college. High schools with a strong college-going culture can serve to bridge the gaps in students' understanding of college planning. But, too often, the students who need this support the most are concentrated in schools where college-going culture is the least present and are expected to navigate the road to college on their own. There is no place where the challenge of transforming the culture of high schools is more evident than in twelfth grade. Chicago Public Schools (CPS) has been a national leader in focusing on college. In 2003, CPS established the Department of Postsecondary Education (now the Office of College and Career Preparation) that focused on improving college counseling supports and providing greater access to information for students in college planning. CPS became the first major school system in the United States to publicly report and track the postsecondary outcomes of graduates. CPS has also been a national leader in expanding Advanced Placement participation, earning a 2010 Advanced Placement district of the year award. These reforms, however, while positive steps, haven't fundamentally reorganized how senior year operates for most students.

The analysis presented in this report suggests that there is much work to do if CPS is to shift the focus of twelfth grade from finishing graduation requirements to preparing for college. Too many students who enter twelfth grade qualified to attend a four-year college are not participating in coursework that would signal to colleges that they are taking an academically focused senior year. Too many students enter senior year unqualified for college or postsecondary training and without a viable pathway to employment. Too often, senior year in CPS looks like it is serving the needs of students in the 1980s rather than the needs of students today.

Across all levels of achievement, students themselves portray their senior year experience as unchallenging and, for some, wasted time. In the most common course-taking pattern, more students are taking an unrequired third physical education course than are taking a fourth year of math. At a time when our national discussion of "senioritis" has been replaced by a discussion of "senior stress," most CPS students describe their senior year as a time when they are not doing homework, not working hard, and not learning much.

There are several reasons why students' academic experiences during senior year have been off the radar. As we saw in this report, CPS core graduation requirements can be completed by the end of eleventh grade, with the exception of English IV. This leaves senior year outside the bounds of the core work of academic departments. Illinois' high stakes test—the primary measure by which high schools are judged—is also given in eleventh grade, providing little incentive for high school educators to focus on twelfth grade beyond making sure students who need credits make them up. Many high schools have tried to fit curriculum to EPAS testing standards, reinforcing a focus on eleventh grade. This has created a misalignment between the needs of students and the practices of high schools. Thus, while CPS has developed an important focus on getting students to apply to college, much less attention has been paid to what twelfth graders need to be ready for college or postsecondary training, how that experience should develop within and across classes, and what the pathway should be for students who are not college bound.

In this report, we examine the current state of twelfth grade in CPS and describe the set of issues that educators must grapple with in order to shift the purpose of senior year from finishing up coursework to preparing for postsecondary opportunities. In particular, this report identifies two groups of students who pose very different sets of challenges: first, students who are not the highest achieving students in the school system but still enter senior year positioned to attend a four-year college, and second, seniors who will graduate but lack the ACT scores and GPAs necessary to have an adequate chance at attending college and doing well once there. The issues raised by these two groups of students are different. They have in common that neither group is being well served during their senior year. What should senior year look like for students who enter senior year with high enough GPAs and ACT scores to be competitive for a four-year college? And what should senior year be for students who enter senior year with such low qualifications that they could graduate but are eligible for only a two-year open enrollment college or a four-year nonselective college? In the remainder of this summary, we focus on five key points that shaped how we think about the challenges these two groups pose for high schools.

Expectations

There is no clear set of expectations or consensus on what seniors who are qualified to attend college should be doing their senior year.

In looking at senior year, there is a central tension in distinguishing between the set of issues relevant only to twelfth grade and the set of issues that are evident in twelfth grade but concern students' entire educational careers. Preparing for college is a process that takes students' entire elementary and high school careers. Virtually all of the academic qualifications that colleges use to evaluate students (ACT scores and GPA) are measures of students' performance at the end of eleventh grade. There is relatively little that can be done as late as senior year that would dramatically alter students' underlying qualifications for college.

At the same time, senior year can also be pivotal for college-going. Students' senior year coursework may shape whether those CPS juniors who aspire to and are qualified to attend college can be competitive in college admissions and ready to meet the new academic and developmental demands of college. For students who aspire to attend college, senior year should be organized around three important tasks: effectively participating in college and financial aid application; engaging in coursework that makes them competitive in college admissions; and engaging in academic and developmental experiences that build college readiness. In our last two reports, *Potholes on the Road to College and Making Hard Work Payoff*, we focused on the first task, demonstrating the myriad of ways in which even higher performing CPS students were not effectively participating in college search, applications, and financial aid. In this report, we turn to the next two tasks, asking whether the courses students take in their senior year matter for their college enrollment and whether senior year in CPS is focused on building college readiness.

The good news is that the highest achieving CPS students—those who enter senior year with high grades and ACT scores that put them within the range of attending a very selective colleges—are generally participating in a rigorous senior year that includes a fourth year of math and one or more AP courses. This group, however, only comprises 7 percent of CPS graduates and is concentrated in selective enrollment high schools and specialized programs (e.g., International Baccalaureate programs) where the expectation is that students will be preparing for and going to college.

In sharp contrast, there seems to be no organizing framework and common set of expectations for students who might be college bound but are not the most highly qualified. Approximately half of CPS students enter senior year with the ACT score and GPA that would give them access to a four-year somewhat selective or selective college. Although these students have a range of college options, they may be academically vulnerable in the transition to college. Nationally, over a quarter of entering college freshman and almost half of African American and Latino freshmen at degree-granting institutions are placed in remedial courses.[60] Yet, many CPS students who are qualified to attend college appear to be doing little academic work during senior year. For example, during their senior year, 40 percent of seniors with access to somewhat selective four-year college took fewer than four core courses in their senior year, 57 percent did not take a math course and nearly two-thirds had not taken an AP course. There is similarly little consensus about what students with access to selective colleges should be taking. Much of these differences in coursetaking, as we will discuss below, can be attributed to differences across high schools in their norms and expectations. The bottom line, however, is that there is no clear consensus in CPS about what courses students should be taking if they are planning on attending a four-year college.

Advanced Placement

Advanced Placement courses may be effective, but one or two courses do not amount to a challenging senior year that is college preparatory.

One strategy for improving college outcomes that CPS has pursued that has had a significant impact on senior year is the investment CPS has made in expanding participation in Advanced Placement courses. CPS students lead the nation in AP participation. In 2007, over 40 percent of all CPS graduates took one or more AP classes during high school. One reading of our findings is that this strategy has paid off.

A key finding in this report is that enrollment in AP courses (and to a lesser extent a fourth year of math) is associated with whether students enroll in a four-year college and, among more qualified students, whether they enroll in a selective four-year college. For example, between two students who enter senior year with similar qualifications to attend a somewhat selective four-year college, the student who takes one or more AP courses is much more likely to attend any four-year college. Likewise, among students who enter senior year with access to selective four-year colleges, taking two or more AP courses increases the likelihood that they enroll in a more selective college. We do not know the mechanisms that drive these results. It could be that high school counselors and teachers give more college guidance support to students in AP courses. It could be that colleges are giving students a boost for taking AP courses—in fact, colleges are quite explicit that they use students' coursetaking in twelfth grade as evidence that students are motivated and taking "rigorous" coursework in making admissions decisions. There is evidence to support both perspectives. But the bottom line is that students who do not take AP are disadvantaged in college applications and admissions.

We find that taking AP courses can increase students' likelihood of enrolling in college; however, we did not find that participation in AP or any other advanced coursework directly affected college retention. Some may see this finding as evidence that AP does not work; we think this is the wrong conclusion. While it seems clear that the College Board has oversold the benefits of AP to students and educators, we found that students' experiences in AP courses were distinct from their experiences in other courses during their senior year. In qualitative interviews, students felt that AP courses were preparing them for college by building the academic skills and academic behaviors that they would need in order to participate in challenging coursework. Students felt that they were held to higher academic standards and were expected to work hard to succeed in the course.

Ultimately AP courses should not be the only challenging courses that students take senior year. We found that even students who described their AP courses as challenging still saw their senior year as unchallenging on balance. This does not mean that AP is not a good strategy. Instead, because AP courses comprise only a fraction of students' schedules and are impractical options for students with weaker skills, AP remains simply an inadequate solution. Perhaps as importantly, treating AP as a panacea for college preparation does not directly engage teachers in the difficult discussion of what skills and academic behaviors students will need in order to do well in college and how those skills and behaviors should be developed over time. Similarly, while there is nothing inherently wrong with the social studies and English electives that comprise a substantial portion of most seniors' schedules, at present these courses lack any common vision for what it means to make students college ready. Investing in improving course quality in the core electives could have large payoffs if the process engages teachers in thinking about the skills and competencies that students should develop in senior year in order to be ready to take on new demands in college.

There is an important window of opportunity to engage teachers in answering these questions. The Common Core State Standards will push high school educators to think critically about the skills high school students should be developing for college and postsecondary training. The critical question is whether educators will use the Common Core to focus on the new test, which will again be given in eleventh grade, or whether they will instead treat the adoption of the Common Core as an opportunity to engage in a broader, ongoing dialogue about college readiness that includes senior year.

Equity and Access

The district needs to pay attention to equity and access in coursework across schools and grapple with the question of whether programmatic and non-core graduation requirements are hindering students.

The prevailing stereotype of senior year is that students' are "coasting to graduation," choosing to take easy courses and glide through. The findings in this report do not support the argument that student choice is driving low levels of advanced coursetaking in senior year. Instead, we find that two important dynamics come together to shape the courses students take senior year. First, the evidence is clear that different high schools are making very different decisions about what courses similarly qualified students should take senior year. Among students who entered senior year positioned to attend a somewhat selective four-year college, the percentage taking an AP class in twelfth grade ranged across high schools from a low of zero to a high of almost 90 percent. We see a similar pattern in coursetaking for fourth-year math and four or more core courses. If taking AP courses makes it more likely that students with comparable achievement attend a four-year college, then students in high schools that do not enroll many students in AP courses are being disadvantaged.

A second problem tied to how high schools program students into senior courses is that for two important groups of students, coursetaking was significantly constrained senior year because of programmatic and non-core graduation requirements. A small but important group of seniors needed the year to complete their graduation requirements, retaking core courses they had failed in previous years. A much larger group of students were taking two or more vocational courses their senior year. In addition to retaking core courses or multiple vocational courses, both of these groups of students often needed to complete fine arts courses required for graduation as well. The combination of these two issues placed a double constraint on students' schedules, effectively crowding out academic coursework.

The career and technical education community has argued that there should not be a tradeoff between college readiness and career preparation. Since this research was conducted, CPS began a significant reorganization of its Career and Technical Education (CTE) programming intended to incorporate best practices in the field and align with industry needs and standards. Given how seniors described their experiences in the ETC program, this change is warranted. Not only did we find that multiple periods of shop constrained students' coursetaking, we found that students described these courses as distinctively poor quality, disorganized, and unchallenging. In these classes, students reported, there was often literally nothing happening. The promise of the new reorganization is to invest in higher-quality programs with clear links to the workplace that provide multiple pathways to careers. However, time in the school day is not unlimited. CTE programs need to ensure that students are not combining college and career in ways that limit their college options. This concern is particularly important as an equity issue, given that African American and, to a lesser extent, Latino CPS students are substantially overrepresented in CTE programs.

What Does College Readiness Mean?

Improving senior year requires paying as much attention to what happens within courses as to what courses students take.

Given the wide variation in students' experiences across high schools, imposing a rule-based solution, such as requiring all students to take a fourth year of math, has a certain appeal. However, the findings of this report suggest that the variation across high schools is actually evidence of a much deeper problem: the underlying lack of clarity among high school educators about what college readiness means and for whom. Coursework requirements may solve the problem of wide variation in students' opportunities across schools; however, such requirements may also create problems, such as putting lower achieving students at risk of not graduating. Most importantly, however, imposing a rule-based solution does not address the overall poor quality and lack of rigor in senior year courses.

The culture of senior year has not substantively changed, even as students' college aspirations have increased and CPS has expanded advanced course offerings. Requiring additional coursework, such as a fourth year of math, without significantly shifting the focus of senior year may become another seemingly simple solution with ultimately little payoff. For students who hope to attend college, senior year must be reinterpreted as more than the end of high school. For these students, senior year should function as a bridge into college. Transforming senior year ultimately requires school leaders, counselors, and teachers to initiate a culture shift in the purpose of senior year. High schools must convey to students and their families that senior year is an important academic year in which students should be pushed to build critical behaviors and skills. As a first step, educators must become engaged in actively deciding not just what courses students should take, but how teaching within and across those courses will prepare students for postsecondary opportunities.

Pathways for Seniors with Low Qualifications

We need a comprehensive strategy that sets students who graduate high school without the likelihood of going to college on a path towards financial stability and viable life choices.

This report identifies many difficult, but important, challenges for CPS educators. Perhaps the most troubling is the high proportion of CPS graduates who leave high school with such low GPAs and ACT scores that they have only the most limited college options and extremely low odds of succeeding in any college. Identifying what the goals of senior year should be for these students is particularly difficult for two reasons.

First, it is a relatively new challenge. Even as recently as 20 years ago, high schools were not expected to send all students to college or link them to employment opportunities. In 1980, more than half of all high school graduates did not enroll in college immediately after high school graduation. Of those, 88 percent were employed. A generation ago, the fact that nearly half of CPS graduates had such limited college options would not have sounded alarms or constituted a call to action. However, in the current economy, there are far fewer low-skilled jobs and the economic returns to completing only a high school diploma are radically eroded.

Second, it is difficult to determine what the goals of senior year should be for students with very low academic achievement because broadly we do not yet understand how to successfully link these students with what job opportunities there are. A recent report by the *Pathways to Prosperity Project* at Harvard University argued that the United States must develop a wider set of options that mix employment and academic training and that add at least one more year of education without having students fall short of the college degree. As the report concludes, the current message of college for all:

> …places far too much emphasis on a single pathway to success: attending and graduating from a four year college after completing an academic program of study in high school …It is long past time that we broaden the range of high-quality pathways that we offer to our young people, beginning in high school.[61]

Currently, however, high schools do not offer that range of pathways. The constellation of problems facing these graduates is further compounded by the fact that, because few of these students will likely work in high school, the primary mechanism by which previous generations built workplace readiness skills has been dismantled. Addressing the needs of these students requires a multi-faceted approach that uses twelfth grade as a transitional experience to link the graduates to employment opportunities in the new economy. High schools, however, cannot do this alone. Building new approaches to postsecondary training and workforce development will require business and workforce development agencies working together with educational institutions at multiple levels.

It is the responsibility of high schools to ensure that students do not enter senior year with such low grades and grade point averages. The average GPA among graduates with the lowest qualifications (those with access to only two-year colleges) was 1.5, meaning that these students only graduated by just passing classes. While extremely low GPAs do not prevent students from graduating, they do not get students into or through college. Very low grades suggest that, during high school, many of these students are not studying, are not engaged or mastering course material, and are unlikely to be developing the kinds of noncognitive academic skills (e.g., the ability to study, work independently, and engage deeply with problems) that are essential for academic success in college and critical in the workplace. High schools must begin to pay attention to what appears to be a culture of passing—communicating more forcefully to students that acquiring these skills is important to their future life chances.

Why Tackle the Problems of Senior Year?

This report has raised a host of complex issues with no easy solutions. The question for educators is: how high should addressing senior year be placed on their list of priorities? At present, high school leaders have few incentives to address these issues. Teachers and principals are not currently held accountable for anything more than ensuring that seniors graduate. At the same time, high school educators are under enormous pressure to raise test scores, reduce dropout rates, increase attendance, and ensure safety. Fixing senior year would not necessarily solve any of those problems. Fixing senior year, it would seem, should rate as a fairly low priority.

But that is not the case if we are interested in college readiness and access. We then need to put first—not last—on the list the question of what should be the goals of senior year. Engaging in deciding what sets of skills students will need to develop in order to make a successful transition from twelfth grade to college, how those skills may be different for different groups of students, and what that means—for not only twelfth grade, but also for grades nine, ten, and eleven—provides an important opportunity to think critically about how we transform high schools from institutions largely focused on getting students high school diplomas to institutions that equip all students for college and postsecondary training. We hope that the analysis and data provided in this report provide useful tools to begin this work for policymakers, educators, and the larger community.

References

Abeles, V. (Director). (2010)
The New York Times Op-Ed: Advanced Pressure [Motion Picture]. A Real Link Film Production.
http://video.nytimes.com/video/2010/01/24/opinion/1247466680941/advanced-pressure.html

Achieve, Inc. (2005)
Rising to the challenge: Are high school graduates prepared for college and work? A study of recent high school graduates, college instructors, and employers. (conducted by Peter D. Hard Research Associates, Public Opinion Strategies). Washington, D.C.: Achieve Inc.

Achieve, Inc. (2008)
Closing the expectations gap 2008. Washington: Achieve, Inc.

Achieve, Inc. (2006)
Closing the expectations gap 2006. Washington: Achieve, Inc.

ACT, Inc. (2004)
Crisis at the core: Preparing all students for college and work. Iowa City, IA:

ACT, Inc. (2005)
Courses count: Preparing students for postsecondary success. Iowa City, IA:

ACT, Inc (2006)
Benefits of a high school core curriculum for students in urban high schools. Retrieved February 15, 2008, from http://www.act.org/research/policymakers/pdf/core_curriculum.pdf

Adelman, C. (2006)
The toolbox revisited: Paths to degree completion from high school through college. Washington, DC: U.S. Department of Education.

Adelman, C. (2004)
Principal indicators of student academic histories in postsecondary education, 1972-2000. Washington, DC: U.S. Department of Education, Institute of Education Statistics.

Adelman, C. (1999)
Answers in the toolbox: Academic intensity, attendance patterns, and bachelor's degree attainment. Washington, DC: U.S. Department of Education, Office of Educational Research and Improvement.

Allensworth, E.M., Correa, M., and Ponisciak, S. (2008)
From High School to the Future: ACT preparation—Too Much, Too Late. Chicago: Consortium on Chicago School Research.

Allensworth, E.M., Takako, N., Montgomery, N., and Lee, V.E. (2009)
College Preparatory Curriculum for All: Academic Consequences of Requiring Algebra and English I for Ninth Graders in Chicago. *Educational Evaluation and Policy Analysis, 31* (4), pp. 367-391.

Association of American Colleges and Universities. (2002)
Greater Expectations: A New Vision for Learning as a Nation Goes to College. Washington: Association of American Colleges and Universities.

Attewell, P., and Domina, T. (2008)
Raising the bar: Curricular intensity and academic performance. *Educational Evaluation and Policy Analysis, 30*, 51-71.

Aud, S., Hussar, W., Planty, M., Bianco, K., Fox, M., and Frohlich, L., et al. (2010)
The Condition of Education 2010 (NCES 2010-028). Washington: National Center for Education Statistics, Institute of Education Sciences, U.S. Department of Education.

Aud, S., Hussar, W., Kena, G., Bianco, K., Frohlich, L., Kemp, J., and Tahan, K. (2011)
The Condition of Education 2011 (NCES 2011-033). U.S. Department of Education, National Center for Education Statistics. Washington, DC: U.S. Government Printing Office.

Bailey, M.J., and Dynarski, S.M. (2011)
Inequality in postsecondary education. In G. J. Duncan and R.J. Murnane (Eds.), *Whither Opportunity* (pp. 117-131). New York: Russell Sage Foundation.

Boyer, E. (1983)
High school: A report on secondary education in America. New York: Harper & Row, Inc.

Bozick, R., and Ingels, S.J. (2008)
Mathematics coursetaking and achievement at the end of high school: Evidence from the educational longitudinal study of 2002. (ELS: 2002) (NCES 2008-319). National Center for Education Statistics, Institute of Education Science, U.S. Department of Education. Washington, DC.

Carnevale, A.P., Smith, N., and Strohl, J. (2010)
Help wanted: Projections of jobs and education requirements through 2018. Georgetown University Center on Education and the Workforce.

Chen, X. (2005)
First generation students in postsecondary education: A look at their college transcripts (NCES 2005–171). U.S. Department of Education, National Center for Education Statistics. Washington, DC: U.S. Government Printing Office.

Coca, V., Johnson, D.W., Kelley-Kemple, T., Roderick, M., Moeller, E., Williams, N., and Moragne, K. (2012)
Working to My Potential: The Postsecondary Experiences of CPS Students in the International Baccalaureate Diploma Programme. Chicago: Consortium on Chicago School Research.

Coca et. al. (2012)
Child Trends Data Bank, http://www.childtrendsdatabank.org/?q=node/374 retrieved May 4, 2012.

The College Board. (2012)
For Students. Retrieved from http://www.collegeboard.com/student/testing/ap/about.html

Common Core State Standards Initiative (2010)
About the Standards http://www.corestandards.org/about-the-standards.

Conley, D. (2007)
Redefining college readiness. Eugene: Educational Policy Improvement Center. Towards a more comprehensive conception of college readiness. Prepared for the Bill and Melinda Gates Foundation.

Crux Market Research, Inc. (2007)
College Board Website. AP and the cost of college. http://professionals.collegeboard.com/profdownload/ap-exam-promo-flyer-2009.pdf

Crux Market Research, Inc. (2006)
College Board Website. http://professionals.collegeboard.com/profdownload/ap-parent-presentation-for-international-schools.pdf

Dodd, F., De Ayala, and Jennings. (2002)
An investigation of the validity of AP grades of 3 and a comparison of AP and non-AP student groups. College Board Research Report No. 2002-2009.

Dorn, S. (1996)
Creating the dropout: An institutional and social history of school failure. Westport: Praeger.

Dougherty, C., Mellor, L., and Jian, S. (2005)
Orange juice or orange drink? Ensuring that 'advanced courses' live up to their labels. National Center for Educational Accountability Study Series Report.

Dougherty, C., Mellor, L., and Jian, S. (2006a)
The Relationship between Advanced Placement and college graduation. Austin, TX: The National Center for Educational Accountability. The University of Texas at Austin.

Duncan, A. (2010)
"The three myths of high school reform." Remarks of U.S. Secretary of Education Arne Duncan to the College Board AP Conference, July 15, 2010, Washington, DC, 2010. Speaker may have deviated from prepared remarks.

Geiser, S., and Santelices, V. (2004)
The role of Advanced Placement and honors courses in college admissions. Berkeley, CA: Center for Studies in Higher Education, University of California, Berkeley. http://ishi.lib.berkeley.edu/cshe/

Goldin, C., and Katz, L. (2008)
The race between education and technology. Cambridge: Harvard University Press.

Heckman, J.J., and Krueger, A.B. (2003)
Inequality in America: What role for human capital policies? Cambridge, MA: MIT Press.

Horn and Carroll. (2001)
U.S. Department of Education. National Center for Education Statistics. *High school academic curriculum and the persistence path through college* NCES 2001-163, by Laura Horn and Lawrence K. Kojaku. Project Officer: C. Dennis Carroll. Washington, DC: 2001.

Jackson, C.K. (2007)
A little now for a lot later: A look at a Texas Advanced Placement program. IRL Collection Working Papers. Ithaca, NY.: Cornell University.

Jackson, C.K. (2009)
A Little Now For a Lot Later. *Journal of Human Resources, 45*(3), pp. 591-639

Joensen, J.S., and Nielsen, H.S. (2009)
"Is there a causal effect of high school math on labor market outcomes?" *Journal of Human Resources, 44*(1), 171-198.

Kemple, J.J., and Willner, C.J. (2008).
Career Academies: Long-Term Impacts on Labor Market Outcomes, Educational Attainment, and Transitions to Adulthood. New York: MDRC

Klopfenstein, K., and Thomas, M.K. (2006)
"The link between Advanced Placement experience and early college success."

Kyburg, R.M., Herthberg-Davis, H., and Callahan, C.M. (2007)
Advanced Placement and International Baccalaureate programs: Optimal learning environments for talented minorities? *Journal of Advanced Academics, 18*(2), 172-215.

Lee, V.E., and Ready, D.D. (2007)
Schools within schools: Possibilities and pitfalls of high school reform. New York, NY: Teachers College Press.

Lichten, W. (2000)
Whither Advanced Placement? *Education Policy Analysis Archives, 8*(29). http://epaa.asu.edu/epaa/v8n29.html

Long, M.C., Conger, D., and Iatarola, P. (2012)
Effects of high school coursetaking on secondary and postsecondary success. *American Educational Research Journal.* Available at http://aer.sagepub.com/content/early/2012/01/30/0002831211431952

Long, M.C., Iatarola, P., and Conger, D. (2009)
Explaining gaps in readiness for college-level math: The role of high school courses. American Education Finance Association.

Loveless, T. (1999)
The tracking wars: State reform meets school policy. Washington, DC: Brookings Institution Press.

Luppescu, S., Allensworth, E.M., Moore, P., de la Torre, M., Murphy, J., with Jagesic, S. (2011)
Trends in Chicago's Schools Across Three Eras of Reform. Chicago: Consortium on Chicago School Research.

Mazzeo, C. (August 2010)
Policy brief, *College prep for all: What we've learned from Chicago's efforts.* Chicago: The Consortium on Chicago School Research.

Mishel, L., and Roy, J. (2006)
Rethinking high school graduation rates and trends. Washington, DC.: Economic Policy Institute.

Montgomery, N., Allensworth, E.M., with Correa, M. (2010)
Passing Through Science: The Effects of Raising Graduation Requirements in Science on Course-Taking and Academic Achievement in Chicago. Chicago: Consortium on Chicago School Research.

National Commission on the High School Senior Year. (2001)
The lost opportunity of a senior year: Finding a better way. A preliminary report. 2001: National Commission on the High School Senior Year.

The New York Times. (2009)
Room for debate: The Advanced Placement juggernaut. Retrieved May 17, 2011, from http://roomfordebate.blogs.nytimes.com/2009/12/20/the-advanced-placement-juggernaut/

Nord, C., Roey, S., Perkins, R., Lyons, R., Lemanski, N., Brown, J., and Schuknect, J. (2011)
The nation's report card: America's high school graduates. Results of the NAEP high school transcript study. National Center for Education Statistics, U.S. Department of Education. Washington, DC: U.S. Government Printing Office.

Pallas, A. and Alexander, K. (1983)
Sex differences in quantitative SAT performance: New evidence on the differential coursework hypothesis. *American Educational Research Journal,* Vol. 20, No. 2 (Summer, 1983), pp. 165-182.

Parsons, L. (2001)
"Reducing Bias in a Propensity Score Matched-Pair Sample Using Greedy Matching Techniques" Paper 214-26, Presented at SUGI 26, April 22-25. Long Beach, CA.

Planty, M., Hussar, W., Snyder, T., Provasnik, S., Kena, G., Dinkes, R., KewalRamani, A., and Kemp, J. (2008).
The Condition of Education 2008 (NCES 2008-031). National Center for Education Statistics, Institute of Education Sciences, U.S. Department of Education. Washington, DC.

Planty, M., Bozick, R., and Ingels, S.J. (2006)
Academic pathways, preparation, and performance: A descriptive overview of the transcripts from the high school graduating class of 2003–2004 (NCES 2007–316). U.S. Department of Education, National Center for Education Statistics. Washington, DC.

Roderick, M., Nagaoka, J., and Allensworth, E. (2006)
From High School to the Future: A First Look at Chicago Public School Graduates' College Enrollment, College Preparation, and Graduation from Four-Year Colleges. Chicago, IL: Consortium on Chicago School Research.

Roderick, M., Nagaoka, J., Coca, V., and Moeller, E. (2008)
From High School to the Future: Potholes on the Road to College. Chicago: Consortium on Chicago School Research.

Roderick, M., Nagaoka, J., Coca, V., and Moeller, E. (2009)
From High School to the Future: Making Hard Work Pay Off. Chicago: Consortium on Chicago School Research.

Proger, Amy R. and Jenny Nagaoka. 2008
Trends in Advanced Placement and International Baccalaureate coursetaking: 1998-2005. Paper presented at the annual proceedings of the American Education Research Association, New York, NY.

Roderick, M., and Stoker, G. (2010)
"Bringing rigor to the study of rigor: Evaluating the efficacy of Advanced Placement as a strategy for increasing college preparation in urban schools" In Judith Meece and Jacquelynne Eccles. *Handbook of Research on Schools, Schooling, and Human Development.* New York, Routledge. 216-234.

Rose, H., and Betts, J. R. (2001)
Math matters: The links between high school curriculum, college graduation, and earnings. San Francisco, CA: Public Policy Institute of California.

Rose, H., and Betts, J.R. (2004)
The effect of high school courses on earnings. *Review of Economics and Statistics, 86,* 497-513.

Sadler, P.M., Sonnert, G., Tai, R.H., and Klopfenstein, K. (eds) (2010)
AP: A critical examination of the Advanced Placement program. Cambridge: Harvard University Press.

Sadler, P.M., and Tai, R.H. (2007)
Advanced Placement exam scores as a predictor of performance in introductory college biology, chemistry, and physics courses. *Science Educator, 16*(2), 1-19.

Shettle, C., Roey, S., Mordica, J., Perkins, R., Nord, C., Teodorovic, J., Brown, J., Lyons, M., Averett, C., and Kastberg, D. (2007)
The nation's report card: America's high school graduates (NCES 2007-467). U.S. Department of Education, National Center for Education Statistics. Washington, DC: U.S. Government Printing Office.

Snyder, T., and Dillow, S. (2011)
Digest of Education Statistics 2010 (NCES 2011-015). Washington, DC: U.S. Department of Education.

Stoker, G.L. (2010)
Closing the gap between educational aspirations and outcomes: Is Advanced Placement (AP) the answer? The University of Chicago. http://search.proquest.com/docview/609291078?accountid=14657

Symonds, W.C., Schwartz, R.B., and Ferguson, R. (2011)
Pathways to prosperity: Meeting the challenge of preparing young Americans for the 21st century. Report issued by the Pathways to Prosperity Project, Harvard Graduate School of Education.

Tai, R.H., Sadler, P.M. and Loehr, J.F. (2005)
Factors influencing success in introductory college chemistry. *Journal of Research in Science Teaching, (42)* 987–1012. doi: 10.1002/tea.20082.

University of Illinois at Urbana-Champaign, Admissions Task Force Report (2009)
http://provost.illinois.edu/admissions/AdmissionsTaskForceReport2009.pdf

U.S. Department of Education, National Center for Education Statistics. (2006)
The condition of education 2006 (NCES 2006-071). Washington, DC: U.S. Government Printing Office.

U.S. Department of Education, National Center for Education Statistics. (2004).
The Condition of Education 2004 (NCES 2004–077). Washington, DC: U.S. Government Printing Office.

U.S. Department of Education, National Center for Education Statistics. (2001)
Bridging the gap: Academic preparation and postsecondary success of first-generation students (NCES 2001-153), by Edward C. Warburton, Rosio Bugarin, and Anne-Marie Nuñez. Project Officer: C. Dennis Carroll. Washington, DC: 2001.

U.S. Department of Education, National Center for Education Statistics. (2002)
Descriptive summary of 1995-1996 beginning postsecondary students: Six years later (NCES 2003-151), by Lutz Berkner, Shirley He, and Emily Forrest Cataldi. Project Officer: Paula Knepper. Washington, DC.

U.S. Department of Education, National Center for Education Statistics. (2003)
Remedial education at degree-granting postsecondary institutions in fall 2000 (NCES 2004-010), by Basmat Parsad and Laurie Lewis. Project Officer: Bernard Greene. Washington, DC.

U.S. Department of Education, National Center for Education Statistics.
High School and Beyond Longitudinal Study of 1980 Sophomores (HS&B-So: 80/82), "High School Transcript Study"; and 1987, 1990, 1994, 1998, 2000, and 2005 High School Transcript Study (HSTS)

Willingham, W. and Morris, M. (1986)
Four years later: A longitudinal study of Advanced Placement students in college. New York: College Board Publications.

Appendix A
Data Used in This Report

Quantitative Data and Sample

Data

This paper draws on data from the Chicago Postsecondary Transition Project, a joint project of the Consortium on Chicago School Research (CCSR), the School of Social Service Administration (SSA) at the University of Chicago, and Chicago Public Schools (CPS). The CCSR database contains complete administrative records for all students since 1992, including birth date, race/ethnicity, special education and bilingual education status, high school course transcripts, and high school achievement test scores. Transcript data allow us to track coursetaking; identify course level (regular, honors, AP); and determine course grades. Because all juniors in Illinois are required to take the ACT, we have ACT scores for all CPS students —not just those who plan to go to college. This data is particularly important for controlling for students' achievement prior to senior year. Also, students' home addresses have been linked to 2000 census data at the block group level. All CPS data are linked by student- and school-specific identification numbers.

As part of the collaboration with the Chicago Postsecondary Transition Project, CCSR also receives college enrollment data from the National Student Clearinghouse (NSC). The NSC is a nonprofit corporation that began in 1993 to assist higher education institutions in verifying enrollment and degree completion. In 2004, NSC expanded its services to high school districts through its new program, "Success Outcomes." In 2005, more than 2,800 colleges participated in the NSC; it covered 91 percent of postsecondary enrollment in the United States. At present, most Illinois colleges participate in NSC's enrollment verification program. CPS is the first major urban school district to participate in this program and produce reports on its graduates. Beginning with the class of 2004, the CPS Department of Postsecondary Education and Student Development (now the Office of College and Career Preparation) used this data to publicly report the college enrollment rates of CPS graduates.

We use NSC data to identify whether former CPS students enrolled in college in the fall after graduation and whether they still were enrolled in college two years after high school graduation. These data are then linked to the Integrated Postsecondary Education Data System (IPEDS) of the National Center for Education Statistics (NCES) and to Barron's selectivity ratings so that we can further describe the characteristics of the colleges to which students have enrolled. Colleges are categorized by their selectivity using the 2005 *Barron's Profiles of American Colleges* rating: (1) nonselective four-year colleges, which combines Barron's "less competitive" and "non-competitive" categories; (2) somewhat selective four-year colleges; (3) selective four-year colleges; and (4) very selective four-year colleges, which combines Barron's two top categories ("most competitive" and "highly competitive").

In a side analysis in Chapter 3 of this report (see *Our Approach to Matching Students and Addressing Selection* on p. 56), we also use information from students' college application process. Since 2004, CPS has had graduating seniors complete the online CPS Senior Exit Questionnaire (SEQ) at the end of the school year. In 2005, the response rate was 93 percent. The SEQ asks students detailed information about what they plan to do after high school graduation, what colleges they applied to and whether they were accepted to college. The SEQ data allows us then to identify the level (four-year versus two-year) and the selectivity of colleges to which students applied and were accepted.

Quantitative Samples

The base sample in this study includes seniors who were in the graduating cohorts of 2003-2009. However, we do not include seniors who were in special education programs, alternative high schools, or charter high schools; nor do we include seniors who took fewer than four classes in their senior year (see Appendix B). Furthermore, in our analyses of college retention, we restrict our sample to students who immediately enrolled in a four-year college after high school and include only cohorts 2003 through 2007 (the cohorts for which we can examine two-year persistence rates).

The analyses for Chapter 3, which includes propensity matching methods, further restrict our sample (see Appendix F).

Qualitative Data, Sample and Methods

Data

Case studies and qualitative analyses presented in this report are drawn from a qualitative sample of 105 students in the Chicago Public Schools, 93 of which had sufficient data on senior year coursework to include in these analyses. We recruited students as juniors from three CPS high schools in the spring of 2005, and they were interviewed throughout high school. The qualitative data used in this report are primarily based on student interviews. Students were interviewed five times throughout their junior and senior years. Students were interviewed twice during spring of junior year: once before and once after taking the ACT. Students were also interviewed three times during senior year: once in October/November; once in February; and finally in May/June, or just before graduation. On average, interviews were completed with 95 percent of the sample at each of the five interview cycles. Interviews were then transcribed, coded, and validated. Though analysis here includes only high school data, interviews have continued through the second year after students graduated from high school.

Three high schools participated in our longitudinal study. The schools were selected because they had college-going rates that were slightly higher than the CPS average. The schools differed by their location, their size, and the racial/ethnic make-up of their student bodies, but they were similar in that each served a predominantly minority student body and each had recently established an International Baccalaureate (IB) program. These schools were not the worst-performing schools in the city; nor did they include any of Chicago's high-performing selective enrollment schools.[62] Rather, they could be described as being "at the margin" of high school reform, serving students with slightly better-than-average incoming achievement, providing access to AP and IB courses, and producing graduates who make a diverse set of post-secondary choices.

The case studies and qualitative analyses also draw on additional sources of data, including linking the students in our qualitative study to the quantitative data sources described earlier (e.g., records from the Chicago Public Schools, National Student Clearinghouse). Our fieldwork also included classroom observations, teacher interviews, and teachers' assessments of student course performance.

Qualitative Sample

There were 105 students who participated in our Qualitative Longitudinal Sample, roughly reflecting the demographic diversity of CPS students. The qualitative sample is gender-balanced (51 percent males, 49 percent females) and reflects the racial/ethnic composition of CPS students (49 percent African American, 47 percent Latino, 2 percent white, 2 percent Asian American). Students in the sample live in different neighborhoods throughout Chicago, entered high school with a range of incoming achievement test scores, and accumulated very different qualifications for college in terms of their grades and ACT scores. Students also participated in a variety of curricular tracks throughout high school. In order to thoroughly understand the outcomes of high-achieving high school graduates, researchers targeted a high proportion of students in the International Baccalaureate (IB) program, as well as students taking honors and AP coursework. Thus, our sample can be characterized as 25 percent IB students, 25 percent honors track/AP students, and 50 percent students taking the standard curriculum.

Due to the intentional over-sampling of students taking IB, AP, and honors coursework, our qualitative sample was much more academically qualified for college than the general CPS population at the end of eleventh grade. In addition, students in the qualitative sample were much more likely to take AP and math courses, which, as we will illustrate later, allowed us to analyze students' experience in AP in greater detail. In addition, because two of the schools we studied had large vocational programs (then called the Education to Career programs or ETC), a much greater share of our sample was enrolled in two or more vocational courses compared to other students throughout the CPS system. These differences are detailed in the table below.

Sample retention was high: by the culmination of the high school interviews, only three students had declined participation in the study. Some students, however, had insufficient interview data regarding their experiences of senior year coursework to accurately code for this analysis. Therefore, the sample analyzed for this report consists of 93 of the original 105 students who enrolled in the study.

TABLE 10

Qualitative sample compared to the system

	CPS Average	Qualitative Sample
(Very) Selective College Access	25%	40%
Somewhat Selective College Access	30%	31%
Nonselective or Two-Year	45%	29%
Took Four or More Core Classes	59%	63%
Took a Fourth Year of Math	36%	47%
Took One or More AP Courses	27%	54%
Took One or More Make-up Courses	35%	7%
Took Two or More Vocational Courses	22%	46%

Qualitative Methods

Information from the longitudinal study presented in this report draws on a qualitative analysis of the 93 student cases from the Qualitative Longitudinal Sample, each consisting of as many as five student interviews (three from senior year). Each case went through an extensive process of coding and validation **(see Table 11** for details about coding for challenge). Researchers read each case in its entirety and assigned ratings for the level of challenge of a student's senior year overall, as well as for each class for which there was sufficient data to assign an individual qualitative code. Cases were coded by one researcher and then validated by a second researcher. Any discrepancies in coding between the two researchers were reconciled as a group by the qualitative research team. Students' academic records were used to determine their qualifications and level of college access using the same rubric used in the quantitative analysis. Each of the case studies shown in the report is representative of a subset of students identified as having a common kind of senior year experience after this process.

To code challenge, we drew on questions in our interviews that asked students about their experience in particular classes (e.g., their reports of how much homework was assigned, their description of the pace and academic demands of the class, and their perception of their learning in that class), as well as their experience across their classes. **Table 11** gives a sense of the type of questions and answers we coded as a part of this analysis.

TABLE 11

Coding for senior year challenge

Question	Responses	Code Considered
Senior Year Overall		
Is senior year harder or easier than previous years of high school?	Easier or the same	Low
	Harder	High
How much homework are you doing this year? Is that more or less than last year?	No homework or virtually no homework; less homework than last year.	Low
	Some homework (approximately weekly); the same as last year	Medium
	Consistent homework (approximately daily); more homework than last year	High
Is your homework difficult or challenging to complete? Is it any harder or easier than last year?	Not challenging; less challenging than last year	Low
	Neither challenging nor easy; the same as last year	Medium
	Challenging; more challenging than last year	High
Are you learning a lot in your classes this year?	No—Not learning anything; learning less than last year	Low
	Yes—Learning college-oriented skills; learning more than last year	High
If I offered you the choice to go back and skip senior year, and you could go straight from junior year to college, would you do it?	Yes—Nothing important learned this year	Low
	No—Learned important things this year	High
Individual Classes Senior Year		
Do you have a lot of homework for this class? How often is homework assigned? How long does it take to complete? How much of it do you do during class time?	No homework or virtually no homework at all; any homework assigned can be finished during the class period	Low
	Some homework (approximately weekly); at least some homework necessary to complete at home	Medium
	Daily homework; projects with clear deadlines; completion of homework required to adequately prepare for class	High
What is that class like? How do you spend your time in that class? What happens on a typical day in that class?	Class is slow moving; class requires little to no participation or attention from student; student is accountable for little of the information imparted in class	Low
	Student is busy at least part of the time in class; information imparted in class is somewhat important (i.e., student takes notes on lectures to use for studying)	Medium
	Student is working productively the entire class period; student is held accountable for information imparted in class	High
Is this class any easier or harder than the classes you've taken in the same subject in previous years?	Easier	Low
	The same	Medium
	Harder	High
Is the work for this class—either during class or work you take home—challenging to complete?	Work is easy or can consistently be done at the last minute; work is the same thing the student did last year; doesn't matter if you miss a day of class	Low
	Work is neither hard nor easy; work is harder but can't describe why; student has to participate in class to some extent	Medium
	Work is hard, and student can describe why; student really has to pay attention in class and/or to the homework in order to understand the concepts; class work or homework requires student to think deeply or in new ways; student believes missing one day of class is risky	High
Are you learning a lot in this class?	No	Low
	Yes	High

We categorized a student as having a high-, medium-, or low level of challenge in senior year according to responses to these questions, including some consideration for the challenge level of individual classes. Specifically, we coded a student as having a high-challenge senior year if s/he: (1) described senior year as more challenging than junior year, (2) felt s/he had learned a great deal in senior year, and (3) depicted at least one of his/her senior year classes as being individually challenging. A student was coded as having a medium-challenge senior year if s/he: (1) described senior year as about equally challenging to previous years of high school but also (2) described at least one class as highly challenging. Finally, a student was coded as having a low-challenge senior year if s/he: (1) described senior year as similar or lower in challenge than previous years and did not describe any class as being individually challenging; *or* (2) described senior year as being clearly less challenging than previous years of high school, regardless of the level of challenge of any individual classes.

Appendix B
Determining Who is a Senior and Who Persists in Four-Year Colleges

Determining Who is a Senior

We use multiple datasets that help us define who is a senior in CPS. **Table 12** displays the various steps we take to create our base sample of students. Our reduced sample accounts for almost 70 percent of all possible seniors (123,783/177,034) in CPS graduating cohorts of 2003-2009.

First, students are considered seniors if they are documented as in the twelfth grade in the CPS administrative files in both fall and spring semesters (**Table 12, Row A**). We omit students who change grades across the semesters (**Table 12, Row B**). However, students who are in the twelfth grade for only one semester (fall or spring) in a given year are counted as seniors. And because we are interested in the specific courses seniors take, we analyze only students who have transcript information. This means we eliminate students who attend charter schools from our analysis because most charters do not report this information to CPS.

To better understand the senior coursework patterns in CPS and what a senior year should look like, we further narrow our sample to those who follow a more traditional pathway of a senior. We also exclude students who repeat the twelfth grade (**Table 12, Row C**) and students who take fewer than four courses in their senior year from our analysis (**Table 12, Row D**). We also omit seniors who are in alternative high schools or special education programs (**Table 12, Rows E and F**). We omit special education students from our analysis because we rely so heavily on GPA and ACT scores to characterize qualifications for college. Grades for students in special education are determined by their Individual Education Plans making GPAs not comparable to non-special education students. In addition, for these students, we do not know if the ACT is an accurate measure of their abilities, thus introducing substantial measurement error. Furthermore, the literature is less clear about the postsecondary options for these students, and we are unclear of what the senior year should look like given their additional needs.

Lastly, because we are interested in college outcomes, we further narrow our sample to include only those seniors who graduated from high school (**Table 12, Row G**).[63] As shown below, the vast majority of students who make it to senior year graduate from high school in the spring.

Determining Persistence in Four-Year Colleges

In order to simplify the complex pathways that students take on their way to a college degree, we look only at the most common path to four-year degree attainment. Consistent with our earlier work, we analyze only students who started their postsecondary career at a four-year college. We avoid looking at two-year enrollees because defining success for these students can be difficult: some students attend a two-year college with the intent of continuing on to a four-year college while others only aspire to a certification or two-year degree. For students who enroll in a four-year college, we can be reasonably certain that success for them would be receiving a bachelor's degree. We further limit our sample to students who enroll in a four-year institution by the fall after they graduate from high school. Thus, students who delay enrollment are not included in our analysis of college enrollment or persistence. While more work needs to be done to look at alternative pathways to four-year college enrollment and graduation, we find that very few students who fail to enroll in college immediately after high school end up enrolling in a four-year college significantly later. Building on this base sample, we determine two-year persistence rates by examining whether students are continuously enrolled in any four-year college or university for the two years following the initial enrollment in a four-year college. 'Continuous enrollment' means that the student has no more than 4.5 months between the end of one term enrollment and the start of the next for the two years following the initial enrollment. This span

TABLE 12

Cohort Year	2000	2001	2002	2003	2004	2005	2006	2007	2008	2009	TOTAL
(A)	Seniors in CPS Administrative Files with Transcript Information										
	15,895	14,392	16,237	16,945	17,816	18,371	18,521	19,627	19,348	19,882	177,034
(B)	Omit Students Who Change Grades Within the Academic Year										
	14,527	13,418	15,205	15,803	16,788	17,462	17,408	18,643	18,328	18,996	166,578
(C)	Omit Repeat Seniors										
	14,124	13,105	14,815	15,322	16,275	16,873	16,777	17,779	17,751	18,354	161,175
(D)	Omit Seniors Taking Fewer than Four Classes										
	13,278	12,465	14,165	14,679	15,569	16,045	16,035	16,661	16,898	17,334	153,129
(E)	Omit Students at Alternative High Schools										
	13,111	12,348	13,989	14,513	15,422	15,944	15,862	16,544	16,676	17,123	151,532
(F)	Omit Seniors in Special Education										
	12,039	11,253	12,545	13,008	13,545	13,887	13,880	14,509	14,537	14,985	134,188
(G)	Omit Seniors Who Did Not Graduate in the Spring										
	11,497	10,536	11,712	12,226	12,590	12,756	12,529	13,015	13,153	13,769	123,783
Types of Analysis Used by Graduating Cohort Year											
Descriptive Only	X	X	X								
College Enrollment				X	X	X	X	X	X	X	
College Persistence				X	X	X	X	X			

of time allows students to take a traditional summer break. Students may transfer between four-year colleges during this time. However, students who transfer to a two-year college are not considered to be continuously enrolled in a four-year college. In cases where students enroll in more than one institution simultaneously, the higher level institution is counted.

Descriptively, we find that 54 percent of students who are continuously enrolled for two years in a four-year college receive a bachelor's degree within six years of graduating high school. While more work needs to be done to improve our understanding of success in college, looking at persistence for two years captures some degree of how a student is performing in college, given the fact that we have no information about students' grades or credit accumulation.

Appendix C
Variables Used in the Analysis

TABLE 13

Variable	Students with Access to Selective Colleges	Students with Access to Somewhat Selective Colleges	Description
Level 1 Individual Characteristics	N: 11,638	N: 18983	
Census Variables of Students' Neighborhood (Based on Geo-Coding Student Addresses to Block Group)			
Concentration of Poverty	-0.06 (0.76)	0.16 (0.76)	Based on 2000 U.S. census information on the block group in which students live on two reverse-coded indicators: (1) the log of the percentage of male residents over age 18 employed one or more weeks during the year, and (2) the log of the percentage of families above the poverty line.
Social Status	-0.14 (0.87)	-0.28 (0.81)	Based on 2000 U.S. census information on two indicators: (1) the log of the percentage of employed persons 16 years old or older who are managers or executives, and (2) the mean level of education among people over 18.
Gender and Race/Ethnicity			
Female	0.65 (0.48)	0.64 (0.48)	Demographic characteristics obtained from official school records
African American	0.31 (0.46)	0.47 (0.5)	
Latino	0.35 (0.48)	0.36 (0.48)	
White	0.21 (0.41)	0.11 (0.31)	
Asian American	0.13 (0.34)	0.05 (0.23)	
Academic Qualifications			
ACT Composite Score	21.43 (3.11)	17.61 (3.05)	Since 2001, the ACT has been part of the Illinois state assessment for high schools. All students in Illinois are required to take the ACT in the spring of their junior year. ACT tests are given in English, reading, math, and science. The rounded average of these four scores is the ACT composite score.
ACT Math	21.01 (3.7)	17.25 (2.96)	ACT Math
Junior Cumulative Core Unweighted GPA	3.19 (0.44)	2.63 (0.44)	
Junior Cumulative Math GPA	3.06 (0.64)	2.40 (0.67)	
Prior Math Courses	5.58 (1.51)	5.56 (1.38)	Number of math courses in student's freshman, sophomore, and junior years
Prior Vocational Courses	3.32 (2.95)	3.66 (2.74)	Number of vocational courses taken in student's freshman, sophomore, and junior years
IB Students	0.05 (0.22)	0.02 (0.15)	

Note: The first number listed in the *Students with Access to Selective Colleges* and *Students with Access to Somewhat Selective Colleges* columns are averages and the numbers in parentheses are standard deviations

Variable	Students with Access to Selective Colleges	Students with Access to Somewhat Selective Colleges	
Level 2 School Variables (N=87 Schools)	N: 11,638	N: 18983	
Selective Enrollment School	N=7	N=7	
Percentage of Prior Year Graduates Attending Four-Year College	64.0 (18.1)	41.7 (14.9)	
School Mean ACT	19.8 (1.8)	16.9 (1.9)	
School Mean GPA	3.31 (0.23)	2.69 (0.21)	

Note: The first number listed in the *Students With Access to Selective Colleges* and *Students With Access to Somewhat Selective Colleges* columns are averages and the numbers in parentheses are standard deviations

Appendix D
Latent Class Analysis

In order to look at a more understandable picture of coursetaking patterns in the senior year, we took two steps in which to categorize seniors. First, we used our qualitative sample of 105 students and coded their senior-year schedules based on course characteristics such as the number of core courses that students were taking, as well as factors like the number of ETC, math, science, and AP courses. This yielded groups that we confidently believed represented our qualitative sample; however, to get a broader and more recent picture of seniors' coursetaking patterns across CPS, we turned to Latent Class Analysis (LCA).

LCA is a statistical model-based approach used to create groups where members (i.e., students) are as similar as possible based on a set of characteristics, in this case courses taken in the senior year. This means that we have a set of diagnostic statistics by which we can judge the quality of the groupings. For each trial of the model, we specified the number of groups into which we thought the students could be grouped. We then tested these models against each other to see which number of groups statistically fit the data the best. For our data, the model determined that six groups was the best fit for the number of overall coursetaking

TABLE 14

Average number of senior classes taken for 2006-2009 graduates by cluster

	CPS Avg N=50,567	Coasters N=15,054	Multiple ETC N=10,065	English AP N=8,158	Non-AP Core N=8,423	Core with Some AP N=4,989	Making Up Courses N=3,878
English IV AP	0.17	0.00	0.00	1.00	0.02	0.04	0.02
Social Science AP	0.17	0.05	0.07	0.39	0.10	0.61	0.03
Science AP	0.12	0.01	0.03	0.26	0.05	0.55	0.04
Math AP	0.11	0.01	0.03	0.23	0.04	0.54	0.06
World Language AP	0.06	0.03	0.01	0.11	0.04	0.17	0.12
English IV Non-AP	0.79	1.03	0.97	0.02	1.00	0.94	0.33
English Elective	0.87	0.92	0.66	0.73	1.47	0.57	0.66
Social Science Non-AP	0.47	0.48	0.20	0.49	0.84	0.34	0.48
Science Non-AP	0.49	0.48	0.24	0.50	0.86	0.47	0.38
Math Non-AP	0.37	0.32	0.20	0.43	0.67	0.39	0.17
World Language Non-AP	0.54	0.55	0.54	0.46	0.70	0.44	0.49
ETC	0.94	0.51	2.64	0.75	0.35	0.35	0.59
Music	0.47	0.66	0.42	0.47	0.22	0.43	0.53
Art	0.46	0.68	0.38	0.47	0.22	0.38	0.50
Physical Education	0.38	0.61	0.32	0.23	0.21	0.27	0.53
Core Makeup*	0.40	0.47	0.21	0.16	0.21	0.10	1.87

Note: Core Make-up does not include making up courses for World Language.

patterns. However, when examining these six groups, we found that two of the groups were both defined by their high levels of AP coursetaking. We combined these two groups in order to streamline the framework of coursetaking patterns. Moreover, these five groups align with the groups we had previously created using our qualitative sample's course schedules.

Not all students' coursework easily fell into a category. Some students' senior year coursetaking shares patterns observed in multiple groups. Thus, we limit our analysis to the students who had at least a 50 percent chance of being in given group. This drops 3.7 percent of our total sample.

TABLE 15

Individual characteristics by cluster

	CPS Avg N=16,582		Coasters N=5,492		Multiple ETC N=1,838		English AP N=2,073		Non-AP Core N=2,060		Core with Some AP N=2,261		Making Up Courses N=2,858	
	Mean	Std	Mean	Std	Mean	Std	Mean	Std	Mean	Std	Mean	Std	Mean	Std
Gender														
Female	57%	0.49	54%	0.50	53%	0.50	68%	0.47	60%	0.49	61%	0.49	53%	0.50
Male	43%	0.49	46%	0.50	47%	0.50	32%	0.47	40%	0.49	39%	0.49	47%	0.50
Race/Ethnicity														
African American	48%	0.50	53%	0.50	58%	0.49	47%	0.50	46%	0.50	36%	0.48	45%	0.50
Latino	36%	0.48	37%	0.48	32%	0.47	30%	0.46	34%	0.48	32%	0.47	42%	0.49
White	11%	0.31	8%	0.27	7%	0.26	13%	0.34	13%	0.33	18%	0.39	9%	0.29
Asian American	5%	0.23	2%	0.15	2%	0.15	9%	0.29	7%	0.25	13%	0.34	4%	0.19
Census Variables of Students' Neighborhoods														
Concentration of Poverty	0.00	1.00	0.11	0.99	0.14	0.94	-0.06	1.00	-0.05	1.07	-0.24	1.00	-0.04	0.96
Social Status	0.00	1.00	-0.10	0.94	-0.11	0.91	0.14	1.06	0.06	1.04	0.24	1.11	-0.06	0.96
Qualifications at the End of Junior Year														
Cumulative Junior GPA	2.35	0.77	2.15	0.66	2.25	0.68	2.93	0.62	2.43	0.71	2.86	0.67	1.91	0.77
ACT Composite	17.7	4.52	16.3	3.45	16.1	3.32	20.2	4.87	18.5	4.47	21.1	5.15	15.7	3.28
Selective Enrollment School														
	14%	0.35	10%	0.30	5%	0.23	20%	0.40	13%	0.34	36%	0.48	6%	0.24

Appendix E
Identifying College Access

College Access Based on Students' Likelihood of Acceptance at Colleges with Different Selectivity Ratings and Academic Qualifications in Students' Junior Year

Throughout this report, we draw on a rubric developed by Roderick, Nagaoka, Coca, and Moeller (2008) that identifies the type (four-year versus two-year) and selectivity of college that students would likely have access to, given their course performance (final unweighted GPA in core classes), their ACT scores, and their involvement in college preparatory AP and IB coursework. Colleges were categorized by their selectivity using *Barron's Profiles of American Colleges* rating,[64] (1) nonselective four-year colleges, which combines Barron's "less competitive" and "non-competitive" categories; (2) somewhat selective four-year colleges; (3) selective four-year colleges; and (4) very selective four-year colleges, which combines Barron's two top categories ("most competitive" and "highly competitive").

Because all CPS juniors take the ACT as part of the state's assessment system for high schools, college qualifications for all CPS juniors were included. The rubric indicates the minimum unweighted GPA and composite ACT scores that CPS graduates would need to have a good chance of being accepted to certain classifications of colleges (**see Table 16**). However, analyses for this report use unweighted GPA at the end of students' junior year to get a sense of what the student may have access to after senior year. Comparisons between cumulative GPA at the end of junior year and at the end of senior year suggest that there is not a great deal of move from one year to the next. Thus, we can be fairly certain that students' college access given their junior qualifications is a good indicator of what they will have access to at the end of their senior year.

The rubric uses cutoffs for each "qualification category" (e.g., access to a selective college) that were determined by using a multivariate analysis that identified the likelihood of acceptance into colleges of various selectivity levels for CPS students by identifying descriptively the modal college attendance patterns of CPS students with different GPA and ACT combinations in prior cohorts. The ACT cutoffs are generally lower than the definitions used in college ratings such as Barron's. This is largely because the rubric is based on the actual college-acceptance and college-going patterns of CPS graduates and their GPAs and ACT scores, and this definition of "qualifications" does not encompass all of the criteria that colleges use in their acceptance decisions. For example, college admissions decisions often rely on class rank, and in low-performing high schools, graduates may have low GPAs, but relatively high class ranks, and still be admitted.

Because all high school graduates have the option of attending a two-year college, graduates with ACT scores and GPAs that fall even below the level necessary for likely admittance to a nonselective four-year college were categorized as being limited to attending two-year colleges. The original rubric also takes the role of advanced coursework (i.e., enrollment in an IB program or taking at least six honors courses and two AP courses) into account when classifying the type of colleges to which students have access. However, since we have not examined the extent to which junior advanced coursetaking impact students' college enrollment patterns, we do not include advanced coursework in junior year as a factor in our adjusted rubric.

TABLE 16

Categories for access to college types based on CPS juniors' GPAs and ACT scores

Composite ACT Score	Unweighted GPA in Core Courses (By the End of Junior Year)				
	Less than 2.0	2.0-2.4	2.5-2.9	3.0-3.4	3.5-4.0
Missing ACT	Two-Year Colleges	Nonselective Four-Year Colleges	Somewhat Selective Colleges	Selective Colleges	Selective Colleges
Less than 18	Two-Year Colleges	Nonselective Four-Year Colleges	Somewhat Selective Colleges	Somewhat Selective Colleges	Selective Colleges
18-20	Nonselective Four-year Colleges	Somewhat Selective Colleges	Somewhat Selective Colleges	Selective Colleges	Selective Colleges
21-23	Somewhat Selective Colleges	Somewhat Selective Colleges	Selective Colleges	Selective Colleges	Selective Colleges
24 or Higher	Somewhat Selective Colleges	Selective Colleges	Selective Colleges	Very Selective Colleges	Very Selective Colleges

Appendix E

Appendix F
Methodology

It is only possible to measure effects of coursetaking if there is variation in coursetaking across similar students. As outlined in Chapter 2, there are two groups of students for whom we see little variation: students who at the end of junior year have very low qualifications to attend college and students who are qualified to attend very selective colleges. For the former group, very few students took any AP classes, a fourth year of math, or four or more core classes. For the latter, the opposite was true: coursework for this group uniformly followed the pattern of at least one AP, four or more core courses, and an advanced math class. As a result, we limit our analysis to students who entered senior year with qualifications to attend somewhat selective and selective four-year colleges. Moreover, we analyze these groups separately to determine if there are differential effects across levels of student qualifications. Each course option was analyzed independent of the other course options for each outcome. This means that for two groups of students, three course options and three outcomes, our analysis was run 18 separate times. This number is doubled to 36 when we account for the fact that we ran these analyses with and without our simulated propensity score matching method.

To illustrate, we use the example of estimating the effect of taking a fourth year of math on the odds of enrolling in a four-year college for a student who would have access to a somewhat selective college. The analysis has three separate steps. First, we start with the schools in the top quartile of participation in fourth-year math among students with access to somewhat selective college (**Equation 1.2**). For each student in those high schools with a high participation rate, we predict the probability of taking advanced math given a student's demographic characteristics, prior math coursetaking, ACT math scores, and junior year cumulative unweighted core GPA. Also included in this equation are terms for that student's school's mean GPA and ACT score. Including this term ensures that when we match students based on this propensity score, they are coming from schools with a similar achievement profile.

We employ a nearest neighbor algorithm to match students based on this real and simulated propensity score. The algorithm uses a greedy matching technique which iterates by taking the two closest matches that have different values of the treatment variable. Because the algorithm takes locally optimal matches, it is possible that our final dataset is not a true optimally matched set. (Parsons n.d.) However, for large datasets, the differences tend to be marginal. While we obviously would like to have as many matches as possible, we create a caliper of .05 outside of which matches are discarded. That is, if a student is more than 5 percent more or less likely to take a match course than her match, that pair of students is not included in the outcome model. Finally, using this matched sample, we estimate the association between taking a fourth-year math course and three different outcomes (**Equation 2**).

We call this method simulated propensity analysis as it employs techniques from instrumental variable (IV) methods as well as simple propensity scoring. The instrumental variable that we have found is geography, or attendance boundaries of high schools, which dictate likelihood of receiving treatment but are not well correlated with college outcomes. However, unlike in most IV analyses, our instrumental variable does not perfectly predict treatment but merely the possibility of receiving treatment. However within the categories of our instrumental variable, it is possible to predict with accuracy the likelihood of receiving treatment. Given that high schools in both the high and low quartiles are similar in other aspects (especially those relating to college outcomes), a simulation of how students from "low" schools would be treated in "high" schools produces a plausible control group.

EQUATION 1.1
Four or More Core Classes (Dummy)

$= \beta_0$ Intercept $+ \beta_1$ Achievement Characteristics
$+ \beta_2$ Previous Vocational Classes $+ \beta_3$ Previous Art or Music Classes
$+ \beta_4$ Previous Core Failures $+ \beta_5$ Demographic Characteristics
$+ \beta_6$ School Level GPA and ACT Scores

EQUATION 1.2
Fourth-Year Math Class (Dummy)

$= \beta_0$ Intercept $= + \beta_1$ Achievement Characteristics
$+ \beta_2$ Previous Math Course Failures $+ \beta_3$ Passed Algebra or Trig
$+ \beta_4$ Demographic Characteristics $+ \beta_5$ School Level GPA and ACT Scores

EQUATION 1.3
Number of AP Classes (Categorial Variable)

$= \beta_0$ Intercept $+ \beta_1$ Achievement Characteristics
$+ \beta_2$ Previous Vocational Classes $+ \beta_3$ Previous Art or Music Classes
$+ \beta_4$ Previous Core Failures $+ \beta_5$ Demographic Characteristics
$+ \beta_6$ IB Status (Dummy) $+ \beta_7$ Number of Previous AP Classes
$+ \beta_8$ School Level GPA and ACT Scores

EQUATION 2
College Outcome

$= \beta_0$ Intercept $+ \beta_1$ Fourth Year Math (Dummy)
$+ \beta_2$ Centered AP Dummies $+ \beta_3$ Centered Four Core Dummy
$+ \beta_4$ Centered Achievement Characteristics $+ \beta_5$ Centered Demographic Characteristics
$+ \beta_6$ Centered High School College-Going Rate from Previous Year $+ e$

Endnotes

Introduction

1. Mishel and Roy (2006).
2. Dorn (1996).
3. Goldin and Katz (2008).
4. In 1980, the Current Population Survey estimated that 50 percent of white, 44 percent of African American, and 50 percent of Hispanic seniors were enrolled in a two- or four-year college in the fall after graduation. By 2008, 72 percent of whites, 56 percent of African Americans, and 64 percent of Hispanic seniors were enrolled (Aud et al. 2010).
5. The percent of seniors in the United States who stated they expected to attain at least some college experience rose from 77.5 percent in 1981-82 to 95 percent in 2003-04, excluding 8 percent of students who stated that they "Do not know" (U.S. Department of Education, National Center for Education Statistics 2006).
6. Roderick, Nagaoka, Coca, and Moeller (2008).
7. Duncan, "The Three Myths of High School Reform," Remarks of U.S. Secretary of Education Arne Duncan to the College Board AP Conference, July 15, 2010, Washington DC, 2010. Speaker may have deviated from prepared remarks.
8. National Commission on High School Senior Year (2001).
9. Snyder and Dillow (2011), Tables 157, 159, 160.
10. *The New York Times* (2009); Abeles, (2010) *The New York Times* Op-Ed.
11. Nord et al. (2011).
12. Association of American Colleges and Universities (2002, p. 14).

Chapter 1

13. In 2004, fully 69 percent of Asian American high school seniors and 54 percent of white seniors had taken at least one course above the level of Algebra II, compared with 42 percent of African Americans and only 34 percent of Latinos. Similarly, fully 84 percent of Asian American seniors and 71 percent of white seniors had taken a more advanced science course compared with approximately 60 percent of Latino and African American seniors. Planty, Bozick, and Ingels, "Academic Pathways, Preparation and Performance—A Descriptive Overview of the Transcripts Form the High School Graduating Class of 2003-04," NCES 2007-316 (Washington: Department of Education, National Center for Education Statistics, 2006).
14. University of Illinois Urbana-Champaign, Admissions Task Force Report (2009).
15. Crux Market Research Inc. (2007), College Board website, AP and the cost of college; Crux Market Research Inc. (2006), College Board website: http://professionals.collegeboard.com/profdownload/ap-parent-presentation-for-international-schools.pdf.
16. Crux Market Research, Inc. (2006), College Board website: http://professionals.collegeboard.com/profdownload/ap-parent-presentation-for-international-schools.pdf.
17. Achieve Inc., *Closing the Expectations Gap 2006* (Washington: Achieve Inc., 2006); Achieve Inc., *Closing the Expectations Gap 2008* (Washington: Achieve Inc., 2008).
18. Snyder and Dillow (2011).
19. Nord et al. (2011).
20. Nord et al. (2011).
21. Nord et al. (2011).
22. Nord et al. (2011).
23. Nord et al. (2011).
24. Shettle et al. (2007); Planty et al. (2006).
25. Nord et al. (2011).
26. Nord et al. (2011).
27. Roderick, Nagaoka, Coca, and Moeller (2008, p.4).

Chapter 2

28. We accounted for schools that allow seniors to take elective English courses, such as African American Literature, in order to fulfill their fourth-year English requirement.

Chapter 2 Supplement

29. CPS only is able to collect Illinois employment data on graduates with valid social security numbers in the CPS Student Information System (about 88 percent of graduates).
30. We count students' post-graduation status in the fall rather than summer to distinguish between students who are employed and not in college and those who are employed and attending college.

31 Outcomes were only slightly better for CPS students who could only qualify for a nonselective college. For these students, 30 percent were not employed and not working, 26 percent were working but not in college, and 21 percent were enrolled in a two-year college. The most significant difference between our two-year only and nonselective four-year group is that 23 percent of the nonselective group did enroll in a four-year college.

32 In 2004, if a person worked full time at the minimum wage rate ($5.50) for six-months, s/he would have made $5,720.

33 Symonds et al. (2011).

Chapter 3

34 ACT, Inc. (2004); ACT, Inc. (2005).

35 ACT, Inc. (2004); U.S. Department of Education, National Center for Education Statistics (2002); Chen (2005); Horn and Carroll (2001); Montgomery, Allensworth, and Correra, (2010); Pallas and Alexander (1983); Rose and Betts (2001); Tai, Sadler, and Loehr (2005); U.S. Department of Education, National Center for Education Statistics (2001).

36 Lee and Ready (2007).

37 ACT, Inc. (2006); Adelman (1999); Adelman (2006); Attewell and Domina (2008); Bozick and Ingels (2008); Horn and Carroll (2001); Planty, Bozick, and Ingels (2006); U.S. Department of Education, National Center for Education Statistics (2001).

38 Kyburg, Herthberg-David, and Callahan (2007); Loveless (1999).

39 Stoker (2010).

40 Attewell and Domina (2008); Joensen and Nielsen (2009); Long, Conger, and Iatarola (2012)

41 Aud et al. (2011), indicator 22.

42 Aud et al. (2011).

43 The U.S. Department of Education estimates are that over one-fifth (22 percent) of first-year entering college students are placed in a remedial math course compared to 14 percent for writing and 11 percent for reading (U.S. Department of Education, National Center for Education Statistics, 2004.)

44 Achieve, Inc. (2005); Conley (2007).

45 College Board website, students.

46 Klopfenstein and Thomas (2006); Sadler and Tai (2007); Long, Conger, and Iatarola (2012); Long, Iatarola, and Conger (2009).

47 Joensen and Neilsen (2009); Rose and Betts (2004).

48 Adelman (2006); Dougherty, Mellor, and Jian (2005); Geiser and Santelices (2004); Klopfenstein and Thomas (2006); Sadler and Tai (2007).

49 Adelman (2006); Dougherty et al. (2005); Klopfenstein and Thomas (2006); Sadler and Tai (2007).

50 Geiser and Santelices (2004); Dougherty et al. (2005); Willingham and Morris (1986).

51 Proger and Nagaoka. (2008).

52 Students who have access to somewhat selective colleges and take no AP courses have a 41.8 percent probability in enrolling in any four-year college. Students who have access to somewhat selective colleges and take one AP course have a 50.4 percent likelihood of enrolling in a four-year college. Thus, the effect of taking one AP course is an 8.5 percentage point increase in the probability of enrolling in a four-year college. The 8.5 percentage point change is an increase of approximately 20 percent of the 41.8 percent probability. Numbers do not sum due to rounding.

53 Match is whether a student enrolled in a college with a selectivity level that a student would likely have been accepted to, given his/her high school qualifications. Roderick et al. (2008, p. 26). *See also College Admissions Interviews, p. 12 and How We Define Senior Courses, p. 20.*

54 Stoker (2010).

55 Long, Iatarola, and Conger (2009).

Chapter 4

56 Mazzeo, Montgomery, and Allensworth, et al. (2010). *Passing Through Science.*

57 Allensworth, Nomi, Montgomery, and Lee (2009).

58 Four students' descriptions of their CTE classes were too vague to code reliably.

Chapter 5

59 Common Core State Standards Initiative (2010).

60 Aud et al. (2011), indicator 22.

61 Symonds et al. (2011)

Appendices

62 Though none of these schools is a selective enrollment school, one did have a long-standing legacy of sending many students to college.

63 CPS only tracks the postsecondary enrollment patterns of students who graduate from CPS.

64 This college ranking system rates four-year colleges on the academic qualifications of the students who attend the college (e.g., ACT or SAT scores, GPA, and class rank), as well as the percentage of applicants who are accepted.

Notes From Boxes

A   Montgomery and Allensworth (2010); Luppescu et al. (2011).

B   Montgomery and Allensworth (2010).

C   Kemple and Willner (2008). Career Academies: Long-Term Impacts on Labor Market Outcomes, Educational Attainment, and Transitions to Adulthood.

D   We characterize college access on the basis of course performance (unweighted, cumulative GPA in core classes) and composite ACT scores. Because the CPS graduation requirements are aligned with the minimum admission requirements of in-state, public, four-year colleges, by definition all graduates should be eligible to attend a four-year college if assessed solely on the basis of their coursework.

E   In addition to college enrollment, we find the rubric is consistent when looking at acceptance at a four-year college.

F   As described by Jackson (2007), schools that adopt the AP incentive program (AP Strategies) receive teacher training from the College Board and a pre-AP curriculum along with monetary support for schools in developing vertical teams to develop and implement pre-AP and AP courses. Student exam fees are supplemented, and students receive between $100 and $500 for each exam score as determined by the schools. Both pre-AP and AP teachers receive annual supplements (approximately $2,000 to $5,000 for lead teachers; and between $500 to $1,000 for pre-AP teachers). AP teachers receive a bonus of between $100 to $500 for each AP score of three or over earned by their students. Donors set the amount of the bonuses for the schools they adopt.

ABOUT THE AUTHORS

MELISSA RODERICK, PHD, is the Hermon Dunlap Smith Professor at SSA and a co-director at CCSR where she leads the organization's postsecondary research. Professor Roderick is also the senior director of the Network for College Success, a network of high schools focused on developing high-quality leadership and student performance in Chicago's high schools. Professor Roderick is an expert in urban school reform, high school reform, high-stakes testing, minority adolescent development, and school transitions. Her new work focuses on understanding the relationship between students' high school careers and preparation, their college selection choices and their postsecondary outcomes through linked quantitative and qualitative research. From 2001 to 2003, Professor Roderick served as Director of Planning and Development for CPS. Professor Roderick has a PhD from the Committee on Public Policy from Harvard University, a master's degree in Public Policy from the John F. Kennedy School of Government at Harvard University, and an AB from Bowdoin College.

VANESSA COCA Vanessa Coca is a second year doctoral student in the Sociology of Education program at Steinhardt School of Culture, Education, and Human Development at New York University. She is also a Research Assistant at the Research Alliance for New York City Schools where she is currently studying the college transitions of New York City public school graduates. Prior to pursuing her doctorate, Vanessa worked as a Senior Research Analyst at the University of Chicago Consortium on Chicago School Research. At CCSR, she studied the college planning decisions of successive cohorts of Chicago Public School graduates and broader issues of college readiness. She is the co-author of a number of CCSR reports including: *From High School to the Future: Potholes on the Road to College* and *From High School to the Future: Making Hard Work Pay Off*. Vanessa's research interests include transitions to college, college choice, and the postsecondary experiences of first-generation college students. She received her Master of Public Policy degree and Bachelor of Arts degree from the University of Chicago.

ELIZA MOELLER is the Lead Qualitative Analyst for the Chicago Postsecondary Transition Project, which is based at the School of Social Service Administration and is a sponsored project of CCSR. She also heads the project's Data Practice Collaborative, which brings researchers together with school leaders to support data-driven, research-based high school reform. She is also the research partner for the College Counselors' Collaborative, a professional learning community of high school counselors across the city who are committed to creating strong college-going cultures in their schools and raising college completion rates in their school communities.

Eliza's primary work at CCSR has been to oversee the implementation and analysis of a longitudinal qualitative study of more than 100 CPS graduates who attended more than 40 postsecondary institutions over the course of three years. These students' high school experiences and college transition stories are at the heart of CCSR's postsecondary research studies, including *Potholes on the Road to College, Making Hard Work Pay Off, Working to My Potential,* and *The Challenge of Senior Year*. Eliza currently oversees a second longitudinal qualitative study that will help inform forthcoming research on college readiness and college choice. Eliza received her BA from the University of Wisconsin-Madison and an MA in Social Service Administration from the University of Chicago.

THOMAS KELLEY-KEMPLE is a research analyst with the Postsecondary Transition Project which is based at the School of Social Service Administration at the University of Chicago and is a sponsored project of CCSR. His current work focuses on senior year coursetaking in CPS High Schools and its effect on college attainment and retention. He received his BA from the University of Chicago in Public Policy.

This report reflects the interpretation of the authors. Although CCSR's Steering Committee provided technical advice, no formal endorsement by these individuals, organizations, or the full Consortium should be assumed.

UCHICAGOCCSR

CONSORTIUM ON CHICAGO SCHOOL RESEARCH

Directors

ELAINE M. ALLENSWORTH
Interim Executive Director
Consortium on Chicago School Research

JENNY NAGAOKA
Deputy Director
Consortium on Chicago School Research

MELISSA RODERICK
Senior Director
Hermon Dunlap Smith Professor
School of Social Service Administration
University of Chicago

PENNY BENDER SEBRING
Founding Director
Consortium on Chicago School Research

Steering Committee

RUANDA GARTH MCCULLOUGH
Co-Chair
Loyola University

MATTHEW STAGNER
Co-Chair
Chapin Hall Center for Children

Institutional Members

CLARICE BERRY
Chicago Principals and Administrators Association

JENNIFER CHEATHAM
Chicago Public Schools

CHRISTOPHER KOCH
Illinois State Board of Education

KAREN G.J. LEWIS
Chicago Teachers Union

Individual Members

VERONICA ANDERSON
Communications Consultant

ANDREW BROY
Illinois Network of Charter Schools

AMIE GREER
Vaughn Occupational High School-CPS

RAQUEL FARMER-HINTON
University of Wisconsin, Milwaukee

REYNA HERNANDEZ
Illinois State Board of Education

TIMOTHY KNOWLES
Urban Education Institute

DENNIS LACEWELL
Urban Prep Charter Academy for Young Men

LILA LEFF
Umoja Student Development Corporation

PETER MARTINEZ
University of Illinois at Chicago

GREGORY MICHIE
Concordia University of Chicago

LISA SCRUGGS
Jenner and Block

LUIS R. SORIA
Ellen Mitchell Elementary School

BRIAN SPITTLE
DePaul University

KATHLEEN ST. LOUIS
Project Exploration

AMY TREADWELL
Chicago New Teacher Center

ARIE J. VAN DER PLOEG
American Institutes for Research

JOSIE YANGUAS
Illinois Resource Center

KIM ZALENT
Business and Professional People for the Public Interest